A Study of the Book of Genesis

A Study
of the
Book of Genesis

**An Introductory Commentary on All
Fifty Chapters of Genesis**

by

Gordon Talbot

Christian Publications, Inc.
Harrisburg, Pennsylvania

Christian Publications, Inc.
25 S. 10th Street, P.O. Box 3404
Harrisburg, PA 17105

The mark of ℘ *vibrant faith*

Library of Congress Catalog Card Number: 81-65578
ISBN: 0-87509-253-5

Contents

Introduction

The first five books of the Old Testament are called the Pentateuch—a transliteration of two Greek words meaning five scrolls. Other passages of Scripture often call the Pentateuch the "book of the law." Since the theme of the law runs through much of Exodus, Leviticus, Numbers, and Deuteronomy, the Jewish practice was to consider the whole Pentateuch as the law. New Testament references to the Old Testament usually used the traditional Jewish division which included Genesis with the books of the law. The Pentateuch covers human history from the creation through the development of the covenant nation, Israel.

Genesis, the name of the first book in this series, is a transliteration of the Greek word meaning generation, or origin. It is a fitting name for a book of beginnings. Genesis is a one-word summary of the content of the book. The writer of Genesis under the inspiration of the Holy Spirit gave the origin of history from the divine viewpoint.

The author, guided by the Holy Spirit, selected only the necessary information to trace the history of God's redemptive acts in the ancient world. The great sweeps of primeval history are covered in the opening chapters. Three-fourths of the book deals with the lifetime of Abraham, Isaac, and Jacob.

Genesis is a book of beginnings—

> The beginning of the universe
> The beginning of man
> The beginning of sin
> The beginning of salvation
> The beginning of nations
> The beginning of Israel
> The beginning of the life of faith
> The beginning of worship
> The beginning of the family
> The beginning of human society

The foundation stones of every great doctrine can be found in Genesis. Christ looked upon the truth in Genesis as normative and on occasion made reference to Genesis to correct the doctrinal deviations of Israel's leaders. When the Pharisees questioned Him on the divorce law as found in the Mosaic system, Jesus referred them to Genesis for the norm. Jesus explained that the more liberal position of the Mosaic teaching was an accommodation to the hardness of men's hearts and did not reflect the highest will of God.

> *But from the beginning of the creation God made them male and female. For this cause shall a man leave his father and mother, and cleave to his wife; and they twain shall be one flesh: so then they are no more twain, but one flesh. What therefore God hath joined together, let not man put asunder (Mark 10:6-9).*

The highest teaching on the sanctity of marriage is the first teaching found in Genesis. It has much to say about marriage and the family. The historical records of the earliest saints and the patriarchs are rich in insights on both the marriage relationship and the home.

Many doctrinal themes run through Genesis. One of the most important is biblical salvation unfolded from the promise of Messiah in Genesis 3:15, through God's covenant with Abraham. Salvation by faith in the substitutionary sacrifice was understood in the early ages of man. The principle of developmental revelation begins in Genesis and comes to completeness in the New Testament.

Divisions of the Book

Genesis can be easily divided into two sections. First, chapters 1 through 11 deal with the general history of the world from creation to the time of Abraham. Second, chapters 12-50 cover the history of Abraham's family.

The book has ten natural divisions, each beginning with the words, "These are the generations." The Hebrew word translated generations means "history" or "account."

The history of Genesis seems always to move from general history to special history, the account of Israel. The writer, under the inspiration of the Holy Spirit, selected from the data available to him the persons and events essential to the history of God's covenant people.

Authorship

Genesis, the first of five books attributed to Moses, the God-appointed leader of Israel, has been under attack by biblical higher criticism like no other part of the Bible. The passing of time has only served to strengthen the traditional position of Mosaic authorship for Genesis, Exodus, Leviticus, Numbers, and Deuteronomy. The discoveries of archaeology have confirmed the historical accuracy of these books. Scholars now concede that the social, economic, and religious life portrayed in Genesis fits the historical period of the patriarchs. Archaeology has proven that a sophisticated civilization existed in the area of the fertile crescent before Abraham and that a monotheism faith was not unusual in that culture. The documentary theory that attempts to prove the Pentateuch a compilation of several writers lacks any empirical evidence. The internal evidence of the Book of Genesis confirms that Moses was its author. Twice the Lord Jesus Christ named Moses the author of the first five books of the Old Testament (John 5:46; Luke 24:27, 44).

Style

Some parts of Genesis are in poetry form. It has been wrongly assumed that they are imaginative literature and not necessarily accurate histories. The New Testament disproves that theory by the fact that Christ and His apostles understood the Genesis record to be historically correct.

Most of the Book of Genesis is in the narrative form and differs from mythology in that it tells of men and women who really lived. Moses no doubt had access to written records and to the oral tradition by which the history of the patriarchs had been preserved. Since writing existed even before the days of Abraham it is conceivable that some written records had been kept of the experiences of Abraham, Isaac, and Jacob. Whatever sources Moses may have used, he was supernaturally guided by the Holy Spirit to select from them only what was true and what was essential to the inspired Scriptures. No oral or written eye-witness accounts existed of the creation. This section of Genesis records a block of history that could only have been known by divine revelation. Here the Creator speaks about His acts of creation.

Whatever sources may have been used by Moses the Book of Genesis had a remarkable unity. It must be treated as a whole and not as a collection of fragments.

The several Hebrew names for God in no way indicate a variation in sources. The names of God in Genesis are always related to some stage of divine revelation and fit into the progress of the book. Elohim was used of God in His role as creator and sovereign over all things. Jehovah was used of God in His eternal self-sufficiency and had special application to man's redemption. These names were given by divine revelation. They were disclosures God gave of His own nature.

From the pages of this book of primeval history come the same kinds of reality that face men and women in today's world. The battle with evil remains. The remedy for it recommended in this ancient book is still valid. The writers of the New Testament found Genesis so relevant they quoted from it sixty times.

The antiquity of Genesis does not detract from its

message to the present age. Understanding Genesis is foundational to all other Bible study.

1

The Birthday of the Universe

Genesis 1:1—2:25

Genesis, as its name implies, is the book of beginnings and from it we learn how the universe came into existence. God took what was formless and dark and changed it into something bright and beautiful. He furnished the earth with vegetation, animal life, and human life and the first family took up residence upon it. Here and here alone can modern man find authoritative evidence regarding his origins.

The writer of the Book of Genesis assumes the existence of God and begins the account with His divine act of Creation. God exists eternally and therefore has no beginning or end. He transcends the material universe. He has created and is separate from and greater than all created things. The Genesis account of Creation rests upon the theological presupposition that an intelligent personal God is the author of the universe.

Creation and Chaos

1:1 *In the beginning God created the heaven and the earth.*

Time had no place in eternity past but began with the Creation. The term "beginning" is time oriented. In this verse it applies to Creation. No date can be set for His Creation of the universe. The inspired Scriptures give only fleeting glimpses of eternity past. Those glimpses are confined to the decrees of God that relate to man's salvation (Eph. 1:4).

Creation is the work of the triune God. The Father was active as creator according to the opening verse of Genesis and verse 2 describes the Holy Spirit at work. The New Testament tells of Christ's involvement in Creation (John 1:1-3; Col. 1:16-17; Heb. 1:1-2).

Since there is a cause-and-effect relationship for everything, how did God create the universe from nothing? He created it from divine energy. Scientists tell us that all matter is energy when it is reduced down to its basic atomic structure. Men have been able to turn matter into various forms of energy, but they have not succeeded in turning energy into various forms of matter.

The word "heaven" used in verse 1 ought to be translated "heavens." The use of the plural suggests that the whole of the universe embracing the solar system and all systems of outer space were created at that time. Only about fifteen hundred stars can be seen with the naked eye. Astronomers with their powerful telescopes and other equipment have discovered innumerable heavenly bodies grouped in huge galaxies in outer space.

1:2a   *And the earth was without form, and void; and darkness was upon the face of the deep.*

There are two ways of approaching this verse. Some Bible scholars feel that God created the earth in some beautiful form but then allowed it to be convulsed into a formless mass. This chaotic condition is thought by those who hold that position to be the result of a divine judgment. They feel that this might explain the geological upheavals that have been discovered and the fossils of extinct animals which scientists try to date hundreds of thousands or even millions of years ago. Others feel that God created the earth as a formless mass and then proceeded to refine it and populate it during the six subsequent days of Creation. They leave the question of how the geological upheavals and fossils appeared unanswered for the time being, although some think there was plenty of time for these to appear if the days of Creation were eras rather than literal twenty-four-hour days.

1:2b   *And the Spirit of God moved upon the face of the waters.*

The Holy Spirit hovered over the waters covering the earth, much as a hen broods over her eggs while waiting for them to hatch. The picture presented here is one of preparation for the creative work soon to be done upon the earth. The Spirit is presented as being in perpetual action. Other Scripture passages indicate some of the particulars of the Spirit's work in Creation (Job 33:4; Ps. 104:30).

The Six Days of Creation

1:3-5 *And God said, Let there be light: and there was light.*

And God saw the light, that it was good: and God divided the light from the darkness.

And God called the light Day, and the darkness he called Night. And the evening and the morning were the first day.

The earth's surface was apparently covered with dense, murky vapors which would not permit the rays of the sun to shine through. God spoke and light was diffused throughout this mass of vapors. The language used implies that the earth rotated on its axis each twenty-four hours to provide daytime and nighttime.

Evangelical scholars have various views on this matter. Some think that each of the six days of Creation was a twenty-four-hour period. Others think that each day could have been an era of time lasting many years. One of the arguments is that Genesis 1:14-18 places the Creation of the sun, moon, and stars on the fourth day, meaning that there could have been no literal twenty-four-hour days before that happened. However, it has been suggested that verses 14-18 simply say that these heavenly bodies became visible from the surface of the earth for the first time, but that they had been created and were shining from the beginning (Gen. 1:1).

1:6-8 *And God said, Let there be a firmament in the midst of the waters, and let it divide the waters from the waters.*

And God made the firmament, and divided the waters which were under the firmament from the waters which were above the firmament: and it was so.

And God called the firmament Heaven. And the evening and the morning were the second day.

The earth's atmosphere now appeared as the heavy forms of water remained on its surface and the lighter forms lifted upward into vaporous clouds suspended above it. Air was needed for most forms of vegetation and animals equipped with lungs which were scheduled to appear on succeeding days.

1:9-13 *And God said, Let the waters under the heaven be gathered together unto one place, and let the dry land appear: and it was so.*

And God called the dry land Earth; and the gathering together of the waters called he Seas: and God saw that it was good.

And God said, Let the earth bring forth grass, the herb yielding seed, and the fruit tree yielding fruit after his kind, whose seed is in itself, upon the earth: and it was so.

And the earth brought forth grass, and herb yielding seed after his kind, and the tree yielding fruit, whose seed was in itself, after his kind: and God saw that it was good.

And the evening and the morning were the third day.

The surface of the earth was completely covered with water, but the Lord commanded land to rise up above it. Since water seeks its own level, it collected at the lower levels. Psalm 104:6-9 seems to describe how such a separation took place. Genesis 1:9 makes it appear as if all of the land was in one mass. It may have been that the continents were all joined together at one time. Scientists think they have evidence that they drifted apart as geological plates shifted. Many of the earthquakes we have today are due to such shifting. It is well known that some islands have been thrust up from the ocean floor by volcanic action, which explains why they are far from the continents.

The wording in verses 11-12 suggests that God brought forth plant life on the earth by causing seeds already there to regerminate. This would suggest that they may have flourished once before. Some might say that this points to a previous time of life which was cut off by a period of chaos (Gen. 1:1-2). Others might argue that God could

15

have placed the seeds in the earth during His act of Creation and then waited to bring forth vegetation for the first time on the third day.

1:14-19 *And God said, Let there be lights in the firmament of the heaven to divide the day from the night; and let them be for signs, and for seasons, and for days, and years:*

And let them be for lights in the firmament of the heaven to give light upon the earth: and it was so.

And God made two great lights; the greater light to rule the day, and the lesser light to rule the night: he made the stars also.

And God set them in the firmament of the heaven to give light upon the earth,

And to rule over the day and over the night, and to divide the light from the darkness: and God saw that it was good.

And the evening and the morning were the fourth day.

Some scholars believe that this section describes the actual Creation of the sun, moon, and stars, while others see this passage as describing the process by which these heavenly bodies became visible from the surface of the earth. The emphasis here is on their function, not on their creation, which Genesis 1:1 would appear to say took place at the beginning. The heavenly bodies were to be used for marking off days, seasons, and years. They were given as signs or tokens of God's providential care. They were to provide light for daytime and nighttime. The sun (which is a star) was placed so closely to earth that its great light rendered stars invisible during the daytime. Its rays reflected off the moon (which is a planet) to give subdued light to the earth during the nighttime at certain periods each month.

1:20-23 *And God said, Let the waters bring forth abundantly the moving creature that hath life, and fowl that may fly above the earth in the open firmament of heaven.*

16

And God created great whales, and every living creature that moveth, which the waters brought forth abundantly, after their kind, and every winged fowl after his kind: and God saw that it was good.

And God blessed them, saying, Be fruitful, and multiply, and fill the waters in the seas, and let fowl multiply in the earth.

And the evening and the morning were the fifth day.

The animal forms which God created on the fifth day were connected with the water and the air, although some of them no doubt crawled out onto the land or touched down on it when that was necessary. Sea creatures of all kinds and birds of all kinds were suddenly created to stock the earth, rather than evolving from lower forms of life as evolutionists try to claim. These verses are a strong defence of the Creation account against the claims of secular and theistic evolutionists.

It is interesting that God commanded these creatures to be fruitful, multiply, and fill the land and seas. It would appear that they could either understand and heed His command or that He communicated this to them by imparting instincts which they could not help but obey.

1:24-27 *And God said, Let the earth bring forth the living creature after his kind, cattle, and creeping thing, and beast of the earth after his kind: and it was so.*

And God made the beast of the earth after his kind, and cattle after their kind, and every thing that creepeth upon the earth after his kind: and God saw that it was good.

And God said, Let us make man in our image, after our likeness: and let them have dominion over the fish of the sea, and over the fowl of the air, and over the cattle, and over all the earth, and over every creeping thing that creepeth upon the earth.

So God created man in his own image, in the image of God created he him; male and female created he them.

The primary work of the sixth day was the Creation of land animals and man. Each was locked into its own par-

17

ticular species, although we know that some modifications within each species have taken place. It is interesting that the Genesis account makes the point repeatedly that God made each kind of animal "after his kind." There was no crossing over from one form of animal life to another and certainly not from animal life to human life.

The use of plural pronouns by God indicates the presence of the three Persons of the Godhead in the plan to make the first man and the first woman. Human beings were to be different from all other creatures in two distinct ways. First, they were to be made in God's image or likeness. Man would have an intelligence superior to that of animals, the ability to communicate freely by language, sensitive emotional capacities, sophisticated social relationships with others, personal consciences, and immortal souls designed to have fellowship with God. Second, they were to have dominion over all of earth's resources.

Verse 27 mentions the Creation of the first man and the first woman only in a general way. Details as to how God did this are reserved for Genesis 2:7 and 21-25.

In addition to what this verse says about the human personality it gives the first doctrinal statement about human sexuality. Verse 27 declares that humanity is bisexual inferring that males and females are equals and that they complement each other.

1:28-31 *And God blessed them, and God said unto them, Be fruitful, and multiply, and replenish the earth, and subdue it: and have dominion over the fish of the sea, and over the fowl of the air, and over every living thing that moveth upon the earth.*

And God said, Behold, I have given you every herb bearing seed, which is upon the face of all the earth, and every tree, in the which is the fruit of a tree yielding seed; to you it shall be for meat.

And to every beast of the earth, and to every fowl of the air, and to every thing that creepeth upon the earth, wherein there is life, I have given every green herb for meat: and it was so.

And God saw every thing that he had made, and,

behold, it was very good. And the evening and the morning were the sixth day.

God gave the command for the first couple to reproduce themselves and fill up the earth with their descendants. The word "replenish" gives the impression that there might have been people on earth previously, but we have no hard evidence of that. The command to multiply and to subdue the earth was tied to the fact that many people would be required to spread out and make such control complete. This may be why God later disapproved of people settling down at Babel. He scattered them out by confusing their language (Gen. 11:1-9).

Verses 29-30 suggest that all of the original animals, as well as the first couple, were to be vegetarians. The word "meat" here might better be translated as "food." The two categories mentioned were plants yielding seeds (such as grains) and fruit-bearing trees, whose seeds were encased in their fruit. It appears that no animals became carnivorous (preying on other creatures and eating their flesh) until after the Fall of man brought the curse of sin upon the earth. Animals will be on friendly terms with each other when the kingdom of Christ is set up sometime in the future (Isa. 11:6-7).

That God looked upon His completed Creation and considered all of it good is most reasonable. All that is disclosed about God in Scripture testifies to His perfections. Consistent with the perfections of His nature God made everything good in Creation.

Creation and God's Rest

2:1, 2 *Thus the heavens and the earth were finished, and all the host of them.*
And on the seventh day God ended his work which he had made; and he rested on the seventh day from all his work which he had made.

God ended His creative work with the Creation of the first human couple. All of the species of living things had been made. From that time forward, plants, animals, and people would increase by reproduction. Minerals would be discovered, unearthed, modified, and used by men, but they would not reproduce themselves.

God did not rest because He was tired. "Hast thou not heard, that the everlasting God, the Lord, the Creator of the ends of the earth, fainteth not, neither is weary?" (Isa. 40:28). That initial Sabbath was the rest of achievement. By sanctifying the seventh day, God provided a model for man to follow for themselves and the animals they domesticate and use for work.

2:3 *And God blessed the seventh day, and sanctified it: because that in it he had rested from all his work which God created and made.*

God set the seventh day apart as a day to be different from the other six in the traditional unit of time known as a week. He did not do this to put a burden upon people. He did it to help them have time for rest and worship. When the Pharisees denounced the disciples of Jesus for husking and eating a few kernels of grain on the Sabbath Day, He replied, "The sabbath was made for man, and not man for the sabbath" (Mark 2:27).

Because Christ rose on Sunday, the first day of the week, that became the Lord's Day for Christians. This basic principle for allotting time to rest from the usual labors and spiritual renewal by worship is still valid for modern man.

Creation and Additional Details

2:4-6 *These are the generations of the heavens and of the earth when they were created, in the day that the Lord God made the earth and the heavens,*
And every plant of the field before it was in the earth, and every herb of the field before it grew: for the Lord God had not caused it to rain upon the earth, and there was not a man to till the ground.
But there went up a mist from the earth, and watered the whole face of the ground.

We now move on to what came from God's original Creation. No shrubs or plants grew until moisture was provided to make their seeds in the ground germinate. That must have happened on the third day of Creation (Gen. 1:11-12). He did not send rain for this, but caused vapor to rise up and moisten the surface of the earth. This was gentler than the rainstorms which came later.

2:7 *And the Lord God formed man of the dust of the ground, and breathed into his nostrils the breath of life; and man became a living soul.*

This provides additional details concerning the Creation of the first man, Adam, as mentioned in Genesis 1:27. There is no hint here of evolvement from lower animal forms. God made Adam from the dust of the earth and then breathed into his nostrils the breath of life to make him a living creature. When God takes away the breath of men or animals, they return to dust (Ps. 104:29). However, the soul of man lives on after death to face an eternity of blessedness or damnation, depending on his response to or rejection of the gospel of Christ. That body of dust will either be resurrected and glorified at Christ's coming (1 Cor. 15:51-53; 1 Thess. 4:13-18), or it will be resurrected to stand before Him at the great white throne judgment (Rev. 20:11-15).

2:8, 9 *And the Lord God planted a garden eastward in Eden; and there he put the man whom he had formed.*
And out of the ground made the Lord God to grow every tree that is pleasant to the sight, and good for food; the tree of life also in the midst of the garden, and the tree of knowledge of good and evil.

The garden of Eden is thought to have been in ancient Mesopotamia. It was a delightful place, perhaps much like a large park. Here Adam was placed to watch over God's Creation. Fruit-bearing trees were natural and plentiful. The tree of life reminded him of God's goodness. The tree of knowledge of good and evil reminded him of his need to be obedient to God.

2:10-14 *And a river went out of Eden to water the*

21

garden; and from thence it was parted, and became into four heads.

The name of the first is Pison: that is it which compasseth the whole land of Havilah, where there is gold;

And the gold of that land is good: there is bdellium and the onyx stone.

And the name of the second river is Gihon: the same is it that compasseth the whole land of Ethiopia.

And the name of the third river is Hiddekel: that is it which goeth toward the east of Assyria. And the fourth river is Euphrates.

A river of Eden flowed into, through, and out of the garden where God had placed Adam. Beyond there it divided into four rivers. The Pison (or Pishon) flowed across or around the land of Havilah located along the border of Babylon. High quality gold was there, as well as bdellium (probably a milky quartz spotted with gold particles) and onyx stone (a form of chalcedony). The Gihon flowed across or around the land of Cush in Mesopotamia. The reason Ethiopia is mentioned may be due to the fact that it was settled by descendants of Cush, the oldest son of Ham and a grandson of Noah. The Hiddekel (Hebrew name) is better known as the Tigris (Assyrian name). It formed the eastern boundary of Mesopotamia. The Euphrates, longest and most important river of Western Asia, formed the western boundary of Mesopotamia. The name of Mesopotamia means "between the rivers," no doubt referring to the Tigris and the Euphrates.

2:15-17 *And the Lord God took the man, and put him into the garden of Eden to dress it and to keep it.*

And the Lord God commanded the man, saying, Of every tree of the garden thou mayest freely eat:

But of the tree of the knowledge of good and evil, thou shalt not eat of it: for in the day that thou eatest thereof thou shalt surely die.

God placed Adam in the garden of Eden and gave them the responsibility to cultivate and care for it. They were permitted to eat of all of the fruit of the trees growing there with one exception. The fruit from the tree of knowledge of good and evil was forbidden them. This fruit would give its eater the ability to know right from wrong. Just the partaking of it would be wrong, for it would show disobedience to God's explicit command. This was man's first moral test while in his original state of innocence. The day in which it was eaten would mark the beginning of physical deterioration eventually ending in death. It is obvious that Adam did not literally die on the day he failed his moral test, for he went on to live until he was nine hundred and thirty years of age (Gen. 5:5). Failing the test first brought spiritual death, for the curse of sin came down upon Adam and his descendants. This basic historical fact about man's fallen condition is essential to understanding the plan of redemption which unfolds throughout the remainder of the Bible. The incarnation of Christ, His death and Resurrection were to destroy the effects of sin. "For as in Adam all die, even so in Christ shall all [who put their faith in Him] be made alive" (1 Cor. 15:22).

2:18-20 *And the Lord God said, It is not good that the man should be alone; I will make him an help meet for him.*

And out of the ground the Lord God formed every beast of the field, and every fowl of the air; and brought them unto Adam to see what he would call them: and whatsoever Adam called every living creature, that was the name thereof.

And Adam gave names to all cattle, and to the fowl of the air, and to every beast of the field; but for Adam there was not found an help meet for him.

God Himself established marriage and the family. The family, then, was the primary social institution from a historical perspective and after all these millenniums still has priority. The social and spiritual well-being of any people is dependent on a wholesome family life. God knew that it was not good for Adam to be alone, so a search for a companion was begun. Various types of animals were paraded before Adam so that he could give them names and become acquainted with them. This experience made him well aware of the fact that none of them could satisfy his need for companionship. It may have been that this procedure made Adam aware of his need and therefore prepared him for the day God would create Eve and present her to him.

> 2:21-25 *And the Lord God caused a deep sleep to fall upon Adam, and he slept: and he took one of his ribs, and closed up the flesh instead thereof;*
> *And the rib, which the Lord God had taken from man, made he a woman, and brought her unto the man.*
> *And Adam said, This is now bone of my bones, and flesh of my flesh: she shall be called Woman, because she was taken out of Man.*
> *Therefore shall a man leave his father and his mother, and shall cleave unto his wife: and they shall be one flesh.*
> *And they were both naked, the man and his wife, and were not ashamed.*

God put Adam into a deep sleep by means of divine anesthetic and then took part of his side out of his body. From this material He expanded and fashioned another human being to provide for Adam a female companion such as each animal already had. She was made in such a way that she would complement him physically and emotionally. Each would be incomplete without the other. Adam was evidently delighted when God presented her to him. He called her Woman. Later he named her Eve, meaning "life-giver," because she was the original mother of the human race (Gen. 3:20).

Jesus quoted from verse 24 when he told the Pharisees that God intended for husbands and wives to remain together (Mark 10:6-9). It is unfortunate that this ideal has often been marred by divorce.

Adam and Eve were naked but were not embarrassed by it in each other's presence. Only after they later yielded to eating the forbidden fruit and lost their original innocence were they ashamed of their lack of clothes (Gen. 3:7).

Summary

God was in complete charge of Creation. He spoke the universe into existence. He made the earth special by furnishing it with water, minerals, vegetation, animal life, and human beings. It was all good, and it brought glory to Him. With the Creation of Adam and Eve, God set the stage for the development of the human race.

Much of the Book of Genesis is occupied with the lives and experiences of three men and their descendants. The first segment of the book deals with Adam and his family. Beginning with chapter 6 Noah's family becomes the center of the narrative. Abraham, the father of the faithful, emerges at chapter 12. The rest of Genesis tells the story of his seed and God's dealings with them. These patriarchs were not perfect by any means, but they increasingly came to know God and His will. Their experiences, both failures and victories, are rich in the spiritual principles they teach. Those same principles are still relevant to those who walk with God today.

2

The Fall of Man

Genesis 3:1-24

Adam and Eve were truly unique in many ways. They were the first human couple and thus the father and mother of the whole human race. They were created mature adults by the hands of God. The home of this primeval pair was a paradise where hard physical labor was not necessary. They were by no means idle but spent their energies in the oversight and care of the garden. The highest privilege they enjoyed was direct communion with God on a daily basis. How long this state of happiness and perfection continued, the Scriptures do not indicate. The third chapter of Genesis preserves the tragic account of the Fall of Adam and Eve and the termination of Edenic bliss. The story of the Fall has many doctrinal overtones. Throughout the Old and New Testament references are made to the event and its aftermath.

Fall from Innocence

3:1a *Now the serpent was more subtil than any beast of the field which the Lord God had made.*

The serpent, as a species, is given only one characteristic in this description. Its subtleness (craftiness, shrewdness, cunning) is mentioned. Jewish tradition claimed that it could walk erect before God cursed it to crawling or slithering for locomotion (Gen. 3:14). It was capable of reasoning and of speech. Eve did not appear to be surprised when a particular serpent talked with her. It must have seemed natural.

From what is written in later Scriptures, it is evident that the serpent was used as a tool of Satan. In fact, Satan has often been referred to as a serpent. Jesus called Satan a liar and the father of lies (John 8:44). As a member of the spirit world, Satan used the serpent to beguile Eve (2 Cor.

11:3-4). He is a fallen angel, but he can give himself the appearance of "an angel of light" (2 Cor. 11:14). Harsh terms are used for him in Revelation 12:9 and 20:2— "dragon," "that old serpent," "the Devil," "Satan, which deceiveth the whole world." His fate is to be the lake of fire (Rev. 20:10).

> 3:1b-3 *And he said unto the woman, Yea, hath God said, Ye shall not eat of every tree of the garden?*
> *And the woman said unto the serpent, We may eat of the fruit of the trees of the garden:*
> *But of the fruit of the tree which is in the midst of the garden, God hath said, Ye shall not eat of it, neither shall ye touch it, lest ye die.*

The cunning of Satan, as he worked through the serpent, was soon apparent. Eve had not had any dealings with evil before, so she was not fortified to withstand this kind of temptation. The serpent first seemed to suggest that Eve might have misunderstood what God had said about the trees of the garden. Eve countered this by stating that she was sure of what God had said. She and Adam were allowed to eat the fruit of all of the trees but the one in the middle of the garden of Eden. This was known as the "tree of the knowledge of good and evil" (Gen. 2:17). We do not know what kind of fruit it produced. Only legend labels its fruit as apples. It stood beside the "tree of life" (Gen. 2:9). The Living Bible refers to it as "the Tree of Conscience." Adam and Eve were later prohibited from eating the fruit of the tree of life, as well.

> 3:4, 5 *And the serpent said unto the woman, Ye shall not surely die:*
> *For God doth know that in the day ye eat thereof, then your eyes shall be opened, and ye shall be as gods, knowing good and evil.*

The serpent assumed the role of a teacher. It told Eve that the fruit of the forbidden tree was not actually poisonous and that it would not cause physical death if it were eaten. The thought was introduced that eating of the fruit

27

would have a beneficial effect. It would make one wise (v. 6) by allowing that person to know the difference between good and evil. Eve had no knowledge of evil, and her curiosity was stirred by this statement. She was told that eating the fruit would upgrade her to the level of God (or gods). She was ambitious for this kind of experience. She failed to ask God if it was all right with Him, for she knew better than to do that. She failed to consult with Adam before doing it. She made the decision on her own after being deceived by the serpent.

> 3:6 *And when the woman saw that the tree was good for food, and that it was pleasant to the eyes, and a tree to be desired to make one wise, she took of the fruit thereof, and did eat, and gave also unto her husband with her; and he did eat.*

Three things made the fruit of the tree of the knowledge of good and evil attractive to Eve. She could see for herself that it was appetizing and beautiful. She believed what the serpent had told her about it having the ability to make her wise. She probably reached out with trembling hands to pluck it from the branch, for she knew in her heart that she was disobeying God's explicit command. Her fear of dying was gone. She bit into it, and it was indeed delicious. It was so good that she offered it to Adam, and he ate of it, too.

There is a question as to Adam's motivation for eating the fruit. Perhaps Eve took it away from the center of the garden and gave it to him in another location. Perhaps he did not realize that it was the forbidden fruit, especially if he was hungry and if it looked similar to other kinds of fruit. While this kind of speculation is interesting, the divine explanation of this event is found in the New Testament.

The reference is found in the pastoral Epistles where Paul was writing to Timothy about the fact that a woman ought to be in submission to her husband. He wrote, "For Adam was first formed, then Eve. And Adam was not deceived, but the woman being deceived was in the transgression" (1 Tim. 2:13-14). It would appear, therefore, that Adam ate the forbidden fruit deliberately, and not because he was deceived about it. It has been suggested by those of a romantic frame of mind that Adam loved Eve so much that he ate the fruit in order to share her fate, whatever that was to be. In any case, they were both now guilty of disobeying the command of God.

The wording here is so simple that we must not overlook its tremendous significance. By his act of disobedience, Adam as the federal head of the human race, brought the curse of sin crashing down upon mankind and on the whole Creation. It would take a "second Adam" to eventually lift that curse. "For as in Adam all die, even so in Christ shall all be made alive" (1 Cor. 15:22).

3:7 *And the eyes of them both were opened, and they knew that they were naked; and they sewed fig leaves together, and made themselves aprons.*

The serpent had told Eve the truth about the level of understanding regarding good and evil she would receive. After eating the forbidden fruit, both Adam and Eve suddenly realized feelings of shame and guilt for the first time. What they felt in their hearts they also found reflected in their view of themselves. They felt uncovered, exposed, and guilty about their nakedness. Stringing together some fig leaves, they made simple skirts to cover their waists and put them on.

Fellowship Broken

3:8 *And they heard the voice of the Lord God walking in the garden in the cool of the day: and Adam and his wife hid themselves from the presence of the Lord God amongst the trees of the garden.*

The implication here is that God came down each evening to fellowship with Adam and Eve. They could hear Him walking in the garden and calling to them. Since God is a Spirit with no body (John 4:24), we wonder how this was possible. As in other cases, this may have been a theophany (physical appearance of God). Their fellowship with their Creator up to this time had been sweet.

That blessed communion was disrupted the very day Adam and Eve fell in sin. Instead of rushing to meet God, as was their usual manner, they hid back in the trees. They were ashamed of themselves. They were filled with remorse. They were afraid. These emotions were strange to them, for they had never felt them before. God kept seeking them, for there was important work to be done with this first pair.

> 3:9, 10 *And the Lord God called unto Adam, and said unto him, Where art thou?*
> *And he said, I heard thy voice in the garden, and I was afraid, because I was naked; and I hid myself.*

The Lord knew, of course, where Adam and Eve were, but He wanted them to reveal themselves to Him. Contact had to be made before corrective measures could be taken. The Lord takes sinful people just as they are, and then the remedial work begins.

Adam replied that his reason for concealment was fear and shame. We do not know why he did not mention Eve. Perhaps he spoke for both of them, since Eve was supposed to be under his protective custody. We can hardly attribute anything too noble to Adam as far as shielding Eve was concerned, for he soon put the blame for his disobedience on her (v. 12). Adam's argument here was weak, for he had covered part of himself with fig leaves and therefore was not entirely naked. It may be that he was unsure of what constituted nakedness and wondered if he should be covered more than he was before God saw him.

> 3:11 *And he said, Who told thee that thou wast naked? Hast thou eaten of the tree, whereof I commanded thee that thou shouldest not eat?*

God knew the answers to these questions, too, but He wanted Adam to confess his sin. This has always been God's way. Confession must precede forgiveness. God's commandment had been disobeyed. A sin had been committed, and God was calling on Adam to admit that he was a sinner. It was not easy for Adam to do it then, and it has not become any easier for his descendants to do it ever since that time. However, it is absolutely necessary to spiritual restoration and blessing.

3:12 *And the man said, The woman whom thou gavest to be with me, she gave me of the tree, and I did eat.*

This was a confession on Adam's part, but notice how he tried to soften his responsibility by blaming Eve for what he did. He even sought to put the blame on the Lord by saying that it was the woman whom *He* had given him that had made him disobedient. Sinful human nature just naturally tries to shift the blame for sin off oneself. It began with the first man, and it has been practiced ever since. God does not want this. He desires an individual to openly admit his sin and be prepared to take the consequences. Because responsibility cannot be shifted, a person deserves whatever judgment and punishment he gets.

3:13 *And the Lord God said unto the woman, What is this that thou hast done? And the woman said, The serpent beguiled me, and I did eat.*

Without recorded comment, the Lord turned to Eve and pursued the thought which had been raised by Adam. This does not imply that God had accepted Adam's excuse. It simply means that God wanted Eve to voice her confession. Following Adam's example, Eve sought to shift blame onto the serpent. The serpent could have tried to put the blame onto Satan, but nothing is said about his attempting that. The serpent, Eve, and Adam now had to await God's decision regarding judgment on them, and it was not long in coming.

Fates Declared

3:14 *And the Lord God said unto the serpent, Because thou hast done this, thou art cursed above all cattle, and above every beast of the field; upon thy belly shalt thou go, and dust shalt thou eat all the days of thy life:*

31

The Jewish legend that serpents once were upright seems to gain support from this verse. The strong implication is that the serpent was drastically humbled from what it was to as low in esteem as it could be. There are some snake lovers in the world, but most people seem to abhor such animals. Signs of their previous beauty may be seen in the markings of snakes and in their smooth, flowing movements. However, just the sight of one slithering along the ground is enough to make many people run away or look for a weapon to use against it. The fear of being injected with poison by the snake's fangs can cause terror. The hissing and rattling associated with some draw negative responses. The very word "snake" has become a byword for despicable behavior. There is revulsion against snakes which can cause death by poison. This is even greater in the case of the boa constrictor, which crushes its victims, swallows them whole, and then takes a long period of time to digest the grotesque bulge in its body.

3:15 *And I will put enmity between thee and the woman, and between thy seed and her seed; it shall bruise thy head, and thou shalt bruise his heel.*

This is generally accepted as the first reference to the Messiah who was to come much later in the history of mankind. The literal serpent was backed by the invisible fallen angel known as Satan. The battle lines were clearly drawn between Christ and Satan at the dawn of time. The drama has been played out in the heavens and on the earth ever since.

People seem to have been divided between the righteous and the unrighteous from the beginning. Abel apparently had no children, but the godly line descended from his brother Seth. Cain killed Abel but was allowed to live, and his descendants constituted an ungodly line. This is not to say that all of Seth's descendants were righteous or that all of Cain's descendants were unrighteous. It does, however, symbolize the fact that men have moved along contrasting tracks throughout the history of the human race.

Satan and his hosts of fallen angels (demons, evil

32

spirits) have persuaded most men to remain in their sins and be part of his army. Christ, the Seed (Descendant) of Eve, marches at the head of the good angels and of the Church which is composed of believers.

These contrary forces are locked in mortal conflict. At His first advent, Christ was hurt by Satan at His Crucifixion, but at the same time He dealt Satan a fatal blow. Having paid the penalty demanded by God by making atonement for sin at Calvary, Christ destroyed Satan's claim to the souls of men.

The final resolution of the long conflict is yet in the future, but the time is coming when Satan will be consigned to the lake of fire forever, and Christ will reign over all. Adam and Eve probably had little or no conception of the implications of what God said to the serpent (and to Satan) in the garden, but they knew that divine judgment had been exercised. Scholars for centuries afterward were to ponder the meaning of God's pronouncement.

> 3:16 *Unto the woman he said, I will greatly multiply thy sorrow and thy conception; in sorrow thou shalt bring forth children; and thy desire shall be to thy husband, and he shall rule over thee.*

The Lord told Eve that she (and other women yet to come) would suffer physical pain and emotional distress in bearing children. In spite of this, she would be drawn to her husband, thus placing herself in the position of going through that suffering repeatedly. She was created to be a "help meet for him" (Gen. 2:20), but now her role as his companion would be a submissive one. Paul used this as an argument for requiring women to be in subjection to their husbands. He coupled with it a promise that they would "be saved [preserved] in childbearing, if they [would] continue in faith and charity and holiness with sobriety" (1 Tim. 2:11-15). The modern women's liberation movement would do well to consider this scriptural teaching. The Bible guards against any male tyranny in marriage. Paul said that men should love their wives, even as Christ loved the Church (Eph. 5:22-33).

> 3:17 *And unto Adam he said, Because thou hast*

hearkened unto the voice of thy wife, and hast eaten of the tree, of which I commanded thee, saying, Thou shalt not eat of it: cursed is the ground for thy sake; in sorrow shalt thou eat of it all the days of thy life;

Adam had previously tended and cultivated the garden of Eden, which means that he had not been indolent (Gen. 2:15). Now he was told that the natural fertility of the ground was cursed. Adam (and his descendants) would have to work hard all of their lives in order to grow enough food to survive. This would be especially true outside of the garden.

3:18 *Thorns also and thistles shall it bring forth to thee; and thou shalt eat the herb of the field;*

For thousands of years most of the people on the earth were engaged in agriculture for their livelihood. That is still true in many parts of the world today, although only about 6 percent of the American population is involved in growing food. Thorns, thistles, and all kinds of weeds have made farmers' lot a hard one. Even with modern pesticides and farming machinery, agriculture is a demanding way of life. In some areas, when crops fail, the people are forced to eat wild plants and grasses. Malnutrition and starvation still plague mankind in some places.

3:19 *In the sweat of thy face shalt thou eat bread, till thou return unto the ground; for out of it wast thou taken: for dust thou art, and unto dust shalt thou return.*

God did not say that Adam would die of starvation, but He said that he would have to work very hard to get the food he needed for survival. In the end he would die and turn back to dust from which he had been made in the first place (Gen. 2:7). This was a far different prospect from what Adam had viewed his life before he fell from innocence.

God had told Adam that "in the day that thou eatest thereof [the forbidden fruit] thou shalt surely die" (Gen. 2:17). The serpent had told Eve, "Ye shall not surely die"

(Gen. 3:4). We are not told how long Eve lived, but we do know that Adam lived for nine hundred and thirty years (Gen. 5:5). This may sound contradictory, but it is not. The day that Adam and Eve disobeyed God, they *began* to die. The curse of sin brought many enemies to mankind. Christ came to destroy them, but "the last enemy that shall be destroyed is death" (1 Cor. 15:26). The fact that Adam took hundreds of years to be claimed by death does not change the fact that he started down that road on the day he fell under the curse of sin.

Future Assured

3:20 *And Adam called his wife's name Eve; because she was the mother of all living.*

Up to this point Eve had simply been called Woman (Gen. 2:23). Now he honored her by calling her Eve, meaning "life-spring," "life-giver," or "life-giving one." It is amazing to think that each of us carries within us genetic links stretching back to this one mother of the human race. No one can take this distinction away from her.

3:21 *Unto Adam also and to his wife did the Lord God make coats of skins, and clothed them.*

This is an interesting verse, even if some commentators give it little or no attention. Up to the time of the Fall, it appears that both people and animals were vegetarians (Gen. 1:29-30—change "meat" to "food"). When the curse came upon the world, the animals came under it, too. Some of them continued to be vegetarians, but others became carnivorous, preying on other animals and consuming them. It may be that God used the hides of animals already slain to make tunics for Adam and Eve to wear. On the other hand, He may have slain animals for this purpose or had Adam and Eve do it. If He slew animals or had them do it, the effect is the same. Animals had to die in order for people to be covered. This took on a spiritual application from that time forward. It culminated in the death of Christ. It was because Christ took our place that we can be covered by His righteousness (2 Cor. 5:21). Righteousness is going to be the eternal clothing of redeemed men and women (Rev. 19:8).

> 3:22, 23 *And the Lord God said, Behold, the man is become as one of us, to know good and evil: and now, lest he put forth his hand, and take also of the tree of life, and eat, and live for ever:*
>
> *Therefore the Lord God sent him forth from the garden of Eden, to till the ground from whence he was taken.*

At first glance this would appear to be a very negative action on God's part. Adam and Eve were expelled from their paradise. We are not told what it was like outside of that special place. The wording implies that it was less attractive and productive. It was going to be an entirely different kind of life for the first couple from what they had known. However, expulsion from the garden is seen by some as an act of divine mercy.

It has been suggested that God drove Adam and Eve out of the garden so that they would not delude themselves into thinking that the fruit from the tree of life could cause them to live forever, a right which they had forfeited by disobedience. On the other hand, a more acceptable view holds that God drove them out in order to prevent them from eating of that tree and thus locking them into an unending life of sin and the miseries that sin brings. Seen in that light, the expulsion could be understood as an act of divine mercy.

Experience has taught us that many of the things which appear to be negative for us are actually positive. God sees the end from the beginning. He knows what is best for us. He may have to restrain us at times for our own good. We chafe under this restraint, but later we praise Him for it. "And we know that all things work together for good to them that love God, to them who are the called according to his purpose" (Rom. 8:28).

> 3:24 *So he drove out the man; and he placed at the east of the garden of Eden Cherubims, and a flaming*

sword which turned every way, to keep the way of the tree of life.

Cherubim is a transliteration of the plural form of a Hebrew word for one kind of angelic being. These mysterious creatures were angels who ministered personally to God the Father. Their presence indicated His presence. Therefore, it may be safe to assume that God himself was posted at the eastern gate of Eden to keep people away from the tree of life. God later told Israel through Moses, "There I will meet with thee [in the holy of holies in the tabernacle], and I will commune with thee from above the mercy seat, from between the two cherubims which are upon the ark of the testimony" (Exod. 25:22). There are many references to cherubim in the Bible, and these may be found by using an exhaustive concordance or Bible dictionary. They were quite different from the fanciful cherubs pictured on typical Valentine Day cards.

Along with the cherubim there was a revolving, flaming sword placed at the east gate of Eden to bar entrance. This may also have been a symbol of God's presence and power. No other gates are mentioned or implied in our text. Whatever arrangement God had for protecting the garden of Eden, this appears to have been the only way to go into it, and this was off-limits to people.

Change has always been part of living. Adam and Eve sadly made their way out of their paradise. They turned to face the uncertain future stretching out before them. They had to adjust to an alien land and a struggle for existence. However, they knew that God was with them. They were called upon to trust God for help in this new and difficult life outside the garden of Eden.

Little is said about them in the remainder of the Book of Genesis. They had two sons named Cain and Abel (Gen. 4:1-2). A son whom they named Seth was born to them when Adam was a hundred and thirty years old (Gen. 5:3). During the next eight centuries they had many more sons and daughters (Gen. 5:4). Adam died at the age of nine hundred and thirty years (Gen. 5:5).

Summary

The events recorded in chapter 3 of Genesis had deep significance not only for Adam and Eve but for the whole human race. Because of what they did, we today are living under the continuing curse of sin, with all which is involved with that condition. Satan, the father of lies, moved the serpent to deceive Eve into eating the forbidden fruit. She, in turn, persuaded Adam to eat it, although he was not deceived.

God questioned the first couple about their disobedience. He declared punishments upon the serpent, Adam, and Eve. Animals were slain to provide them with coverings, a fitting symbol of the covering for sin which Christ would one day provide by His death on the cross. God mercifully expelled Adam and Eve from the garden of Eden to prevent them from eating of the tree of life and thus perpetuating themselves in an endless state of sinfulness. As they left, He went with them to help them adjust to their new life.

3

The Sons of Adam

Genesis 4:1—5:32

In Genesis 4 three of Adam's sons were born. Their lives and actions illustrate the conflict between the godly and the ungodly seed. Chapters 4 and 5 relate a number of "firsts" in human history. The first sin offerings were made, one of which was acceptable, while the other was not. The first murder came as a result of Cain's rejection. Glimpses are given of the first crafts and art forms. The first city was built by Cain and his family.

Genesis 5 relates the death of Adam, the first of its kind and gives the first biblical genealogy. From an historical perspective these chapters trace the godly line to the time of Noah and the great Flood. The tragic murder of Cain produced a problem in perpetuating the godly seed. God intervened by giving Adam, Seth who took up Abel's place in the line of true believers.

Sin Offerings

4:1 *And Adam knew Eve his wife; and she conceived, and bare Cain, and said, I have gotten a man from the Lord.*

Adam and Eve had been created as full-grown individuals by the Lord. All others were to come into existence by birth from human parents. The one exception, of course, was the virgin birth of Jesus. He was conceived in Mary by the Holy Spirit, and not by a human father. Jesus, however, was born of woman and became truly incarnate in human flesh.

Adam "knew" Eve in the most intimate way (sexual intercourse). This passage gives a helpful insight into the biblical understanding of sex within the marriage relationship. The Hebrew word for knowledge implies the exercise of the affections. The increase of understanding regarding the marriage partner deepens the affections and enriches the physical aspect of the relationship. She conceived and Cain was born. His name meant "possession," "acquisition," "created," or "gotten." Eve explained that she had "gotten a man from the Lord." She seemed happy about it. It may have been that Eve thought Cain was the promised Messiah. This could be the reason of her great joy at his birth. She would eventually learn that Cain was basically ungodly and not the promised deliverer.

4:2 *And she again bare his brother Abel. And Abel was a keeper of sheep, but Cain was a tiller of the ground.*

The second child born to Adam and Eve was named Abel. His name meant "exhalation," "fleeting breath," "vapor," "that which ascends," or "transitoriness." We are not told why this name was chosen for him. No indication is given as to how she felt about this second son. When they had both grown to maturity, Abel became a shepherd, while Cain became a farmer growing crops. These were two of the most important occupations throughout history until modern times. In many parts of the third world they still have priority.

4:3-5a *And in process of time it came to pass, that Cain brought of the fruit of the ground an offering unto the Lord.*
And Abel, he also brought of the firstlings of his flock and of the fat thereof. And the Lord had respect unto Abel and to his offering:
But unto Cain and to his offering he had not respect.

Although this is the first record of the presentation of offerings to the Lord, no doubt Adam and Eve had done this previously. The principle of substitutionary sacrifice had been taught them by the Lord and Adam and Eve had taught this truth to their sons. It seemed natural for Cain to bring grain as his offering. Later under Levitical law such offerings were received by the Lord for certain purposes but they were inappropriate for a sin offering. Abel

40

brought animal sacrifices, the offering of which required the death of the victim. Without the shedding of blood there is no remission of sins. The blood sacrifice continued through Old Testament days until Christ presented Himself as the fulfillment of all true sacrifices.

Cain apparently did not take seriously the necessity for the shedding of blood, and the death of the sacrificial animal. However, the problem with Cain seemed to be more than the kind of offering he brought. His attitudes and actions were evil. Jesus called Abel "righteous" (Matt. 23:35). The writer of the Epistle to the Hebrews did, too (Heb. 11:4). John claimed that Abel's works were "righteous," but that Cain's works were "evil" (1 John 3:12). Since righteousness is by faith, Abel was righteous in that he presented the slain sacrifice in obedient faith. Cain's disobedience indicates his lack of faith.

> 4:5*b*-7 *And Cain was very wroth, and his countenance fell.*
> *And the Lord said unto Cain, Why art thou wroth? and why is thy countenance fallen?*
> *If thou doest well, shalt thou not be accepted? and if thou doest not well, sin lieth at the door. And unto thee shall be his desire, and thou shalt rule over him.*

We are not told *how* God showed approval of Abel's sacrifice or withheld it from Cain's sacrifice. Perhaps flame came down to consume the animal sacrifice of Abel. In any case, Cain was very angry at the rejection of his offering. He showed the kind of negative heart attitude which made him unacceptable to the Lord. What was in his heart showed on his face.

Now God dealt firmly but gently with Cain. He said that corrective measures could be taken. Otherwise, Cain stood in jeopardy of being consumed by his sinful emotion. Interpretation of verse 7 is not unanimous. Some would say it meant that sin was a monster waiting to devour Cain. Others would say that an animal suitable for a sin offering crouched at the door, and Cain could overpower it and offer it up to the Lord as a suitable sacrifice. We are not told what Cain did in response to the remarks made by God to him. From what is recorded next, it is apparent that Cain was unwilling to solve his sin problem.

Sin of Murder

> 4:8 *And Cain talked with Abel his brother: and it came to pass, when they were in the field, that Cain rose up against Abel his brother, and slew him.*

The wording here does not tell us what kind of a conversation Cain had with Abel. Perhaps it was an argument. Perhaps it was at least outwardly peaceful. Perhaps Cain invited Abel to take a walk out in his field. Once they were alone, Cain overcame Abel and slew him. Blood was shed (v. 11), although there is no mention of Cain using a weapon. Thus began the sin of murder, which, after thousands of years, still remains a major crime problem. It is usually categorized as premeditated or spontaneous. We are not told which kind this was.

> 4:9, 10 *And the Lord said unto Cain, Where is Abel thy brother? And he said, I know not: Am I my brother's keeper?*
> *And he said, What hast thou done? the voice of thy brother's blood crieth unto me from the ground.*

The Lord knew what had happened, but He posed as one searching for Abel. This gave Cain an opportunity to confess his sin and seek God's forgiveness. Cain not only refused to confess, but he lied to the Lord. He then added insult to injury by asking if God expected him to watch over his brother as a shepherd takes care of a sheep. The Lord now became more direct, asking Cain what he had done to Abel, but Cain again refused to confess his sin. The Lord gave the spilled blood of Abel a personality of its own by stating that it cried out for vengeance to Him. At that moment Cain must have realized that he could not deceive God.

> 4:11, 12 *And now art thou cursed from the earth, which hath opened her mouth to receive thy brother's blood from thy hand;*

When thou tillest the ground, it shall not henceforth yield unto thee her strength; a fugitive and a vagabond shalt thou be in the earth.

It is interesting that the sentence on Adam for eating the forbidden fruit was a curse on the ground, making it difficult to grow food from it, and that a similar sentence was imposed on Cain. It appears that his normal occupation of farmer was going to be so difficult that he would choose to become a wandering nomad, perhaps caring for the animals which Abel used to have. We do not know why God did not require Cain's life, for that was to be the punishment for murder after the great Flood (Gen. 9:6). Perhaps it was due to the scarcity of men on the earth that God allowed Cain to continue living.

4:13, 14 *And Cain said unto the Lord, My punishment is greater than I can bear.*
Behold, thou hast driven me out this day from the face of the earth; and from thy face shall I be hid; and I shall be a fugitive and a vagabond in the earth; and it shall come to pass, that every one that findeth me shall slay me.

Cain's remarks reveal some interesting things about his twisted personality. He did not seem to be remorseful for murdering Abel. He was upset over the fact that he was caught and punished. He did not seem to be grateful that his life had been spared. He resented being separated from human society. He felt that God would abandon him when he stopped farming and left his settled way of life. He was afraid that whoever he met as a wanderer would try to kill him. Whatever people there were, were closely related, for there had not yet been much time for the world's population to build up. Cain's inner weaknesses included the inability to face up to his punishment as a man should.

4:15 *And the Lord said unto him, Therefore whosoever slayeth Cain, vengeance shall be taken on him sevenfold. And the Lord set a mark upon Cain, lest any finding him should kill him.*

God listened to Cain's plea and then decided to provide protection for him. The reason for this remains a mystery. The Lord promised to take a sevenfold vengeance on anyone killing Cain. This probably meant that anyone bold enough to slay Cain would himself die, along with six other members of his family. No one knows what the "mark" or "sign" was which God placed upon Cain to warn men to leave him alone. Ideas range from some physical mark to a ferocious appearance. It worked, for he went on to build a city east of Eden.

Signs of Development

4:16, 17 *And Cain went out from the presence of the Lord, and dwelt in the land of Nod, on the east of Eden. And Cain knew his wife; and she conceived, and bare Enoch: and he builded a city and called the name of the city, after the name of his son, Enoch.*

Evidently the area called Eden was the place of God's blessing, even though the curse of sin was on it. Adam and Eve had been driven out of the garden of Eden, but Cain and his wife were driven out of Eden altogether. They went eastward to the land they named Nod, which means "wandering," "flight," or "exile." They were there long enough for Cain's wife to conceive and bear a son named Enoch (but *not* the same Enoch mentioned in Gen. 5:21-24). They remained there long enough for Cain to direct the building of a community called Enoch in honor of his son. We do not know how long Cain lived there, but he seemed to have settled down for a long period. Perhaps God rescinded the requirement that he be a perpetual vagabond. The location of the city of Enoch in the land of Nod is not known. It has been suggested that it may have been Petra in Arabia.

4:18 *And unto Enoch was born Irad: and Irad begat Mehujael: and Mehujael begat Methusael: and Methusael begat Lamech.*

We know nothing of the first four men mentioned here. It is interesting that two of them had their names end in

44

"el." This was probably a contraction of the Hebrew name for God, Elohim. It may have indicated a continuing recognition of the existence and power of God in the minds of Cain's descendants.

> 4:19-22 *And Lamech took unto him two wives: the name of the one was Adah, and the name of the other Zillah.*
>
> *And Adah bare Jabel: he was the father of such as dwell in tents, and of such as have cattle.*
>
> *And his brother's name was Jubal: he was the father of all such as handle the harp and organ.*
>
> *And Zillah, she also bare Tubal-cain, an instructor of every artificer in brass and iron: and the sister of Tubal-cain was Naamah.*

The Lamech mentioned here was *not* the same as the one mentioned in Genesis 5:28-31. He was the first recorded polygamist, having two wives, Adah and Zillah. His son Jabal (by Adah) was probably a nomad, living in tents and moving his herd around to find sufficient forage. His son Jubal (by Adah) made and performed on musical instruments such as the harp (or lyre) and the organ (or pipe or flute). His son Tubal-cain (by Zillah) was a smith who forged tools (and perhaps weapons) of brass (bronze) and of iron. The men are mentioned as if their descendants followed them in their special vocations. Lamech's daughter Naamah (by Zillah) is named here, but no details regarding her are given.

The fact that these skills are mentioned in this passage helps us to realize that there was the development of an advanced civilization in the earliest times. No doubt the evidences of this were lost in the tremendous upheavals of the great Flood which came later in Noah's time. It helps to counteract the teaching that the first people on the earth were merely some kind of half-animals in an evolutionary chain. There is no proof that these people were substantially any different in physical appearance and mental accomplishments than those of later civilizations.

4:23, 24 *And Lamech said unto his wives, Adah and Zillah, Hear my voice; ye wives of Lamech, hearken unto my speech: for I have slain a man to my wounding, and a young man to my hurt.*

If Cain shall be avenged sevenfold, truly Lamech seventy and sevenfold.

Verse 23 is interpreted a couple of ways. Some think that it means Lamech was boasting to his wives that he had slain a young man for wounding him and perhaps another one for merely striking him. Others believe that it means Lamech accidentally slew a young man who was threatening his life, so that it was a case of self-defense. In any case, Lamech argued that if the murder of Abel by Cain was followed by a divine promise that anyone slaying Cain would receive a sevenfold retribution, then anyone slaying Lamech would receive a seventy-sevenfold retribution. Since this passage in Hebrew takes the form of poetry, Lamech may have been the world's first poet. It does seem to have the repetition typical of Hebrew poetry. Note how he said to his wives, "Hear my voice" and "Hearken unto my speech." Because of this repetition, he may have been referring to only one young man here, instead of two, when he mentioned "a man to my wounding" and "a young man to my hurt."

Seth's Birth

4:25 *And Adam knew his wife again; and she bare a son, and called his name Seth: For God, said she, hath appointed me another seed instead of Abel, whom Cain slew.*

The name Seth meant "appointed," "substituted," "granted," or "given." It is clear here that Eve considered Seth to be a replacement from God for righteous Abel. The genealogy given in Luke 3:23-38 would seem to imply that Seth was at the head of a line of people stretching from Adam to Jesus. Except for Jesus, these people were not perfect, but they were the righteous line as opposed to the wicked line descending from Cain. This is *not* meant to imply that righteousness or wickedness is inherited, for

46

the Bible teaches otherwise (Ezek. 18:1-22). It *does* mean that the influence of individuals on their descendants can make a difference in the way that they live.

> 4:26 *And to Seth, to him also there was born a son; and he called his name Enos: then began men to call upon the name of the Lord.*

Interpretations of this verse vary. One thought is that some men began to be called by the name of the Lord, perhaps in contempt for their righteous ways. Another thought is that Enos (or Enosh) was the first to gather people together for public worship in the name of the Lord. Whichever is right, there appears to have been a time of spiritual revival under Enos.

> 5:1, 2 *This is the book of the generations of Adam. In the day that God created man, in the likeness of God made he him;*
> *Male and female created he them; and blessed them, and called their name Adam, in the day when they were created.*

The language used here is very similar to that which is found in Genesis 1:27. Moses, the author of the book, seemed to want to present a brief review of Adam as he prepared to record his death (v. 5). Perhaps he also wanted to remind his readers of the fact that man had been made in God's likeness and that people could still experience divine blessings on their lives, in spite of the failures they had experienced thus far.

> 5:3, 4 *And Adam lived an hundred and thirty years, and begat a son in his own likeness, after his image; and called his name Seth:*
> *And the days of Adam after he had begotten Seth were eight hundred years: and he begat sons and daughters:*

Seth was born to Adam and Eve when Adam (and probably Eve) were one hundred and thirty years old. Evidently Seth was much like Adam in appearance, spirituality, or both. For the next eight centuries Adam lived, and during that long period of time he continued to produce more children. Although we assume that Eve was the mother of all of these, we cannot be sure, for we are not told when she died or stopped bearing children.

The Bible does not tell us why people lived long lives at that time in history. Various suggestions have been put forward. Perhaps the human race in its original purity was much stronger than in later generations. Perhaps the cloud cover over the earth before the great Flood strained out damaging rays from the sun. The Lord chose to give them long lives, and we may just have to leave it at that, rather than speculating further.

> 5:5 *And all the days that Adam lived were nine hundred and thirty years: and he died.*

God had promised Adam back in the garden of Eden that "in the day that thou eatest thereof [the forbidden fruit] thou shalt surely die" (Gen. 2:17). As mentioned before, this did not mean that Adam would die physically on that specific day. However, the process of dying began on that day, and it culminated when Adam was nine hundred and thirty years old. He was truly unique, and no one will ever have the same experiences which he had. His body turned to dust, as God had predicted (Gen. 3:19). His soul went into Sheol to the place of the righteous dead, there to be comforted and to wait for release into the presence of God following the Atonement made by Christ at Calvary (Luke 16:22, 25; Rom. 3:23-26; Eph. 4:8-10). Some day we shall see him and have opportunity to discuss those early days, unless Isaiah 65:17 means that such memories will literally be erased.

Seth's Descendants

> 5:6-8 *And Seth lived an hundred and five years, and begat Enos:*
> *And Seth lived after he begat Enos eight hundred and seven years, and begat sons and daughters:*
> *And all the days of Seth were nine hundred and twelve years: and he died.*

The birth of Enos was mentioned back in Genesis 4:26, but it is repeated here in the summary of Seth. Of all his sons and daughters, Enos was apparently the most outstanding. Seth is mentioned only once more in the Bible, and that is only in a genealogy (Luke 3:38), but he was a righteous man and at the head of a long line of righteous men. Some think that these were the "sons of God" mentioned in Genesis 6:2 and 4, which we will consider in the next lesson.

5:9-11 *And Enos lived ninety years, and begat Cainan:*

And Enos lived after he begat Cainan eight hundred and fifteen years, and begat sons and daughters:

And all the days of Enos were nine hundred and five years: and he died.

It was during the lifetime of Enos that men began to call upon the name of the Lord (Gen. 4:26). This might also be translated that men began to call themselves by the name of Jehovah. It seems apparent that Seth influenced Enos to live righteously.

5:12-14 *And Cainan lived seventy years, and begat Mahalaleel:*

And Cainan lived after he begat Mahalaleel eight hundred and forty years, and begat sons and daughters:

And all the days of Cainan were nine hundred and ten years: and he died.

Cainan was also called Kenan (1 Chron. 1:2). There seems to be no further information about him. The fact that he gave his son a name ending in "el" (a contraction of *Elohim*, a name for God) would indicate that Cainan still recognized the Lord.

5:15-17 *And Mahalaleel lived sixty and five years, and begat Jared:*

And Mahalaleel lived after he begat Jared eight hundred and thirty years, and begat sons and daughters:

And all the days of Mahalaleel were eight hundred

ninety and five years: and he died.

The name Mahalaleel meant "praise of God." He was called Maleleel in Luke 3:37. We know nothing else about him.

> 5:18-20 *And Jared lived an hundred sixty and two years, and he begat Enoch:*
> *And Jared lived after he begat Enoch eight hundred years, and begat sons and daughters:*
> *And all the days of Jared were nine hundred sixty and two years: and he died.*

His name was spelled Jered in 1 Chronicles 1:2. We know nothing more about him. He did produce an unusual son.

> 5:21-24 *And Enoch lived sixty and five years, and begat Methuselah:*
> *And Enoch walked with God after he begat Methuselah three hundred years, and begat sons and daughters:*
> *And all the days of Enoch were three hundred sixty and five years:*
> *And Enoch walked with God: and he was not; for God took him.*

He was called Henoch in 1 Chronicles 1:3. He may have been named after Cain's first son (Gen. 4:17). He and Noah were noted for the fact that they "walked with God" (Gen. 5:24; 6:9). Enoch was honored in Hebrews 11:5—"By faith Enoch was translated that he should not see death; and was not found, because God had translated him: for before his translation he had this testimony, that he pleased God." Some might see him as a foretype of the saints who will be translated to heaven at the Second Coming of Christ without having to die (1 Thess. 4:17).

> 5:25-27 *And Methuselah lived an hundred eighty and seven years, and begat Lamech:*
> *And Methuselah lived after he begat Lamech seven*

hundred eighty and two years, and begat sons and daughters.

And all the days of Methuselah were nine hundred sixty and nine years: and he died.

He was called Methusala in Luke 3:37. His name meant "man of the javelin." As far as we know, he was the man who lived the longest in human history. He died in the same year that the great Flood of Noah's time came upon the earth.

5:28-31 *And Lamech lived an hundred eighty and two years, and begat a son:*

And he called his name Noah, saying, This same shall comfort us concerning our work and toil of our hands, because of the ground which the Lord hath cursed.

And Lamech lived after he begat Noah five hundred ninety and five years, and begat sons and daughters:

And all the days of Lamech were seven hundred seventy and seven years: and he died.

He may have been named after the descendant of Cain mentioned in Genesis 4:18-24. He named his son Noah, which meant "rest," "relief," or "comfort." He evidently felt that this son would somehow get the curse of sin lifted from the earth and thus make life easier for those who had to till it. Actually, it was in Noah's time that the great Deluge was to come which wiped out the human race, with the exception of the eight people in Noah's family.

5:32 *And Noah was five hundred years old: and Noah begat Shem, Ham, and Japheth.*

As was the case with the other patriarchs, Noah probably had many sons and daughters born to him earlier. If so, then they must have died either before the Flood or in it. If not, then he was very old before fathering his first children—Shem, Ham, and Japheth. They were born about twenty years after God had told Noah that the Flood was coming. They no doubt helped him build the great ark when they were old enough to do so. There was to be a period of warning lasting a hundred and twenty years before the Flood came (Gen. 6:3). Noah was "a preacher of righteousness" during that time (2 Pet. 2:5), but only his wife, his three sons, and their wives seemed to heed his warnings.

Shem was called Sem in Luke 3:36. He was the only one listed of Noah's three sons, apparently because he was the one through whom the Messiah was to come. He is believed to be the father of the Semitic race. Ham was Noah's youngest son. He is believed to be the father of the Canaanites and people who lived in the northeastern parts of Africa (but not necessarily Negroes). Japheth was Noah's oldest son. He is believed to be the father of people who later inhabited Macedonia (upper Greece) and Asia Minor (Turkey).

Summary

In the space of just two chapters, we have seen the human race expand rapidly from the original couple, Adam and Eve, to a large population of untold numbers. We have learned that worship of God was practiced with sacrifices involving the death of animals. We have learned of the first death of a human being, the murder of Abel by his brother Cain. We have learned of the continuing consequences of sin through God's punishment of Cain, although this was tempered by divine mercy.

We know that the descendants of Cain developed the pastoral way of life, the musical arts, and the metalworking craft. We know that God replaced Abel with Seth, in order that the righteous line might continue. We have traced this line down through several generations to righteous Noah. This line would continue until the Messiah came many centuries later. God knew exactly what He was doing in all of this, and His purposes were being fulfilled according to His divine calendar.

4

The Great Flood

Genesis 6:1—8:14

The system for disseminating moisture to sustain life in the garden of Eden was apparently different than in the post-flood era. "But there went up a mist from the earth, and watered the whole face of the ground" (Gen. 2:6). We do not know if the curse of sin caused by Adam's fall affected this watering system or not. Some conclude that rain did not fall until the time of the Flood in the six hundredth year of Noah's life (Gen. 7:11). At that time it came down in great torrents and the fountains of the deep were opened. The face of the earth was covered with water which destroyed the earth's inhabitants, except for those eight persons who floated above the Deluge in the safety of the ark. Before considering the facts regarding the Flood the writer of Genesis explains the cause of this drastic act of divine judgment. The whole of civilization in that day had become permeated with evil. The level of wickedness was so great that judgment was the only alternative.

The decay of pre-flood culture was the direct result of spiritual decline.

6:1-2 *And it came to pass, when men began to multiply on the face of the earth, and daughters were born unto them,*
That the sons of God saw the daughters of men that they were fair; and they took them wives of all which they chose.

Who were "the daughters of men," and who were "the sons of God"? One view is that these women were human beings and that these men were supernatural beings such as angels. Such a view seems unlikely, for Jesus himself said that angels do not marry (Matt. 22:30). The writer of Hebrews said that angels are spirits (Heb. 1:14), although

53

we know that they sometimes assumed human forms when ministering on the earth. A more acceptable view is that the women were in the line of Cain and were unrighteous, whereas the men were in the line of Seth and were righteous.

These two verses do not mention anything evil, but verse 3 reveals that great evil was generated on the earth by the mixed marriages between the men and women of these two lines.

A Period of Probation

6:3 *And the Lord said, My spirit shall not always strive with man, for that he also is flesh: yet his days shall be an hundred and twenty years.*

This verse is not easy to interpret and must not be taken out of its context. One view is that God's Spirit sought to control men from outside. Another view is that God's Spirit was abiding in men and keeping them alive. Withdrawal of God's Spirit in either case would result in the extinction of men. However, men would have a grace period of one hundred and twenty years in which to repent and seek forgiveness from God. However, God's decision regarding this seems to have been made in Adam's time (Gen. 3:22-24). The more acceptable view appears to be that God would warn men through Noah's preaching for a hundred and twenty years while he was building the ark. Then general destruction of the human race would take place, except for Noah and the members of his family (cf. 1 Pet. 3:20).

6:4 *There were giants in the earth in those days; and also after that, when the sons of God came in unto the daughters of men, and they bare children to them, the same became mighty men which were of old, men of renown.*

We know that there were giants in the time of Moses, for the Israelite spies saw them in Canaan and called them "the sons of Anak" (Num. 13:33). Og, King of Bashan, had an iron bedstead nine cubits long and four cubits wide (about fourteen by six feet), according to Deuteronomy 3:11, which mentions that he was the last of such giants like the Anakim. Goliath of Gath in Philistia, whom David slew, was the most famous of biblical giants (1 Sam. 17:49). The Hebrew terms for giant include one which refers to ferocious warriors, men likely to make great names for themselves in battle, and perhaps that was what was meant in Genesis 6:4.

> 6:5-7 *And God saw that the wickedness of man was great in the earth, and that every imagination of the thoughts of his heart was only evil continually.*
> *And it repented the Lord that he had made man on the earth, and it grieved him at his heart.*
> *And the Lord said, I will destroy man whom I have created from the face of the earth; both man, and beast, and the creeping thing, and the fowls of the air; for it repenteth me that I have made them.*

God became grieved at the extent of human depravity. The people of the pre-flood days had given over completely to sin. Not only were their actions corrupt but their thoughts and imaginations were equally as wicked as their actions. It was probably true that every evil imaginable had been committed. Satan cleverly persuaded men to disregard the safeguards against evil and fully indulge their distorted appetites. There was no interruption to the flow of sin. The description here seems to parallel the Romans passage (Rom. 1—3).

God is of purer eyes than to behold iniquity. It is hard for us to comprehend the sorrow He felt at man's condition.

There is a theological problem connected with the use of the verb "repented" in verses 6 and 7. The root meaning of repentance is "to change the mind." The Scripture says, that God does not change His mind (Mal. 3:6). There is no need for Him to do so, since He knows all things from start to finish. What verses 6 and 7 mean is that He decided to act in a way which would *appear* to men that He had changed His mind, but He *actually* was going to work according to a predetermined plan.

The Grace of God

> 6:8-10 *But Noah found grace in the eyes of the Lord. These are the generations of Noah: Noah was a just man and perfect in his generations, and Noah walked with God.*
>
> *And Noah begat three sons, Shem, Ham, and Japheth.*

God always has a remnant of righteous people in every generation, but this surely must have been the smallest remnant of all time. Noah and his wife, plus their three sons and their wives, stood alone in an ungodly culture doomed to certain judgment. He looked at Noah and his family with love. He was gracious toward them. Noah was noted for his righteousness, his sincere and blameless life, and his determination to walk according to God's will. He maintained close fellowship with the Lord and acted honorably toward others. Noah set the pace, and because of his integrity his family followed him.

We do not know if children were born to Shem, Ham, and Japheth before the Flood. None is mentioned. However, after the Flood, they were told to "be fruitful, and multiply, and replenish the earth" (Gen. 9:1). It is likely that God planned it this way, so that the family was compact and able to ride out the Flood in the ark with ample room for the eight persons aboard and all of the animals and provisions required for the duration of the Flood.

God's Decision to Judge Mankind

> 6:11-13 *The earth also was corrupt before God, and the earth was filled with violence.*
>
> *And God looked upon the earth, and, behold, it was corrupt; for all flesh had corrupted his way upon the earth.*
>
> *And God said unto Noah, The end of all flesh is come before me; for the earth is filled with violence through them; and, behold, I will destroy them with the earth.*

God was thoroughly disgusted with the sinfulness

56

which permeated every aspect of human life. He was prepared to destroy the human race for the most part and begin anew with Noah and his family. The world of that day had already been warned by the ministry of Enoch. "Enoch. . .the seventh from Adam, prophesied of these [apostate teachers], saying, Behold, the Lord cometh with ten thousands of his saints, To execute judgment upon all, and to convince all that are ungodly among them of all their ungodly deeds which they have ungodly committed, and of all their hard speeches [things] which ungodly sinners have spoken against him" (Jude 14-15). He had warned them through Noah, "a preacher of righteousness" (2 Pet. 2:5). This is probably what is meant when it says in 1 Peter 3:18-20 that Christ went by the Holy Spirit and preached to "the spirits in prison. . .spirits of those who, long before in the days of Noah, had refused to listen to God, though he waited patiently for them while Noah was building the ark" (Living Bible).

Instructions for Building the Ark

6:14-16 *Make thee an ark of gopher wood; rooms shalt thou make in the ark, and shalt pitch it within and without with pitch.*

And this is the fashion which thou shalt make it of: The length of the ark shall be three hundred cubits, the breadth of it fifty cubits, and the height of it thirty cubits.

A window shalt thou make to the ark, and in a cubit shalt thou finish it above; and the door of the ark shalt thou set in the side thereof; with lower, second, and third stories shalt thou make it.

The ark was not to be a ship with a keel or rudder. It had no need of any means of locomotion. It could be compared to a huge barge, ready to go up and down and to drift in any direction. A cubit is about 18 inches. Therefore, God directed Noah to build the ark approximately 450 feet long, 75 feet wide, and 45 feet high. He was to seal it with pitch inside and outside to make it watertight. Noah was instructed to use gopher (cypress) wood in the construction of the ark. Compartments were to be built on its three decks for his family, a host of animals, and the food needed for all of them to eat.

The ark was to have a window eighteen inches high running around its circumference at the top. This means a series of windows which could be used to let in fresh air, light, and perhaps rainwater when needed. They could also be used for letting out stale air and waste products as required. The one door was to be set in the side. God himself would shut it when all of the occupants were inside (Gen. 7:16). This would prevent anyone from gaining entrance when the Flood waters came for they would have lost their opportunity to be saved. The ark has often been used as a type of salvation from sin.

The project facing Noah and his three sons in building this vessel was a great one. Designing it, securing materials for it, building it, and equipping it presented tremendous challenges to them. It was to be the size of a battleship. The scoffing of their neighbors and friends added psychological pressure to their already difficult task. They must have been tempted many times to abandon the project but they kept working.

God's Covenant with Noah

> 6:17-18 *And, behold, I, even I, do bring a flood of waters upon the earth, to destroy all flesh, wherein is the breath of life, from under heaven; and every thing that is in the earth shall die.*
>
> *But with thee will I establish my covenant; and thou shalt come into the ark, thou, and thy sons, and thy wife, and thy sons' wives with thee.*

God announced to Noah in advance that He was going to unleash supernatural power to bring a flood which would cover the earth. Some modern scholars have attempted to build a case for limiting the Flood of Noah's time to the geographical region of the Near East. The language of this passage speaks clearly to a universal flood. All human and animal life would perish as a result of this judgment except for the occupants of the ark. His promise would protect them from harm. It seems obvious that many sea creatures would survive, since they would be in their natural element, but many may also have perished in the upheavals and disruptions which took place.

6:19-21 *And of every living thing of all flesh, two of every sort shalt thou bring into the ark, to keep them alive with thee; they shall be male and female.*

Of fowls after their kind, and of cattle after their kind, of every creeping thing of the earth after his kind, two of every sort shall come unto thee, to keep them alive.

And take thou unto thee of all food that is eaten, and thou shalt gather it to thee; and it shall be for food for thee, and for them.

Noah and his sons had to collect lumber and pitch for building the ark, but that was not all. They also had to collect representative land animals, birds, and reptiles to form a continuing link for surviving the Flood. They had to collect enough food to feed themselves, their wives, and the animals on board the ark. It is interesting to note that the animals God mentioned were to come to Noah, perhaps driven there by the Lord himself. That would certainly have simplified the task. It is also possible that there were many fewer species of animals at that time, so that the number of them could be accommodated in the ark.

6:22 *Thus did Noah according to all that God commanded him, so did he.*

A healthy fear (or reverence) for God motivated Noah to do all that he was told to do. "By faith Noah, being warned of God of things not seen as yet, moved with fear, prepared an ark to the saving of his house; by the which he condemned the world, and became heir of the righteousness which is by faith" (Heb. 11:7).

Safe in the Ark

7:1-5 *And the Lord said unto Noah, Come thou and all thy house into the ark; for thee have I seen righteous before me in this generation.*

*Of every clean beast thou shalt take to thee by sevens,
the male and his female: and of beasts that are not clean
by two, the male and his female.*

*Of fowls also of the air by sevens, the male and the
female; to keep seed alive upon the face of all the earth.*

*For yet seven days, and I will cause it to rain upon the
earth forty days and forty nights; and every living substance that I have made will I destroy from off the face
of the earth.*

*And Noah did according unto all that the Lord com-
manded him.*

Some scholars interpret the number of seven as meaning three pairs of clean animals, plus a seventh animal for
sacrifice. Another possible interpretation is that God told
Noah to take seven pairs of each kind of clean animals
with him. Though the Levitical laws regarding clean and
unclean animals had not yet been given Noah had received some understanding of the principle of ceremonial
cleanness. This concept was to be fully developed in the
Mosaic law.

God gave Noah notice one week in advance of the Flood.
This allowed for an orderly preparation for their long stay
in the ark. God's dealings with Noah reflect His tender
mercies. There was a gentleness about the divine directive
to enter the ark. It took the form of an invitation.

7:6-9 *And Noah was six hundred years old when the
flood of waters was upon the earth.*

*And Noah went in, and his sons, and his wife, and his
sons' wives with him, into the ark, because of the waters
of the flood.*

*Of clean beasts, and of beasts that are not clean, and
of fowls, and of every thing that creepeth upon the
earth,*

*There went in two and two unto Noah into the ark, the
male and the female, as God had commanded Noah.*

The other people on the earth did not seem to be alarmed
about the calamity soon to break upon them, although
Noah had warned them about it. This generation of people
are representative of those who neglect the warnings of

impending judgment. Jesus declared that the same attitude would prevail among many at the time of the end. "In the days that were before the flood they were eating and drinking, marrying and giving in marriage, until the day that Noe [Noah] entered into the ark" (Matt. 24:38). The patience of God was now coming to an end.

7:10-12 *And it came to pass after seven days, that the waters of the flood were upon the earth.*

In the six hundredth year of Noah's life, in the second month, the seventeenth day of the month, the same day were all the foundations of the great deep broken up, and the windows of heaven were opened.

And the rain was upon the earth forty days and forty nights.

God had given the people ample warning, of the coming judgment. When Noah and his family were safe in the ark, the Flood came. Those on the outside of the ark may have realized what was happening and then tried to do something about it, but it was too late. The waters beneath the earth's surface were turned loose to surge upward. The saturated clouds above the earth were allowed to drop their burden. A continuous rain poured down for almost seven weeks. The world had not had anything like it before has not seen anything like it since that time. The inspired record indicates that this Flood was a massive deluge which argues for a universal flood rather than a local one.

7:13-16 *In the selfsame day entered Noah, and Shem, and Ham, and Japheth, the sons of Noah, and Noah's wife, and the three wives of his sons with them, into the ark;*

They and every beast after his kind, and all the cattle after their kind, and every creeping thing that creepeth upon the earth after his kind, and every fowl after his kind, every bird of every sort.

And they went in unto Noah into the ark, two and two of all flesh, wherein is the breath of life.

And they that went in, went in male and female of all

flesh, as God had commanded him: and the Lord shut him in.

This appears to be a summary, for there is nothing new in it, except the final statement. This says that the *Lord* closed the door of the ark. The implication is that the door was shut in such a way (or perhaps guarded by Him in such a way) that no one could panic and get out, and no one could storm it and get in.

The Devastation of the Earth

7:17-20 *And the flood was forty days upon the earth; and the waters increased, and bare up the ark, and it was lift up above the earth.*
And the waters prevailed, and were increased greatly upon the earth; and the ark went upon the face of the waters.
And the waters prevailed exceedingly upon the earth; and all the high hills, that were under the whole heaven, were covered.
Fifteen cubits upward did the waters prevail; and the mountains were covered.

These details about the extent of the disaster were given for a purpose. They lend support to the concept of a universal flood. The water rose until it covered even the highest points to a depth of twenty-two-and-a-half feet. This does not sound as if it were describing an area flood, but one which was worldwide. In the face of such total destruction, even the massive ark must have looked tiny and frail. However, the Lord protected it with His sovereign hand. Gradually elevated, it bobbed on the water's surface, carrying in it the seeds of a new world of men and animals. Noah and his wife were as much the parents of the human race as were Adam and Eve, at least in the sense that all people since their time have descended from them.

7:21-24 *And all flesh died that moved upon the earth, both of fowl, and of cattle, and of beast, and of every creeping thing that creepeth upon the earth, and every man:*

All in whose nostrils was the breath of life, of all that was in the dry land, died.

And every living substance was destroyed which was upon the face of the ground, both man, and cattle, and the creeping things, and the fowl of the heaven; and they were destroyed from the earth: and Noah only remained alive, and they that were with him in the ark.

And the waters prevailed upon the earth an hundred and fifty days.

For a period of five months the flood waters did their divinely appointed work. Guilty people died. Innocent animals caught up in the judgment on guilty people also died. Some strong birds may have managed to fly above the waters for a time, but they too weakened and fell to be claimed by the waters. Vegetation must have been flattened or buried by the weight of the water or the shifting of earth and sand. Eradication of civilization was so complete that a new beginning would have to be made.

Judgment Completed

8:1-5 *And God remembered Noah, and every living thing, and all the cattle that was with him in the ark: and God made a wind to pass over the earth, and the waters asswaged;*

The fountains also of the deep and the windows of heaven were stopped, and the rain from heaven was restrained;

And the waters returned from off the earth continually: and after the end of the hundred and fifty days the waters were abated.

And the ark rested in the seventh month, on the seventeenth day of the month, upon the mountains of Ararat.

And the waters decreased continually until the tenth month: in the tenth month, on the first day of the month, were the tops of the mountains seen.

When the destruction of the earth was complete, God put the next stage of His plan into action. The flood waters

63

were abated and slowly the earth began to dry out. The mighty springs of the deep were again sealed up and the rain from above ceased. God sent a strong wind to speed up the evaporation of the flood waters.

The ark came gently to rest on a mountain somewhere in eastern Turkey (Armenia). The Tigris and Euphrates Rivers find their sources in this area. Ararat is more the name of a region than of a particular mountain, although some claim that it is Ara Dagh, a mountain with one peak almost 18,000 feet high and another about 13,500 feet high. In any case, it appears that the ark drifted several hundred miles from the area east of Eden in which most people lived following the expulsion of Adam and Eve from the garden of Eden. It would seem natural for Noah and his descendants to follow the river valleys southward again until they came to the "plain in the land of Shinar" located between the Tigris and Euphrates Rivers in Mesopotamia (Iraq).

8:6-12 *And it came to pass at the end of forty days, that Noah opened the window of the ark which he had made:*

And he sent forth a raven, which went forth to and fro, until the waters were dried up from off the earth.

Also he sent forth a dove from him, to see if the waters were abated from off the face of the ground;

But the dove found no rest for the sole of her foot, and she returned unto him into the ark, for the waters were on the face of the whole earth: then he put forth his hand, and took her, and pulled her in unto him into the ark.

And he stayed yet other seven days; and again he sent forth the dove out of the ark;

And the dove came in to him in the evening: and, lo, in her mouth was an olive leaf pluckt off: so Noah knew that the waters were abated from off the earth.

And he stayed yet other seven days; and sent forth the dove; which returned not again unto him any more.

Forty days after the ark came to rest on the earth, Noah sent a raven out. This bird preferred solitude and was content to fly back and forth over the waters and not return to the ark. It may have perched occasionally on the roof of the ark, on dead carcasses floating on the water, or on floating logs or other debris. Noah next sent out a female dove, which came back to enjoy the comforts of the ark. A week later Noah sent her out again, and this time she came back with an olive leaf in her bill, a sign that trees were reviving again. When he sent her out a week after that, she did not return. His assessment was that it was time to disembark, but he waited for instructions from the Lord before doing that.

> 8:13-14 *And it came to pass in the six hundredth and first year, in the first month, the first day of the month, the waters were dried up from off the earth: and Noah removed the covering of the ark, and looked, and, behold, the face of the ground was dry.*
> *And in the second month, on the seven and twentieth day of the month, was the earth dried.*

The Flood began in the six hundredth year of Noah's life, on the seventeenth day of the second month (May). The first month in the Hebrew calendar was April. The Flood had receded, and the ground was dry in the six hundred and first year of Noah's life, on the twenty-seventh day of the second month (May). Therefore, the ark was occupied for over a year. No doubt Noah's family and the animals were happy to be released from their confinement in the ark. The crisis was over and thanks to God's grace mankind could enjoy a new beginning.

Summary

The earth's population had been so corrupted by sin that God decided to destroy it and begin anew with Noah and his family. This righteous man followed God's instructions for the construction of the ark in which he, his family, and representatives from the animal kingdom would be saved from the judgment of the Flood. During the century it took Noah and his sons to build the ark, the people were repeatedly warned to turn from their sins or face destruction. At the divinely appointed time Noah, his family and the animals entered the ark, God shut the door and the Deluge came. A little over a year later, the flood waters subsided and the inhabitants of the ark were ready to come out and replenish the earth. God was giving the human race a second opportunity to follow His will.

5

The Post-Flood Era

Genesis 8:15—11:9

God had wiped the slate clean. The earth had been devastated by the Flood. Its population had been decimated, and the land animals destroyed with the exception of those preserved in the ark as representatives of the various species of animals. Noah and his family were now to have the privilege and the responsibility for writing a new chapter in the history of mankind.

8:15-19 *And God spoke unto Noah, saying,*
Go forth of the ark, thou, and thy wife, and thy sons, and thy sons' wives with thee.
Bring forth with thee every living thing that is with thee, of all flesh, both of fowl, and of cattle, and of every creeping thing that creepeth upon the earth; that they may breed abundantly in the earth, and be fruitful, and multiply upon the earth.
And Noah went forth, and his sons, and his wife, and his sons' wives with him:
Every beast, every creeping thing, and every fowl, and whatsoever creepeth upon the earth, after their kinds, went forth out of the ark.

After being shut up in the ark for over a year, Noah and his family showed no anxiety but patiently waited until the Lord gave the command to disembark. It is difficult to imagine their state of mind as they descended the ramp to begin a new way of life.

Noah Worships

8:20-22 *And Noah builded an altar unto the Lord; and took of every clean beast, and of every clean fowl, and offered burnt offerings on the altar.*
And the Lord smelled a sweet savour; and the Lord

*said in his heart, I will not again curse the ground any
more for man's sake; for the imagination of man's heart
is evil from his youth; neither will I again smite any-
more every thing living, as I have done.*

*While the earth remaineth, seedtime and harvest, and
cold and heat, and summer and winter, and day and
night shall not cease.*

Noah's first action upon leaving the ark was to worship
the God by whose grace he and his family had been
spared. He constructed an altar, and offered as sacrifices
some of the "clean" animals and birds from the ark. The
Lord was pleased with Noah's offerings and indicated his
acceptance by the revelation of a new covenant to be made
with Noah and his family.

It is difficult to know how much to read into verses 21-
22. Lamech, Noah's father, had said of his son, "This
same shall comfort us concerning our work and toil of our
hands, because of the ground which the Lord hath cursed"
(Gen. 5:29). Six centuries later the Lord declared, "I will
not again curse the ground any more for man's sake." It
seems most consistent with the context that Lamech's
prophecy was fulfilled in God's promise to Noah that He
would never again destroy the earth by a universal flood.
The curse placed on the earth as a result of the Fall of man
in Eden could not have been lifted at this time since the
Scriptures elsewhere speak of it as yet future (Rom. 8:20-
23). The lifting of the curse awaits the Second Coming of
Christ.

The covenant God made with Noah was based on His
mercy. In spite of human depravity God determined to
bless man with a world where the laws of nature would be
dependable. The language of this passage introduces a
new factor of climate not previously mentioned in Scripture. Apparently the order of the seasons and the climate
were considerably different than the pre-flood days.

Instructions for Noah's Family

9:1-4 *And God blessed Noah and his sons, and said
unto them, Be fruitful, and multiply, and replenish the
earth.*

68

And the fear of you and the dread of you shall be upon
every beast of the earth, and upon every fowl of the air,
upon all that moveth upon the earth, and upon all the
fishes of the sea; into your hand are they delivered.

Every moving thing that liveth shall be meat for you;
even as the green herb have I given you all things.

But flesh with the life thereof, which is the blood
thereof, shall ye not eat.

The wording in this passage is similar to that found in
the instructions God gave to Adam and Eve (Gen. 1:28-29).
Noah and his family were directed to populate the earth
by human reproduction. It would appear that from the
time of Adam until after the Flood men were vegetarians.
The terms of this covenant permitted Noah the use of
animals and fish for food, along with plant food. One
restriction was imposed on the use of animal flesh as food.
The blood of animals was to be drained from them before
the meat was eaten. Since the blood represented life it was
considered sacred. The blood sacrifices of the Old Testament prefigured the shed blood of Christ which represents
the pouring out of His life for the sins of men. It has also
been suggested that the prohibition against eating blood
prevented men from consuming animals while they were
still alive, a horrible pagan practice.

9:5-7 *And surely your blood of your lives will I re-*
quire; at the hand of every beast will I require it, and at
the hand of man; at the hand of every man's brother will
I require the life of man.

Whoso sheddeth man's blood, by man shall his blood
be shed: for in the image of God made he man.

And you, be ye fruitful, and multiply; bring forth
abundantly in the earth, and multiply therein.

This brief passage is very significant for at least two
basic reasons. First, it provides the foundation for the
practice of capital punishment. Any man or beast guilty
of murdering a person was to be executed. Obviously, this
law had reference to deliberate killing, not to accidental
killing. It did not prohibit legal executions or the slayings
required in defensive warfare or personal self-defense.

Second, it provides the foundation for human government. It was "at the hand of every man's brother [fellow-
man]" that God would require the life of a murderer. The
reason for execution of murderers was that their victims
were made in the image or likeness of God himself. Even
unbelieving government officials are given power by God
to execute murderers and to exercise other necessary
functions of government (Rom. 13:1-4). Government according to Scripture was instituted by God for the welfare
of man.

The Sign of the Rainbow

9:8-11 *And God spake unto Noah, and to his sons
with him, saying,*
*And I, behold, I establish my covenant with you, and
with your seed after you;*
*And with every living creature that is with you, of the
fowl, of the cattle, and of every beast of the earth with
you; from all that go out of the ark, to every beast of the
earth.*
*And I will establish my covenant with you; neither
shall all flesh be cut off any more by the waters of a
flood; neither shall there any more be a flood to destroy
the earth.*

The covenant which God established here involved a
promise to people, animals, and the earth itself. God said
that He would not use another universal flood to judge
men. This promise is still in effect today, whether people
love and serve the Lord or not. It is one evidence of His
providential grace. That does not mean that the earth will
never come under judgment again. The medium of divine
judgment on the earth at the end of time will be fire (2 Pet.
3:10-13).

9:12-17 *And God said, This is the token of the
covenant which I make between me and you and every
living creature that is with you, for perpetual generations:*
*I do set my bow in the cloud, and it shall be for a token
of a covenant between me and the earth.*
And it shall come to pass, when I bring a cloud over

the earth, that the bow shall be seen in the cloud:

*And I will remember my covenant, which is between
me and you and every living creature of all flesh; and
the waters shall no more become a flood to destroy all
flesh.*

*And the bow shall be in the cloud; and I will look upon
it, that I may remember the everlasting covenant
between God and every living creature of all flesh that is
upon the earth.*

*And God said unto Noah, This is the token of the
covenant, which I have established between me and all
flesh that is upon the earth.*

God designated the rainbow as a visible sign of His
promise not to destroy the earth again by a universal
flood. The statement that the bow would remind Him of
His promise is perplexing, for He never forgets anything
and therefore needs no reminders. Perhaps it means that
the rainbow serves as a reminder to *men* that God's
promise is valid and will be upheld.

9:18-19 *And the sons of Noah, that went forth of the
ark, were Shem, and Ham, and Japheth: for Ham is the
father of Canaan.*

*These are the three sons of Noah: and of them was the
whole earth overspread.*

Noah and his wife evidently had no more children after
bearing Shem, Ham, and Japheth. From these three sons
and their wives came all of the people of the earth.

Noah's Failure

9:20-23 *And Noah began to be an husbandman,
and he planted a vineyard:*

*And he drank of the wine, and was drunken; and he
was uncovered within his tent.*

*And Ham, the father of Canaan, saw the nakedness
of his father, and told his two brethren without.*

*And Shem and Japheth took a garment, and laid it
upon both their shoulders,and went backward, and
covered the nakedness of their father; and their faces*

71

were backward, and they saw not their father's nakedness.

The discovery of Noah's nakedness was not the offense, but Ham's disrespect for his father. He broke the fifth commandment. Although the decalogue had not yet been given the family of Noah had light enough to know that paternal respect was essential. It was wrong of Noah to become drunk but Ham was guilty of sin because he had used this unfortunate incident as a means of ridicule. Shem and Japheth showed proper respect toward their father by the way they managed to cover him with a robe until he was sober.

Since this is the first mention of a vineyard or wine in the Bible, it may have been that Noah was the first to grow grapes and did not realize that their fermented juice would make him intoxicated. In that case, he could not be considered guilty of deliberate drunkenness. It would clear him of the one blot on his otherwise clean record of righteousness. The Scripture makes no moral judgment of Noah's action.

> 9:24-27 *And Noah awoke from his wine, and knew what his younger son had done unto him.*
>
> *And he said, Cursed be Canaan; a servant of servants shall he be unto his brethren.*
>
> *And he said, Blessed be the Lord God of Shem; and Canaan shall be his servant.*
>
> *God shall enlarge Japheth, and he shall dwell in the tents of Shem; and Canaan shall be his servant.*

Noah, upon learning of Ham's action, uttered a prophecy upon Canaan, one of Ham's sons. The prophecy related only to Canaan and not to all of Ham's sons. It was the descendants of Canaan that God destroyed when He gave Palestine to the sons of Abraham. This passage should not be used to support the idea that black people were destined to become perpetual slaves of white people or any other people. The Canaanites who descended from Ham's son, Canaan, settled Palestine. They were later slain or made servants by the Israelites who came out of Egypt and possessed their land.

Shem was the second and middle son of Noah. He became the father of the Semites who settled much of the Middle East. The Hebrews were his descendants and consequently the Messiah came from his line.

Japheth was the first and eldest son of Noah. He became the father of the Gentile nations which settled Europe and a large part of Asia. In accordance with Noah's prophecy his descendants were scattered far and wide and became both powerful and prosperous. The meaning of Japheth dwelling "in the tents of Shem" is uncertain. Some think that it means Japheth's descendants secured most of their civilization from the Semites. Others relate this phrase to the blessing of God which will come upon the Gentiles through redemption.

> 9:28-29 *And Noah lived after the flood three hundred and fifty years.*
>
> *And all the days of Noah were nine hundred and fifty years: and he died.*

Noah lived a very long life, only nineteen years less than the oldest man, Methuselah, who died at the age of nine hundred and sixty-nine (Gen. 5:27). He was one of the great spiritual leaders of the ancient world, the link between the pre-flood and post-flood periods. There is a sense in which he was the father of us all.

The Genesis of the Nations

> 10:1-5 *Now these are the generations of the sons of Noah, Shem, Ham, and Japheth: and unto them were sons born after the flood.*
>
> *The sons of Japheth; Gomer, and Magog, and Madai, and Javan, and Tubal, and Meschech, and Tiras.*
>
> *And the sons of Gomer; Ashkenaz, and Riphath, and Togarmah.*
>
> *And the sons of Javan; Elishah, and Tarshish, Kittim, and Dodanim.*
>
> *By these were the isles of the Gentiles divided in their lands; every one after his tongue, after their families, in their nations.*

Seven of Japheth's sons are named in this record—Gomer, Magog, Madai, Javan, Tubal, Meshech, and Tiras. Two of Japheth's grandsons are named and seven great-grandsons. Japheth's descendants settled on islands and coasts along the European continent. Tarshish may have been Spain, Kittim may have been Cyprus, and Dodanim (or Rodanim) may have been Rhodes. These people no doubt penetrated inland, settling much of Europe and up into the area now occupied by Russia.

10:6-12 *And the sons of Ham; Cush, and Mizraim, and Phut, and Canaan.*

And the sons of Cush; Seba, and Havilah, and Sabtah, and Raamah, and Sabtechah: and the sons of Raamah; Sheba, and Dedan.

And Cush begat Nimrod: he began to be a mighty one in the earth.

He was a mighty hunter before the Lord; wherefore it is said, Even as Nimrod the mighty hunter before the Lord.

And the beginning of his kingdom was Babel, and Erech, and Accad, and Calneh, in the land of Shinar.

Out of that land went forth Asshur, and builded Nineveh, and the city Rehoboth, and Calah,

And Resen between Nineveh and Calah: the same is a great city.

Some principle of selection must have been followed by the compiler of this genealogy. The descendants of only three of Ham's four sons are listed. Four sons are named for Ham—Cush, Mizraim, Phut, and Canaan. Only three of them have their sons named—Cush, Mizraim, and Canaan. Considerable attention is given to the descendants of Cush and Canaan, a little to Mizraim's descendants, and none to those of Phut. Cush is thought to be Ethiopia, Mizraim to be Egypt, Phut to be Libya, and Canaan to be Palestine.

Cush had a son named Nimrod, a mighty hunter. He may have been the first king on the earth. He moved from Babylon to Assyria and built settlements, including Nineveh.

74

10:13-14   *And Mizraim begat Ludim, and Anamim, and Lehabim, and Naphtuhim,*
And Pathrusim, and Casluhim, (out of whom came Philistim,) and Caphtorim.

The Philistines which came out of Philistim (v. 14) were always hostile toward the Israelites. At times when Israel was spiritually apostate, Jehovah used the Philistines to subjugate them. It is possible that the descendants of the Philistines migrated from Crete to settle the coastline of Southwestern Palestine. Mizraim probably is the ancient name of upper and lower Egypt.

10:15-20   *And Canaan begat Sidon his firstborn, and Heth,*
And the Jebusite, and the Amorite, and the Girgasite,
And the Hivite, and the Arkite, and the Sinite,
And the Arvadite, and the Zemarite, and the Hamathite; and afterward were the families of the Canaanites spread abroad.
And the border of the Canaanites was from Sidon, as thou comest to Gerar, unto Gaza; as thou goest, unto Sodom, and Gomorrah, and Admah, and Zeboim, even unto Lasha.
These are the sons of Ham, after their families, after their tongues, in their countries, and in their nations.

Perhaps the most famous name in this list is Heth. He was the father of the Hittites, who developed a powerful kingdom which lasted from 1600 to 700 B.C. The descendants of Canaan spread out to cover all of Palestine from Sidon on the Phoenician coast southward to Philistia and eastward to the cities in the Jordan Valley.

10:21-23   *Unto Shem also, the father of all the children of Eber, the brother of Japheth the elder, even to him were children born.*
The children of Shem; Elam, and Asshur, and Arphaxad, and Lud, and Aram.
And the children of Aram; Uz, and Hul, and Gether, and Mash.

Since Genesis is the inspired record of the godly line the genealogy of Shem is given last. The remainder of the book focuses on his descendants. Five sons are named for Shem—Elam, Asshur, Arphaxad, Lud, and Aram. Only two of them have their sons named—Aram and Arphaxad. Four sons are named for Aram, but nothing distinctive is mentioned about them.

> 10:24-25 *And Arphaxad begat Salah; and Salah begat Eber.*
> *And unto Eber were born two sons: the name of one was Peleg; for in his days was the earth divided; and his brother's name was Joktan.*

The most important name in this list is that of Eber the grandson of Shem. His name means "across" or the region "across the river." Eber was the father of the Hebrews. The Israelites were from the Hebrew line.

Eber named his first son Peleg which means "divisions." It may be that Eber gave his son this name to commemorate the division of the people that occurred following the confusion of languages at Babel.

> 10:26-30 *And Joktan begat Almodad, and Sheleph, and Hazarmaveth, and Jerah,*
> *And Hadoram, and Uzal, and Diklah,*
> *And Obal, and Abimael, and Sheba,*
> *And Ophir, and Havilah, and Jobab: all these were the sons of Joktan.*
> *And their dwelling was from Mesha, as thou goest unto Sephar a mount of the east.*

Joktan, Eber's son and Peleg's brother, had thirteen sons. Mesha was located in southern Arabia. Sephar was also in Arabia and the boundary of the Semites to the east at that time. Joktan is thought to be the patriarch of many of the Arabic tribes.

> 10:31-32 *These are the sons of Shem, after their families, after their tongues, in their lands, after their nations.*
> *These are the families of the sons of Noah, after their*

*generations, in their nations: and by these were the
nations divided in the earth after the flood.*

The names mentioned in this chapter represent not just
individuals, but ethnic groups as well. This selective
genealogy puts the history of the post-flood era into a
capsule form. The roots of all the nations and ethnic
groups in the world can be traced to one of Noah's three
sons. Seventy names make up this primitive table of the
nations.

Disobedience in Shinar

11:1-4 *And the whole earth was of one language, and
of one speech.*
*And it came to pass, as they journeyed from the east,
that they found a plain in the land of Shinar; and they
dwelt there.*
*And they said one to another, Go to, let us make brick,
and burn them thoroughly. And they had brick for
stone, and slime had they for morter.*
*And they said, Go to, let us build us a city and a tower,
whose top may reach unto heaven; and let us make us a
name, lest we be scattered abroad upon the face of the
whole earth.*

It would appear that in verse 2 Moses goes back in time
to the movement of Noah's family from Ararat in
Armenia down the Tigris-Euphrates River Valleys. The
build up of population and the scattering out of people had
not yet taken place. All of the existing people of the world
used one language for communication. A better translation here might be that the people journeyed eastward,
rather than "from the east." Actually, they were probably
moving in a southeasterly direction. Coming to Mesopotamia, which means "between the rivers," they decided to
settle down in the land of Shinar where a fertile plain
would make life easy. One of the towns Nimrod built there
was called Babel, probably after the event we are now
studying took place. The country of Iraq may have gotten
its name from the city of Erech, which Nimrod also built
(Gen. 10:10). The name Babylon may be traced to the

Akkadian *babilu*, meaning "gate of God." Perhaps the tower the people wanted to build was intended to be a religious monument to the Lord, reaching upward like a spire on a church. Around it they wanted to build a city and settle down together.

The Judgment of Confusion

> 11:5-9 *And the Lord came down to see the city and the tower, which the children of men builded.*
>
> *And the Lord said, Behold, the people is one, and they have all one language; and this they begin to do: and now nothing will be restrained from them, which they have imagined to do.*
>
> *Go to, let us go down, and there confound their language, that they may not understand one another's speech.*
>
> *So the Lord scattered them abroad from thence upon the face of all the earth: and they left off to build the city.*
>
> *Therefore is the name of it called Babel; because the Lord did there confound the language of all the earth: and from thence did the Lord scatter them abroad upon the face of all the earth.*

The language of verses 6 and 7 implies that the whole Trinity acted in this situation. The Godhead were not pleased with the people's intention to settle in one place, rather than populate the whole earth as they had been told to do. To curtail this rebellion the Lord confused their languages. A universal language had prevailed until this act of judgment took place. It may be that the diversity of new languages followed family or clan lines, since they could no longer understand each other. The great building projects stopped and groups with mutual languages began to move away to new locations. This may be the division mentioned in Eber's time, when he named his son Peleg to signify the scattering of people (Gen. 10:25). When people refuse to do God's will voluntarily, He may force them to do it, anyway. It is far better to walk with the Lord, as Enoch and Noah did, rather than behind Him or ahead of Him.

Summary

Noah and his family came out of the ark to face a renewed earth. Sinful men had perished in the great Flood, so they did not have to cope with them. They had animals which were ready to multiply and be used as food. Vegetation was already beginning to flourish. Human government was instituted. God promised never to destroy the earth by a great flood again. Everything pointed to a good future.

Sinful natures still inhabited each person, and this was manifested in the lack of respect shown to Noah. A curse was put upon Ham through his son Canaan when Noah predicted that his descendants would become servants. Noah passed off the scene, but his sons reproduced themselves and the world population began to grow. The human attempt to thwart the purpose of God was overcome by God's intervention in the confusion of languages. Man was subsequently forced to scatter out and populate the earth as God had originally commanded.

6

Abram Crosses Over

Genesis 11:10—13:4

Abram, later renamed Abraham, was the first Hebrew, which means "one who crosses over." He was a Semite tracing his roots to the line of Shem, son of Noah. He was a man of great faith at a time when the majority of men around him were pagans. Historically Abram was the father of the Jewish race and of other nations in the Near East. About one-fourth of the Book of Genesis is occupied with this unusual man of faith.

11:10-11 *These are the generations of Shem: Shem was an hundred years old, and begat Arphaxad two years after the flood:*
And Shem lived after he begat Arphaxad five hundred years, and begat sons and daughters.

We know that Shem had five sons—Elam, Asshur, Arphaxad, Lud, and Aram (Gen. 10:22). He may have had other unnamed sons, and he did have unnamed daughters, according to Genesis 11:11. The only descendants of Shem traced in chapter 11 are those leading to Abram. The writer of Genesis from this point exercises a principle of selection of genealogical materials that relate to Abram or his descendants. Old Testament history is admittedly concerned with the affairs of the godly line from which Christ was destined to come.

11:12-13 *And Arphaxad lived five and thirty years, and begat Salah:*
And Arphaxad lived after he begat Salah four hundred and three years, and begat sons and daughters.

Born just two years after the flood, Arphaxad lived a long life and was blessed with many children. Only one of his sons is listed in this genealogy (cf. Gen. 10:24).

11:14-15 *And Salah lived thirty years, and begat Eber:*
And Salah lived after he begat Eber four hundred and three years, and begat sons and daughters.

Salah had other sons and daughters, but the only one named was his son Eber (cf. Gen. 10:24).

11:16-17 *And Eber lived four and thirty years and begat Peleg:*
And Eber lived after he begat Peleg four hundred and thirty years, and begat sons and daughters.

Eber had other children, but the only ones named were his sons Peleg and Joktan (cf. Gen. 10:25).

11:18-19 *And Peleg lived thirty years, and begat Reu:*
And Peleg lived after he begat Reu two hundred and nine years, and begat sons and daughters.

Eber named his son Peleg to signify "division," for it was at that time that the people of the earth were scattered abroad, probably from their concentration at Babel (cf. Gen. 11:25). Peleg had other children, but only Reu was named in his genealogy.

11:20-21 *And Reu lived two and thirty years, and begat Serug:*
And Reu lived after he begat Serug two hundred and seven years, and begat sons and daughters.

Notice that with almost every generation the life span was shorter. While no reason is given for this change it could be assumed that the effect of sin was taking its toll.

11:22-23 *And Serug lived thirty years, and begat Nahor:*
And Serug lived after he begat Nahor two hundred years, and begat sons and daughters.

The sons of Shem, Ham, and Japheth had been required

81

to marry their sisters or cousins, but as the generations increased there were many opportunities for marriage choices of Serug's children. Only Nahor, Abram's grandfather, was listed in the record.

11:24-25 *And Nahor lived nine and twenty years, and begat Terah:*
And Nahor lived after he begat Terah an hundred and nineteen years, and begat sons and daughters.

From Nahor's children Terah is selected by the inspired writer as he traces the line of the faithful from generation to generation. Terah's name was important because he was the father of Abram. We do not know how Moses obtained this genealogical information. It may have been passed down orally from one generation to another or in written form, or it may have come to him by divine revelation. Whatever the method used he was empowered by the Holy Spirit to write an accurate record. It is interesting to note that Abram came from the godly line of Seth, Adam's son (Gen. 5:6-32; 11:10-26).

11:26-28 *And Terah lived seventy years, and begat Abram, Nahor, and Haran.*
Now these are the generations of Terah: Terah begat Abram, Nahor, and Haran; and Haran begat Lot.
And Haran died before his father Terah in the land of his nativity, in Ur of the Chaldees.

We do not know if Terah had other children or not. Only Abram, Nahor, and Haran are named. Nahor was probably named after his grandfather (vv. 22-25). He and Terah were evidently as much believers in Jehovah as Abram was, for Laban later referred to Him as "the God of Abraham, and the God of Nahor, [and] the God of their father [Terah]" (Gen. 31:53).

Haran died while the family was living in Ur. He left at least three children behind—a son named Lot (v. 27) and two daughters named Milcah and Iscah (v. 29).

11:29-30 *And Abram and Nahor took them wives: the name of Abram's wife was Sarai; and the name of*

Nahor's wife, Milcah, the daughter of Haran, the father
of Milcah, and the father of Iscah.
But Sarai was barren; she had no child.

The reference to the wives of the patriarchs is a new
feature of the genealogy introduced at this point. It was no
doubt because these women were to have important roles
in the subsequent unfolding of the plan of God that they
are mentioned here. It appears that Abram married his
half-sister, Sarai, for they had a common father but different mothers (Gen. 20:12). Nahor seems to have married his
orphaned niece, Milcah. Marriage to such close relatives
may have taken place because these men did not want to
marry pagan women around them. Marriage to close relatives had been fairly common in early generations, so it
would not have the same stigma that it has in our times.
Sarai, later to be renamed Sarah, was unable to bear children. This must have been a source of grief to her and
Abram. It may have been mentioned here to enhance the
miracle which God wrought in allowing her to bear Isaac
in her old age (Gen. 17:19; 21:1-2).

11:31-32   *And Terah took Abram his son, and Lot the*
son of Haran his sons's son, and Sarai his daughter in
law, his son Abram's wife; and they went forth with
them from Ur of the Chaldees, to go into the land of
Canaan; and they came unto Haran, and dwelt there.
And the days of Terah were two hundred and five
years: and Terah died in Haran.

Ur was a well-developed city in ancient times. Located
on or near the Persian Gulf, it was a center of culture and
commerce. However, it was a place of rank idolatry, with
special emphasis on the moon god, *Sin.* Righteous Terah
and members of his family must have vexed their righteous souls day by day in that environment. The Lord
evidently told Terah and his family to move out of Ur,
although later references focus on God calling Abram out
of that city (Gen. 15:7; Neh. 9:7).

Genesis 11:31, in retrospect, states that Terah and his
family went forth from Ur of the Chaldees to go into the
land of Canaan. It was not clear to them at the beginning

of their journey that they were ultimately going to Palestine at the other end of the Fertile Crescent. Even when Abram left Haran, he did not know what his destination was. "By faith Abraham, when he was called to go out into a place which he should after receive for an inheritance, obeyed; and he went out, not knowing whither he went" (Heb. 11:8).

Ur was at the southern end of Mesopotamia (Iraq), and Haran was at the northern end of it. Though Terah and his family were moved some five hundred and fifty miles from Ur, they were still in their home country. The moon god was worshipped in Haran, as it was in Ur. Perhaps the family (or clan) settled there because of Terah's age. He was unable to journey any farther. Some Bible scholars have concluded that Abram's time at Haran was "wasted years," but the Scripture says nothing to confirm that position. Abram as an obedient son remained with his father and took increased responsibilities during Terah's declining years. The Lord waited until Terah's death before renewing the call for Abram to go to a new land, as we shall see in chapter 12.

12:1 *Now the Lord had said unto Abram, Get thee out of thy country, and from thy kindred, and from thy father's house, unto a land that I will shew thee:*

Mesopotamia was located between the Tigris and Euphrates Rivers. To the west was the awesome Arabian Desert, a natural barrier to travel. When God told Abram to leave Haran, He may have pointed him in a westerly direction and left it at that for the time being. The old trade route would carry the caravan over the top of the Fertile Crescent before turning southward into Palestine. Abram prepared himself and his family to carry out God's will. They set out expecting God to lead them.

Promise of Blessing

12:2-3 *And I will make of thee a great nation, and I will bless thee, and make thy name great; and thou shalt be a blessing:*
And I will bless them that bless thee, and curse him

that curseth thee: and in thee shall all families of the earth be blessed.

It must have been difficult for Abram and Sarai to contemplate leaving Mesopotamia, their clan, and their closest relatives. We who live in a Western culture know little about the cohesion in an "extended family" which has prevailed in much of the world since ancient times. Abram and Sarai did not have the means of communication and transportation which we have today. To leave home might mean that they would never see it again. They probably could have remained in Haran and done very well as heads of the clan, but God told them to leave it all behind.

Along with the divine directive came a promise of blessing. God said that Abram's family would become a great nation. Imagine how that prediction must have sounded to this aged and barren couple! How could Abram father a nation? Though confounded by the magnitude of this promise they continued to believe and obey God.

They no doubt felt threatened by the prospect of going to a strange land, but God quieted their fear with a promise to protect them. He promised to bless those who treated them well and to curse any who mistreated them. Subsequent history of the patriarchs and their descendants show that He fulfilled this promise. God made this promise for the whole Jewish race, although many who got out of His will paid a high price for their sins.

It is certainly true that the descendants of Abram have blessed "all families of the earth" by their intelligence and talents. Jews seem to have contributed more to various fields of human endeavor than their comparatively small numbers would warrant. The heart of God's promise that Abram's seed would bless the world is its Messianic application (Gal. 3:8). It is not likely that Abram fully realized the implications of God's promise. The Lord Jesus Christ was born of Abram's family and by His death and resurrection has provided salvation for all who believe. The children of Abram have been a blessing to the world in the gift of the Old Testament and the Messiah.

12:4-6 *So Abram departed, as the Lord had spoken*

*unto him: and Lot went with him: and Abram was
seventy and five years old when he departed out of
Haran.*

*And Abram took Sarai his wife, and Lot his brother's
son, and all their substance that they had gathered, and
the souls that they had gotten in Haran; and they went
forth to go into the land of Canaan; and into the land of
Canaan they came.*

*And Abram passed through the land unto the place of
Sichem, unto the plain of Moreh. And the Canaanite
was then in the land.*

Abram was a great pioneer of faith in God. He had no
Scriptures and none of the helpful literature which we
take for granted today. He was leaving all that was familiar and going to what was new and strange. He may have
had a sense of adventure to draw him onward, but it was
the command of God which counted most.

We do not know if God told Abram to take Lot and his
household with him. Nothing is said about this. It
probably was his own personal decision. Perhaps he could
not bear to think of leaving all of his relatives behind.
Perhaps he wanted the added protection of Lot and his
servants in the event they encountered bandits along the
way. Abram and Lot later separated in Canaan, with Lot
choosing to dwell in wicked Sodom (Gen. 13:12-13). He
would probably have done better to remain behind in
Haran, considering how things turned out for him and his
family when Sodom was destroyed by divine fire (Gen.
19).

Abram was seventy-five years old when he left Haran.
Sarai was ten years younger (Gen. 17:17). Sarai was to live
until she was one hundred and twenty-seven (Gen. 23:1).
Abram was to live until he was one hundred and seventy-
five (Gen. 25:7). Thus, Sarai's life was only about half
over, and Abram's life was only three-sevenths over. We
might say that they were in the "prime of life."

The journey to Canaan was about 350-400 miles from
Haran. Sichem (or Shechem) was located in the central
part of Canaan about forty miles north of what later came
to be known as Jerusalem. The plain of Moreh was a good
place to camp for a while, with its grove of oak or terebinth

trees and its view of Mount Gerizim and Mount Ebal. Canaanites were living in the land, but they were probably split up into nomadic groups moving about to find forage for their herds and thus posed no threat to Abram and Lot.

Another Divine Visitation

12:7-9 *And the Lord appeared unto Abram, and said, Unto thy seed will I give this land: and there builded he an altar unto the Lord, who appeared unto him.*

And he removed from thence unto a mountain on the east of Bethel, and pitched his tent, having Bethel on the west, and Hai on the east: and there he builded an altar unto the Lord, and called upon the name of the Lord.

And Abram journeyed, going on still toward the south.

The covenant which God gave to Abram included a promise that he would become a multitude of people and also have a homeland for the people. It is this covenant on which Jews today base their claim to Palestine. Tremendous pressures are brought against the modern state of Israel to give part of this away to create a state for Palestinian refugees, but it is being resisted. Dispossessed many times over the centuries, the Israelis are determined not to be pushed around. The clash of wills in the Middle East has a direct bearing on world politics.

In order to examine the land of Canaan, as well as to find food for their increasing flocks, Abram and Lot kept on the move. They pitched camp at a mountain near Bethel, which at that time was probably named Luz (Gen. 28:19). Hai was the town called Ai when the Israelites conquested it after the Exodus (Josh. 8:28). Moving continually southward, Abram found a scarcity of food for the herds. Famine was stalking the inhabitants of Canaan.

Famine

12:10 *And there was a famine in the land: and*

87

Abram went down into Egypt to sojourn there; for the famine was grievous in the land.

Some people criticize Abram for leaving the land of Canaan and going down to Egypt at this time. They argue that he should have stayed in the land of promise and trusted the Lord to take care of him there. They imply that Abram had a lapse of faith in this situation and that he would not have gotten into difficulty in Egypt if he had stayed in Canaan where he belonged. However, there is nothing in the passage which states that God forbade Abram from going to Egypt to avoid the famine in Canaan. In fact, when Jacob later was ready to take his clan and leave another famine in Canaan to join his long lost son in Egypt, the Lord said to him, "Fear not to go down into Egypt; for I will there make of thee a great nation" (Gen. 46:3). It is also possible that God wanted Abram to go to Egypt in order that He might use the Pharaoh there to enrich Abram (Gen. 12:16; 13:2). This would be one means by which the Lord could fulfill His promise to bless Abram in a material way (Gen. 12:2). The verb "sojourn" implied that Abram planned to be in Egypt only for a temporary period before returning to Canaan. He did not intend to forsake the land of promise permanently.

12:11-13 *And it came to pass, when he was come near to enter into Egypt, that he said unto Sarai his wife, Behold now, I know that thou art a fair woman to look upon:*
Therefore it shall come to pass, when the Egyptians shall see thee, that they shall say, This is his wife: and they will kill me, but they will save thee alive.
Say, I pray thee, thou art my sister: that it may be well with me for thy sake; and my soul shall live because of thee.

This passage does show Abram motivated by fear, rather than by faith, as he sought for a way to protect himself. After leaving Haran, he had arranged with Sarai to deliberately deceive foreigners wherever he and she went by having her say that she was his sister and hide

88

the fact that she was his wife (Gen. 20:13). He had evidently known something of the customs in Palestine and
Egypt. A ruler felt justified in adding any beautiful
woman to his harem, provided he paid her nearest relative
a large dowry. Abram was also afraid that he himself
would be slain, if a ruler desired Sarai and discovered that
he was her husband.

Note how Abram appealed to Sarai's sense of fear as
they approached Egypt. He began by flattering her in
saying that she was a fair woman to look upon. He implied
that the Egyptians would find her irresistible (even
though she was about sixty-five years old). He suggested
that they would kill him, if they discovered that he was
her husband, and that she would then be made part of a
harem in a foreign land. He rationalized that she really
was his sister, although she was actually his half-sister.
He told her that the planned deception was necessary for
preserving his life and her future welfare. He later used
the same deception with Abimilech, the king of Gerar
(Gen. 20:1-12). Abram's deliberate use of deception revealed an unfortunate lack of faith in God for deliverance
in his threatening circumstances. As with all other
human beings, there were times when Abram did not
measure up to the high standards which please the Lord.

12:14-16 *And it came to pass, that, when Abram was
come into Egypt, the Egyptians beheld the woman that
she was very fair.*

*The princes also of Pharaoh saw her, and commended
her before Pharaoh: and the woman was taken into
Pharaoh's house.*

*And he entreated Abram well for her sake: and he had
sheep, and oxen, and he asses, and menservants, and
maidservants, and she asses, and camels.*

Abram was right about the reaction of the virile
Egyptians to the sight of the well-preserved Sarai. The
princes of the kingdom told the Pharaoh that a likely
prospect for his harem had arrived. He listened to them,
he summoned Abram and Sarai to appear before him, and
a deal was arranged. Abram watched while his beloved
Sarai was taken away to the Pharaoh's house. Then he

was presented with many animals and slaves in payment. Silver and gold may also have been given to him here (Gen. 13:2).

We can only speculate as to what went through Abram's mind at this time. He reasoned that this course of action was justified since his household and that of Lot were desperately in need of food. He did not want to leave Sarai in the Pharaoh's possession. He wanted to take her back to Canaan when the time to leave came. How did he plan to get her back? Perhaps he thought that he could arrange for her to escape. Perhaps he thought that God would somehow intervene and restore her to him. He may even have known what was about to happen to the Pharaoh and his household because of Sarai's presence among them.

Divine Intervention

12:17-20 And the Lord plagued Pharaoh and his house with great plagues because of Sarai Abram's wife.

And Pharaoh called Abram, and said, What is this that thou hast done unto me? why didst thou not tell me that she was thy wife?

Why saidst thou, She is my sister? so I might have taken her to me to wife: now therefore behold thy wife, take her, and go thy way.

And Pharaoh commanded his men concerning him: and they sent him away, and his wife, and all that he had.

There was usually an extended period of preparation before a woman would actually become the wife of an ancient ruler. She had not been in his palace very long before serious diseases began to afflict the royal household. The ruler probably called his counselors together to ask what might be wrong. They may have suggested that the only new variant in the situation was the presence of Sarai. These superstitious pagans may have decided that the god of the Hebrews was punishing the Pharaoh for his action. He concluded that Sarai must be more than a sister to Abram; she must be his wife, too. Of course, it may be that Sarai or some other Hebrew let the information slip out and be known to the Pharaoh.

The ruler was highly offended at Abram's deception, and he had a right to be. Now he showed that he was a far more honorable person than Abram had thought him to be. The Pharaoh did not kill Abram, Sarai, or any other member of the Hebrew clan. He did not take back the possessions which he had lavished on Abram. All that he did was to banish them from his kingdom under an armed escort. God's intervention had spared the Hebrews and they returned to the land of promise far richer than when they entered Egypt.

13:1-2 *And Abram went up out of Egypt, he, and his wife, and all that he had, and Lot with him, into the south.*
And Abram was very rich in cattle, in silver, and in gold.

The shortest route from Egypt to Canaan would have been across the northern part of the Sinai Peninsula. It was a hot, dusty, and tiresome journey. It must have been refreshing to come to the hill country in the southern part of Palestine. Progress was slow, for the caravan could not travel any faster than the slowest person or animal could go. When an oasis was reached, the caravan might camp there for several days or weeks before moving on to the next one.

Wealth in those times was counted primarily by the possessions of slaves, herds of various animals, gold, silver, and fine clothing. Abram was rich by these standards. We might expect the caravan to be bothered by roving robbers, but there were apparently enough men in the combined households of Abram and Lot to offer sufficient protection from such an eventuality. We know that it was not long afterward that Abram was able to muster three hundred and eighteen men in his own household, arm them with weapons, and lead them in an operation to rescue Lot and his household who had been kidnapped and taken northward to Syria (Gen. 14:14-16). This gives us some idea of the enormous size of these households.

Back to Bethel

13:3-4 *And he went on his journeys from the south even to Bethel, unto the place where his tent had been at the beginning, between Bethel and Hai.*

Unto the place of the altar, which he had made there at the first: and there Abram called on the name of the Lord.

Moving from place to place up through the southern part of Canaan, Abram finally came to the spot where he had rested when he first entered Palestine. Although he was still a stranger in this new land, he began to sense that it was his home. The altar he had previously built, probably with large stones, was still there. He prayed to Jehovah and no doubt offered up animal sacrifices to Him to atone for sins and to give thanks for protection and enrichment.

At Bethel, Abram was able to reflect on the life of faith he had been following. He may have retraced in his mind the journey from Ur and sought to better understand God's purpose for him and his household. When Terah died God renewed His call to Abram to leave his country and kindred and go out to a new land which would be shown to him. Bolstered by divine promises of blessing, Abram, Lot, and their households headed westward and then southward across the Fertile Crescent.

It was in Canaan that God told Abram that his descendants were going to inherit the land. Because of famine conditions, the Hebrews went down into Egypt to seek food. Abram's deception of the Pharaoh concerning Sarai led to a stern rebuke and banishment, but it also increased Abram's wealth. He returned to Canaan and renewed his worship of Jehovah at the altar he had built there.

7

Lot Chooses Sodom

Genesis 13:5—14:24

Prosperity can sometimes bring bane along with blessing. The herds of Abram and Lot had increased to the point where they taxed the available pasture lands. Dissension had broken out among the herdsmen. To solve the problems brought on by their prosperity a peaceful separation was decided. Lot headed for the Jordan Valley and Abram remained in the hill country to the west near Hebron. The character of Lot is reflected in his choice.

13:5-7 *And Lot also, which went with Abram, had flocks, and herds, and tents.*

And the land was not able to bear them, that they might dwell together: for their substance was great, so that they could not dwell together.

And there was a strife between the herdmen of Abram's cattle and the herdmen of Lot's cattle: and the Canaanite and the Perizzite dwelled then in the land.

The word "tents" implies the presence of many servants. These servants, charged with caring for the livestock, began to argue with one another over which flocks and herds would get the pasture lands and the available water. The presence of Canaanites and Perizzites roving about the area posed a threat to Abram and Lot. They, too, wanted pastures and water for their livestock. If Abram and Lot fought each other, these pagans might move in and overcome them.

The Separation

13:8-9 *And Abram said unto Lot, Let there be no strife, I pray thee, between me and thee, and between my herdmen and thy herdmen; for we be brethren.*

Is not the whole land before thee? separate thyself, I

*pray thee, from me: if thou wilt take the left hand, then I
will go to the right; or if thou depart to the right hand,
then I will go to the left.*

Abram was a wise man. He saw no value in continued
contention between himself and Lot or between their
herdmen. Since they were kinsmen Abram thought it inappropriate for them to fight with each other and lose
integrity before the pagans.

Abram graciously offered Lot the first choice of the
territory. There were many locations in Canaan where he
might take his household and find adequate room for ex-
pansion of his flocks and herds. Once Lot had selected a
place Abram would go elsewhere and settle.

13:10-11 *And Lot lifted up his eyes, and beheld all
the plain of Jordan, that it was well watered every
where, before the Lord destroyed Sodom and Gomorrah,
even as the garden of the Lord, like the land of Egypt, as
thou comest unto Zoar.*

*Then Lot chose him all the plain of Jordan; and Lot
journeyed east: and they separated themselves the one
from the other.*

Standing on a hill east of Bethel, Lot looked down the
Jordan Valley. The Jordan River provided it with water,
so that trees grew along its banks and broad pastures
stretched out beyond them on either side. The natural
riches of that valley are here compared to the garden of
Eden in which Adam and Eve had originally lived. Its
fertility was like the Nile Valley in Egypt. Before the Lord
rained fire and brimstone down upon Sodom and
Gomorrah, this fertile valley probably extended to the
area of the Dead Sea as far south as Zoar. Recent arch-
aeological excavations give indications that Zoar is
buried under water at the southeastern part of the Dead
Sea. Zoar means "little," and may have been the place to
which Lot fled when Sodom was destroyed (Gen. 19:20-22).
The town named Zoar shown just south of the Dead Sea on
Bible maps may have been named as a replacement for
the one under water.

We cannot help but be disturbed by two things about

Lot. He should have deferred to his Uncle Abram and insisted that Abram take first choice of a place to live, but he did not. He should have investigated the people in the Jordan Valley and Dead Sea Valley before deciding to live among them, but apparently he did not or he chose to live among them in spite of their sinfulness.

13:12-13 *Abram dwelled in the land of Canaan, and Lot dwelled in the cities of the plain, and pitched his tent toward Sodom.*
But the men of Sodom were wicked and sinners before the Lord exceedingly.

Although we think of all of Palestine as Canaan, it was the area between the Jordan River and the Mediterranean Sea which appears to be meant here, especially the hill country. Abram located about ten miles north of Jerusalem in the area of Bethel, while Lot made his way to the cities of the Jordan Valley and Dead Sea Valley and finally pitched his tent near Sodom. He eventually became a leader in that city and had a house there (Gen. 19:1-2). This is hard to understand, because he was a just and righteous man who was vexed (irritated) daily by the filthy behavior of the wicked people who lived there (2 Pet. 2:7-8). He evidently felt that the opportunities to prosper materially there were worth putting himself and his family into spiritual peril. The only other possibility would seem to be that he thought he might be a good influence in an evil situation, but we have no evidence to support this. Homosexuality was so rampant in Sodom, as illustrated in Genesis 19:4-9, that the term sodomy has been a synonym for it ever since.

The Promise Renewed

13:14-15 *And the Lord said unto Abram, after that Lot was separated from him, Lift up now thine eyes, and look from the place where thou art northward, and southward, and eastward, and westward:*
For all the land which thou seest, to thee will I give it, and to thy seed for ever.

The promise to inherit the land made earlier to Abram was confirmed as he resettled in Canaan (Gen. 12:7). This land was to become the possession of Abram and his descendants forever. Palestine gets its name from Philistia which was located in southwestern Palestine by the Mediterranean Sea in what is now the Gaza Strip. The larger territory eventually took on the name of this smaller region. God told Abram to look in all four directions from his vantage point in the hill country. By this he was assured that the entire land would become the possession of his descendants. It would be centuries later before this prediction would be fulfilled.

> 13:16 *And I will make thy seed as the dust of the earth: so that if a man can number the dust of the earth, then shall thy seed also be numbered.*

God followed the promise regarding the land with a prediction of the numerical size of the nation that was to come from the line of Abram. His descendants would become in number as the "stars" in the sky (Gen. 15:5) and the "[grains of] sand which is upon the sea shore" (Gen. 22:17). Although there are only approximately fourteen million Jews in the world today, countless others have lived on the earth before them since Abram's time. The concept of having even a single million descendants would have been mind-boggling to Abram, who lived at a time when populations were much smaller than they are now.

> 13:17-18 *Arise, walk through the land in the length of it and in the breadth of it; for I will give it unto thee.*
> *Then Abram removed his tent, and came and dwelt in the plain of Mamre, which is in Hebron, and built there an altar unto the Lord.*

Abram was not only instructed to look at the land but he was to walk through it. As he walked he was to assess the full extent of his inheritance. There is a sense in which walking through the land was an exercise of faith. Abram, though an alien, was claiming the land according to God's promise. The Lord's promise to give Abram this land could not be implemented until His promise to make him a nation came true. It was in Egypt that this nation was to be produced (Gen. 46:3). At the time that Jacob went down to join Joseph in Egypt, there were only seventy people in the Hebrew clan (Gen. 46:26-27). Waiting for God to fulfill His promises sometimes requires great patience on the part of men, but the Lord does not look at time as we do (2 Pet. 3:8).

Mamre was the name of an Amorite who had two brothers named Eshcol and Aner. These were allies of Abram after he moved to the plain of Mamre just north of Hebron in the hill country of southern Canaan (Gen. 14:13, 24). It was there that Abram built another altar, probably of large stones, in order that he might offer up sacrifices to Jehovah.

The Rescue of Lot

14:1-4 *And it came to pass in the days of Amraphel king of Shinar, Arioch king of Ellasar, Chedorlaomer king of Elam, and Tidal king of nations;*

That these made war with Bera king of Sodom, and with Birsha king of Gomorrah, Shinab king of Admah, and Shemeber king of Zeboiim, and the king of Bela, which is Zoar.

All these were joined together in the vale of Siddim, which is the salt sea.

Twelve years they served Chedorlaomer, and in the thirteenth year they rebelled.

A confederation of four kings in the east had subdued the people from Mesopotamia to Canaan. These alien rulers were Amraphel, king of Shinar (northern Mesopotamia), Arioch, king of Ellasar (Babylonia), Chedorlaomer, king of Elam (a mountain region near the head of the Persian Gulf) and Tidal, king of nations. Tidal may have been chief of a roving band of people. Berkeley suggests that he may have been Tudhul, king of Gutium northeast of Babylonia. The leader of this confederation was Chedorlaomer.

The kings of the Dead Sea Valley are named in verse 2. The fact that they had grown tired of giving allegiance to

Chedorlaomer and his allies for twelve years and rebelled against him in the thirteenth year is mentioned in verse 4. The fact they prepared to meet him in battle in the Valley of Siddim (Salt or Dead Sea Valley) is mentioned in verse 3. Before studying that battle, however, let us see what Chedorlaomer and his allies did to nations living in the area south of the Dead Sea. The account of that campaign is found in verses 5-7. Then the account of the war with the Dead Sea Valley kings is found in verses 8-11

> *14:5-7 And in the fourteenth year came Chedor-laomer, and the kings that were with him, and smote the Rephaims in Ashteroth Karnaim, and the Zuzims in Ham, and the Emims in Shaveh Kiriathaim.*
>
> *And the Horites in their mount Seir, unto El-paran, which is by the wilderness.*
>
> *And they returned, and came to En-mishpat, which is Kadesh, and smote all the country of the Amalekites, and also the Amorites, that dwelt in Hazezon-tamar.*

The bloodthirsty kings of the east went on a rampage in the area south of Canaan. They evidently came down the eastern side of the Jordan Valley, sweeping everything before them and bypassing the cities in the Dead Sea Valley for the time being. They conquered the Rephaims in Ashteroth Karnaim, the Zuzims in Ham, the Emims in Shaveh Kiriathaim, and the Horites from Mount Seir down to El-paran on the border of the wilderness in the central part of the Sinai Peninsula. On their way back, they overcame people in En-mishpat (or Kadesh), an area which was later settled by the Amalekites, descendants of Esau. They also subdued the Amorites in Hazezon-tamar.

What apparently happened was that when the Dead Sea Valley kings rebelled against Chedorlaomer and his allies, the kings of the east decided to come to Palestine and teach these rebels a lesson that they would not forget. This presented an opportunity for the kings of the east to expand their dominion by subduing nations to the south of Palestine. Then they planned to deal with the rebellious Dead Sea Valley kings while on their way home. Thus the stage was set for a confrontation between the kings of the east and the kings of the Dead Sea Valley.

14:8-11 *And there went out the king of Sodom, and the king of Gomorrah, and the king of Admah, and the king of Zeboiim, and the king of Bela (the same is Zoar;) and they joined battle with them in the vale of Siddim;*

With Chedorlaomer the king of Elam, and with Tidal king of nations, and Amraphel king of Shinar, and Arioch king of Ellasar; four kings with five.

And the vale of Siddim was full of slimepits; and the kings of Sodom and Gomorrah fled, and fell there; and they that remained fled to the mountain

And they took all the goods of Sodom and Gomorrah, and all their victuals, and went their way.

The five kings of the Dead Sea Valley were Bera, king of Sodom; Birsha, king of Gomorrah; Shinab, king of Admah; Shemeber, king of Zeboiim; and an unnamed king of Bela (or Zoar). They met the combined army of the four kings of the east, but they surely were no match for these battle-hardened warriors. In the rout which took place, the kings of Sodom and Gomorrah fled, but they fell into slime pits in the area. They have also been called asphalt pits, bitumen pits (with the petroleum removed), and tar pits. The other three kings escaped to a mountain nearby. We do not know if the king of Sodom mentioned in verses 17 and 21-22 was the one mentioned here (having been rescued somehow) or if he was a replacement chosen by the time Abraham returned. The kings of the east plundered Sodom and Gomorrah, taking their treasures, food (or provisions), and many captives with them as they moved northward to return to Mesopotamia.

14:12-16 *And they took Lot, Abram's brother's son, who dwelt in Sodom, and his goods, and departed.*

And there came one that had escaped, and told Abram the Hebrew; for he dwelt in the plain of Mamre the Amorite, brother of Eshcol, and brother of Aner: and these were confederate with Abram.

And when Abram heard that his brother was taken captive, he armed his trained servants, born in his own house, three hundred and eighteen, and pursued them unto Dan.

And he divided himself against them, he and his

servants, by night, and smote them, and pursued them
unto Hobah, which is on the left hand of Damascus.
And he brought back all the goods, and also brought
again his brother Lot, and his goods, and the women
also, and the people.

We do not normally think of Abram as a warrior, but he rose to the challenge here.

Someone who escaped the massacre at the slime pits reached Abram near Hebron and reported the capture of Lot. It was a time for action, because Abram cared about Lot and his family. He did not want them to be made slaves for the rest of their lives. If he had been a harsh man, he might have decided that Lot was getting what he deserved for aligning himself with the wicked people of Sodom, but Abram's heart was tender.

Abram consulted hurriedly with his friends—Mamre, Eshcol, and Aner—and they raised an army from their own households to attempt a rescue. There were an amazing three hundred and eighteen men from Abram's household alone! This army could travel lightly and more quickly than the army of the kings from the east. Abram and his men caught up with them at Leshem (Josh. 19:47) or Laish (Judg. 18:7) near Mount Hermon north of Canaan. This was later renamed Dan after it was conquered and settled by that tribe of Israelites following the Exodus.

Dividing his forces into at least two smaller groups, Abram attacked at night and routed them. He and his men pursued them as far north as Hobah, west of Damascus, Syria, a distance of about a hundred miles. It was a stunning victory for men who had had little or no experience in fighting. No doubt the Lord gave them this victory. Abram returned to Canaan triumphantly, leading his nephew Lot and all of the captives taken, along with the booty which the enemy had taken. Word of this exploit preceded him and he and his men were given a hero's welcome as they returned to the valley.

14:17   *And the king of Sodom went out to meet him*
after his return from the slaughter of Chedorlaomer,

*and of the kings that were with him, at the valley of
Shaveh, which is the king's dale.*

The king of Sodom is not named here, making us
wonder if it was Bera (v. 2) or a replacement. He came up to
the Valley of Shaveh, also called the King's Dale (or
Valley). It was probably a plain near Salem (later to be
renamed Jerusalem). Abram had to be careful how he
related to the king of Sodom, for he was very different
from him in beliefs and practices.

The Blessing of Melchizedek

14:18-20 *And Melchizedek king of Salem brought
forth bread and wine: and he was the priest of the most
high God.*
*And he blessed him, and said, Blessed be Abram of
the most high God, possessor of heaven and earth:*
*And blessed be the most high God, which hath
delivered thine enemies into thy hand. And he gave him
tithes of all.*

Melchizedek, the king of Salem, also came to recognize
Abram for his victory. Melchizedek was a mysterious
person. He was not only the king of Salem, but he was also
a priest of the most high God. Somehow the concept of
Jehovah, the true God, had penetrated the heart of this
man. This is the first time that the term "priest" is used in
the Bible. The writer of the epistle to the Hebrews later
called Christ "a priest for ever after the order of Melchis-
edec," as did the Psalmist in Psalm 110:4. The parallels
drawn between Christ and Melchizedek in Hebrews 7:1-10
are so striking that some scholars maintain that Melchizedek may not have been a historical figure but a preincar-
national appearance of Christ. While this is a possibility,
it seems more likely that Melchizedek was a historical
person. He served as a type of the priesthood of Christ and
it is to this that the writer to the Hebrews made reference.
We do not know if the bread and wine brought out by
Melchizedek were merely for ceremonial use in
celebrating Abram's victory, or if this king gave refresh-
ments to Abram's whole army and the captives he had

rescued. It was an act of kindness in either case. Melchizedek used the occasion to bless both Abram and the most high God who had given Abram his victory over the kings of the east. In response, Abram offered Melchizedek a tenth of all of the spoils of war which he had brought back with him. This is the first mention of tithes in the Bible.

14:21-24 *And the king of Sodom said unto Abram, Give me the persons, and take the goods to thyself.*

And Abram said to the king of Sodom, I have lift up mine hand unto the Lord, the most high God, the possessor of heaven and earth,

That I will not take from a thread even to a shoe-latchet, and that I will not take any thing that is thine, lest thou shouldest say, I have made Abram rich:

Save only that which the young men have eaten, and the portion of the men which went with me, Aner, Eshcol, and Mamre; let them take their portion.

The king of Sodom was so grateful for what Abram had done that he asked only for the return of his people who had been rescued from the enemy. He was willing to let Abram keep all of the loot taken from Sodom. Abram refused to take any of it, except what had been required for feeding his soldiers and what he felt was the just share of his allies—Aner, Eshcol, and Mamre. He would not accept even one thread of raiment or one sandal strap from the pagan king of Sodom. He raised his hand in sworn testimony to the one true God that he had made this decision so that no one could ever say that he had been enriched by this man. Abram graciously refrained from condemning the king of Sodom for the kind of wickedness that he tolerated in his depraved city, but by his act he made his intention clear.

Lot and his family went back to live in Sodom after this experience. Evidently they had not learned from it that they ought to find another place to live where they could worship and serve Jehovah in righteousness and be free from the evil distractions and dangers of that place. Even if they wanted to be close enough to maintain a testimony for the Lord there, they could have moved outside of the city itself. It appears that whatever the comforts, cultural advantages, and business opportunities of the city were, they were sufficient to cause them to remain in that hostile spiritual vacuum.

Abram might have concluded that his increased importance in that part of Canaan was the means by which God would allow him to start taking control of the land promised to him. However, he did not take advantage of his military superiority and assume political control over the area. He evidently felt that his role was to remain separated from the prevailing paganism of the land and to maintain a pure testimony for Jehovah there.

The prosperity which came to Abram and Lot in Canaan brought with it the problems of limited resources and dissension. They could not live together and have sufficient pasturage and water for the people and animals of both households. They separated peacefully, with Abram remaining in the hill country west of the Jordan River and Lot moving to the Jordan Valley.

The Lord confirmed His covenant promises to Abram, telling him again that He would give him the land of Canaan and a multitude of descendants to populate it. Abram moved from Bethel southward to the plain of Mamre near Hebron.

Abram was learning to walk by faith. The testings Jehovah permitted only served to strengthen him. He was evermore aware that the covenant promises must be fulfilled in God's time and in God's way.

8

Abram's Struggles of Faith

Genesis 15:1—17:27

Hebrews 11:6 says, "He that cometh to God must believe that he is [or exists], and that he is a rewarder of them that diligently seek him." Faith is sometimes a long process accompanied by many testings. Abram grew impatient when the years passed by and he did not have a child. How was he to be the father of a nation? How could God's promise be fulfilled? Though a man of faith Abram found himself yielding to the frustration this situation of his childlessness imposed. Once again the Lord visited Abram and confirmed in a dramatic way His promise.

15:1-3 *After these things the word of the Lord came unto Abram in a vision, saying, Fear not, Abram: I am thy shield, and thy exceeding great reward.*

And Abram said, Lord God, what wilt thou give me, seeing I go childless, and the steward of my house is this Eliezer of Damascus?

And Abram said, Behold, to me thou hast given no seed: and, lo, one born in my house is mine heir.

God reassured Abram that He would protect him. Abram may have been afraid that he would die without bearing a child, since he was now over eighty years old. He did not want to have to leave his inheritance to his chief servant, Eliezer of Damascus, a slave born and raised in his own household. He wondered what good any riches given to him by the Lord would be, if he could not pass them on to a son.

15:4-6 *And, behold, the word of the Lord came unto him, saying, This shall not be thine heir; but he that shall come forth out of thine own bowels shall be thine heir.*

And he brought him forth abroad, and said, Look now

toward heaven, and tell the stars, if thou be able to number them: and he said unto him, So shall thy seed be.

And he believed in the Lord; and he counted it to him for righteousness.

The Lord quickly reassured Abram that He was going to fulfill His promise to make of him a great nation (Gen. 12:2). Abram's first heir was to be his own son not an adopted one. God sent him out of his tent to look up at the star-filled sky, and then He promised Abram that his descendants were to be more in number than the stars. Since we know that Abram could only see about fifteen hundred stars with the naked eye, the number of his descendants was going to far exceed what he saw. Abram believed what God told him, and the Lord set that to his spiritual account as righteousness. Thus, even before the Law was given through Moses, and before salvation came through the Atonement for sin made by Christ, it was faith which put people into right relationship with God. Works alone have never been able to do this (Eph. 2:8-9).

15:7-8 *And he said unto him, I am the Lord that brought thee out of Ur of the Chaldees, to give thee this land to inherit it.*

And he said, Lord God, whereby shall I know that I shall inherit it?

The two parts of the covenant God made with Abram seem to be consistently mentioned together (Gen. 12:2, 7; 15:5, 7; 17:6, 8). First, God promised to give Abram many descendants, and second, He promised to give them the land of Canaan. The Lord reminded Abram that He had moved him all the way from the other end of the Fertile Crescent so that he would be located in Canaan. Abram wanted some proof that he would indeed inherit this land, so he asked for it. God responded to this request.

15:9-11 *And he said unto him, Take me an heifer of three years old, and a she goat of three years old, and a ram of three years old, and a turtledove, and a young pigeon.*

And he took unto him all these, and divided them in the midst, and laid each piece one against the other: but the birds divided he not.

And when the fowls came down upon the carcasses, Abram drove them away.

As he had been directed, Abram searched through his animals and selected a young cow, a female goat, a ram (male sheep), a turtledove, and a pigeon. The three animals were split into two halves and the halves were arranged in a line opposite each other. The two birds were not cut up but were placed opposite each other. While Abram waited the next directive the vultures (or other birds of prey) swooped down to feast on the carcasses of the slain animals and birds, but Abram shooed them away. He continued guarding the sacrifices until evening. Abram, as in every step of his spiritual journey, had to learn the patience and struggles associated with walking by faith.

15:12-17 *And when the sun was going down, a deep sleep fell upon Abram; and, lo, an horror of great darkness fell upon him.*

And he said unto Abram, Know of a surety that thy seed shall be a stranger in a land that is not their's, and shall serve them; and they shall afflict them four hundred years;

And also that nation, whom they shall serve, will I judge: and afterward shall they come out with great substance.

And thou shalt go to thy fathers in peace; thou shalt be buried in a good old age.

But in the fourth generation they shall come hither again: for the iniquity of the Amorites is not yet full.

And it came to pass, that, when the sun went down, and it was dark, behold a smoking furnace, and a burning lamp that passed between those pieces.

At sunset the Lord put Abram into a deep sleep. He was overwhelmed by a vision of fear and great darkness. Then the Lord told him that his descendants would become slaves in a foreign land, which we know was ancient

Egypt. God told Abram that they would be released after four centuries, referring to the Exodus of the Israelites. Involved in that release would come divine judgment (the ten plagues) and the enrichment of Abram's descendants (the "spoiling" of Egypt). The fulfillment of this prophecy is recorded in Exodus 1—12.

The Lord assured Abram that he himself would live to a ripe old age and die a natural death. That prophecy's fulfillment is recorded in Genesis 25:7-8.

The Lord told Abram that in the fourth generation his descendants would return to conquer Canaan. The Amorites are mentioned as inhabiting the land, a general reference to the various nations there. After four centuries these depraved people would be ripe for divine judgment under the onslaught of the Israelites. Although we normally think of a generation spanning twenty or thirty years, it was longer in this case. Moses, who led the Israelites out of Egypt was the fourth in line from Jacob—Levi, Kohath, Amram, Moses (Gen. 46:8, 11; Exod. 6:18, 20).

The passing of the smoking fire pot and flaming torch between the split carcasses of the animals and the birds represented Jehovah.

The procedure of walking between several sacrifices was a common way of establishing a contract in ancient times. Both parties were ordinarily required to walk through the pieces if the contract was to be valid. But God did not ask Abram to walk through. God alone passed through and indicated that He alone had power to keep the covenant. The use of a physical mode to designate the presence of Jehovah occurred again in Bible times. When Israel was in the wilderness His presence was manifest in a pillar of fire (Exod. 13:21).

15:18-21 *In the same day the Lord made a covenant with Abram, saying, Unto thy seed have I given this land, from the river of Egypt unto the great river, the river Euphrates:*

The Kenites, and the Kenizzites, and the Kadmonites,

And the Hittites, and the Perizzites, and the Rephaims,

And the Amorites, and the Canaanites, and the Girgashites, and the Jebusites.

God repeated His promise to give to Abram's descendants the land of Palestine. Its southern border would be an area between Egypt and Canaan. Some scholars believe that "the river of Egypt" here refers to the Nile, but others think it refers to a lesser stream (or even a wadi) much closer to the southern border of Judah. The extent of territory as far as the Euphrates River is more difficult to explain. Even under Solomon's reign the kingdom of Israel did not reach that far. The more likely interpretation is that the boundaries of Israel described in this passage apply to the nation in the future when its fortunes will be restored.

The Kenites and Kenizzites have been lost to history, although some think they may have descended from Esau. We know nothing about the Kadmonites, either. The Hittites were descendants of Noah's son, Ham, through Canaan's second son, Heth. Archaeologists have discovered the remains of their culture. The Perizzites are mentioned only in biblical documents (Pentateuch, Joshua, Judges). The Rephaims were giants. The Amorites were prominent before Israel conquered Canaan. They may have controlled large parts of Mesopotamia and Syria for a time, with a capital at Haran. Defeated by the Hittites, they settled in Canaan and may have ruled Egypt for a time. The Canaanites seem to have lived throughout Palestine and Phoenicia. The Girgashites were descendants of Ham. Tradition says that they fled to Africa after being conquered by the Israelites. The Jebusites lived for a long time in the vicinity of Jerusalem until displaced by David when he made it the capital of his united kingdom. He bought the threshing floor or Araunah the Jebusite for a temple site (2 Sam. 24:18-25).

The Lapse of Faith

16:1-4a *Now Sarai Abram's wife bare him no children: and she had an handmaid, an Egyptian, whose name was Hagar.*

And Sarai said unto Abram, Behold now, the Lord hath restrained me from bearing: I pray thee, go in unto my maid; it may be that I may obtain children by her. And Abram hearkened to the voice of Sarai.

108

And Sarai Abram's wife took Hagar her maid the Egyptian, after Abram had dwelt ten years in the land of Canaan, and gave her to her husband Abram to be his wife.

And he went in unto Hagar, and she conceived:. . .

Abram was seventy-five years old when he came from Haran to Canaan (Gen. 12:4). Now he was eighty-five, and Sarai had not been able to conceive a child. Realizing Abram's concern for an heir, Sarai devised her own plan for solving the problem. She offered Hagar, an Egyptian slave obtained from the Pharaoh (Gen. 12:16), to her husband as a secondary wife (or concubine). Since Hagar was her personal property, she felt that Abram could have the child he desperately wanted in this indirect way. The arrangement was common enough in pagan cultures, but it was not what God wanted for Abram and Sarai. However, He permitted it to be done as the free choice of this couple, perhaps to teach them a lesson the hard way. Abram's compliance with this plan brought him no end of suffering. How much easier it would have been had he waited for God's time. The schemes of the flesh cannot take the place of obedience and trust.

16:4b-6   . . .and when she saw that she had conceived, her mistress was despised in her eyes.

And Sarai said unto Abram, My wrong be upon thee: I have given my maid into thy bosom; and when she saw that she had conceived, I was despised in her eyes: the Lord judge between me and thee.

But Abram said unto Sarai, Behold, thy maid is in thine hand; do to her as it pleaseth thee. And when Sarai dealt hardly with her, she fled from her face.

The consequences of Sarai's and Abram's bad decision soon appeared. Hagar, the slave, had disdain for her mistress, probably making snide remarks about her barrenness. Sarai complained to Abram, as if she wanted him to punish Hagar, but Abram told *her* to do it. Sarai's treatment of Hagar was evidently so severe that she ran away into the wilderness. Abram's and Sarai's disobedience touched the lives of others. Those who get

109

out of the will of God generally do not suffer alone.

> 16:7-9 *And the angel of the Lord found her by a fountain of water in the wilderness, by the fountain in the way to Shur.*
> *And he said, Hagar, Sarai's maid, whence camest thou? and whither wilt thou go? And she said, I flee from the face of my mistress Sarai.*
> *And the angel of the Lord said unto her, Return to thy mistress, and submit thyself under her hands.*

Hagar somehow made her way about a hundred and fifty miles to Shur, where there was a spring of water and a wall built by the Egyptians for defense. Weary from her journey and void of resources, Hagar was at the edge of despair when the angel of the Lord appeared to her. The "angel of the Lord" here is thought by some to have been Christ himself in pre-incarnate form. He asked Hagar where she came from and where she was going, and she readily told the stranger about her problem. The angel directed her to go back to Sarai and be submissive to her, rather than going to Egypt. Nothing could be gained by running from God's dealings. Hagar too had to learn that walking by faith meant ready submission to one's circumstances no matter how unpleasant they may be.

> 16:10-12 *And the angel of the Lord said unto her, I will multiply thy seed exceedingly, that it shall not be numbered for multitude.*
> *And the angel of the Lord said unto her, Behold, thou art with child, and shalt bear a son, and shalt call his name Ishmael; because the Lord hath heard thy affliction.*
> *And he will be a wild man; his hand will be against every man, and every man's hand against him: and he shall dwell in the presence of all his brethren.*

The language of verse 10 supports the interpretation that the divine visitant here was an appearance of Christ in a human form, for the angel said that *He* would give Hagar many descendants. He had supernatural knowledge for He knew she was pregnant, that she would

110

bear a son, and that the child was to be named Ishmael (Hebrew for "God hears"). Ishmael's character according to the "angel of the Lord" would be that of a fiercely independent person, roaming the deserts. Some think that he was father of the Arabs or Bedouins who lived as nomads in the Middle East and North Africa. Others might restrict his descendants more to the Arabian and Sinai Peninsulas.

> 16:13-16 *And she called the name of the Lord that spake unto her, Thou God seest me: for she said, Have I also here looked after him that seeth me?*
>
> *Wherefore the well was called Beer-lahai-roi; behold, it is between Kadesh and Bered.*
>
> *And Hagar bare Abram a son: and Abram called his son's name, which Hagar bare, Ishmael.*
>
> *And Abram was fourscore and six years old, when Hagar bare Ishmael to Abram.*

Further support is found here for the contention that it was the eternal Christ in human form who appeared to Hagar. The slave girl's encounter with the Lord of glory demonstrates the truth that redemption brings extraordinary blessing to very ordinary people. When all human eyes may be turned from the suffering of a poor slave His all-seeing eyes still see and He cares. Hagar had found God through her sufferings. Her perception of Him was enlarged. The immediate effect of her experience was to return to Abram's tent and humbly submit to Sarai.

Abram's New Name

> 17:1-7 *And when Abram was ninety years old, and nine, the Lord appeared to Abram, and said unto him, I am the Almighty God; walk before me, and be thou perfect.*
>
> *And I will make my covenant between me and thee, and will multiply thee exceedingly.*
>
> *And Abram fell on his face: and God talked with him, saying,*
>
> *As for me, behold, my covenant is with thee, and thou shalt be a father of many nations.*

111

*Neither shall thy name any more be called Abram,
but thy name shall be Abraham; for a father of many
nations have I made thee.*

*And I will make thee exceeding fruitful, and I will
make nations of thee, and kings shall come out of thee.*

*And I will establish my covenant between me and
thee and thy seed after thee in their generations for an
everlasting covenant, to be a God unto thee, and to thy
seed after thee.*

Abram had been waiting twenty-four years for God to
give him the promised son.

The Lord appeared to Abram and revealed Himself by a
new name, *El Shaddai,* meaning "Almighty God." He
wanted Abram to realize that He was still able to perform
a miracle in this case. As El Shaddai He was able to fulfill
His promises. He is also able to empower those in a right
relationship to Him. God was now calling Abram to a life
of sanctification. He was to walk before God and be perfect. The long delay in the fulfillment of the promise was
serving the purpose of God in bringing Abram to spiritual
maturity. Each divine visitation brought a deepening of
his walk with God. Each struggle of faith enriched his life.
To remind Abram that he was being enlarged spiritually
God changed his name from Abram ("high father") to
Abraham ("father of many nations"). Kings would be
numbered among his descendants. We will later see that
Abraham had Isaac through Sarah (Gen. 21:1-2) and six
more sons through Keturah, whom he married after
Sarah's death (Gen. 25:1-2). Thus, through eight sons he
was to father many nations.

17:8 *And I will give unto thee, and to thy seed after
thee, the land wherein thou art a stranger, all the land of
Canaan, for an everlasting possession; and I will be
their God.*

On the occasion of this divine visitation Abraham re-
ceives assurance of a family and a homeland for them.
Palestine was promised to Isaac, the covenant son, not to
the other seven sons of Abraham. All of the blessings of
the Abrahamic covenant were to be fulfilled in the de-

scendants of Isaac. The Gentiles dominated Palestine from the time of the Assyrian and Babylonian conquests in the eighth through sixth centuries before Christ right up to the formation of the modern state of Israel in 1948. Even now we cannot say that Israel is in close fellowship with God, for the Jews still refuse in a large part to accept Jesus Christ as God's Son and their Messiah. The promise of God's regathering of the earth's Jews to Palestine and the promise of His being in close fellowship with them is yet in the future (Jer. 31:31-34; Ezek. 36:24-28). It will happen only after they see Christ for who He really is and then turn to Him for cleansing (Zech. 12:10—13:1).

The Covenant Sign

17:9-14 *And God said unto Abraham, Thou shalt keep my covenant therefore, thou, and thy seed after thee in their generations.*

This is my covenant, which ye shall keep, between me and you and thy seed after thee; Every man child among you shall be circumcised.

And ye shall circumcise the flesh of your foreskin; and it shall be a token of the covenant betwixt me and you.

And he that is eight days old shall be circumcised among you, every man child in your generations, he that is born in the house, or bought with money of any stranger, which is not of thy seed.

He that is born in thy house, and he that is bought with thy money, must needs be circumcised: and my covenant shall be in your flesh for an everlasting covenant.

And the uncircumcised man child whose flesh of his foreskin is not circumcised, that soul shall be cut off from his people; he hath broken my covenant.

Circumcision was not a new concept. Other people practiced it in Canaan and Egypt particularly. The significance of God's command to Abraham was that circumcision was to be the physical signs of an inner relationship to Himself. Every male in his household had to submit to it, whether he was freeborn or a slave, whether he was a Hebrew or a foreigner. The ceremony was to take place on the male child's eighth day after birth. The pagans circumcised the males in the puberty rituals of their religion. The circumcision of infants practiced by the Hebrews came by revelation and was distinctly different. The prophets understood the physical sign to signify the circumcision of the heart. Any who refused to be circumcised, or to have his son circumcised, was to be cast out and treated as if he were a pagan.

17:15-19 *And God said unto Abraham, As for Sarai thy wife, thou shalt not call her name Sarai, but Sarah shall her name be.*

And I will bless her, and give thee a son also of her: yea, I will bless her, and she shall be a mother of nations; kings of people shall be of her.

Then Abraham fell upon his face, and laughed, and said in his heart, Shall a child be born unto him that is an hundred years old? and shall Sarah, that is ninety years old, bear?

And Abraham said unto God, O that Ishmael might live before thee!

And God said, Sarah thy wife shall bear thee a son indeed; and thou shalt call his name Isaac: and I will establish my covenant with him for an everlasting covenant, and with his seed after him.

The meaning of Sarai is uncertain, but the name Sarah means "princess." What is meant here by saying that she would be a "mother of nations" and that "kings of people shall be of her" is uncertain, for she appears to have had only one son, Isaac. A measure of unbelief appears to have afflicted both Abraham and Sarah at the thought of bearing a son in their old age. In both cases (Gen. 17:17; 18:11-15) this produced inner laughter. In the second case, it is clear that God was displeased, so that may have been true of the first, also.

Abraham proceeded to suggest to the Lord that Ishmael be accepted as the covenant son, but God rejected that idea. He made it crystal clear that the covenant promises would apply only to a natural son to be born to them (Isaac) and to his descendants.

17:20 *And as for Ishmael, I have heard thee: Behold, I have blessed him, and will make him fruitful, and will multiply him exceedingly; twelve princes shall he beget, and I will make him a great nation.*

Although Ishmael could not qualify as the covenant son, he did receive the divine promise of blessing. He was to be compensated by becoming the father of a nation with twelve princes (Gen. 25:12-18).

17:21-22 *But my covenant will I establish with Isaac, which Sarah shall bear unto thee at this set time in the next year.*
And he left off talking with him, and God went up from Abraham.

God evidently appeared to Abraham in some bodily form here, just as chapter 18 shows Him doing at a later time. Since God the Father is a Spirit without a body (John 4:24), some might reason that this was Christ in pre-incarnate form.

17:23 *And Abraham took Ishmael his son, and all that were born in his house, and all that were bought with his money, every male among the men of Abraham's house; and circumcised the flesh of their foreskin in the selfsame day, as God had said unto him.*

God's conversation is recorded in Genesis 17:1-22. As soon as it ended, Abraham sent out word to all the men in his household that they should assemble. He then circumcised all boys and men to show immediate obedience to the Lord's command. Abraham's prompt obedience in the circumcision of his household that very day seems to indicate some progress in the school of faith. Now Abraham was ready for divine blessings.

17:24-27 *And Abraham was ninety years old and nine, when he was circumcised in the flesh of his foreskin.*
And Ishmael his son was thirteen years old, when he was circumcised in the flesh of his foreskin.

115

In the selfsame day was Abraham circumcised, and Ishmael his son.

And all the men of his house, born in the house, and bought with money of the stranger, were circumcised with him.

In these three chapters we have seen the impatience of Abram manifested in discouragement. The Lord told him that his chief steward, Eliezer, was not to be his heir. but a son who would be born of Abram himself. God predicted that Abram's descendants would become a nation and lay claim to Canaan, although they would spend four centuries and become slaves in a foreign land (Egypt) before claiming Canaan from the Amorites and other pagans living there.

When Abram was eighty-five years old, he accepted the offer by Sarai of her maid Hagar as a concubine, hoping to have a son in that way who could become his covenant heir. This act of impatience caused much trouble. Sarai punished Hagar for mocking her. Hagar fled toward Egypt, but she was met by the angel of Jehovah and persuaded to return to Canaan and be submissive to Sarai. Ishmael was born when Abram was eighty-six years old.

Thirteen more years went by, and still no son was born to Abram and Sarai. Abram seems to have become desperate about the situation, but God appeared to him and announced that the covenant was still going to be fulfilled. Abram's name was changed to Abraham. Sarai's name was changed to Sarah. Blessing was pronounced upon Ishmael, but God made it very clear that a son would be born to Abraham and Sarah the next year, and he alone would be the covenant son, the son of promise, and his name would be Isaac. Abraham immediately called all the males of his household together and circumcised them and himself. His faith had been renewed.

9

Abraham and Lot in Contrast

Genesis 18:1—19:38

The underlying theme of this section of Genesis is the practical outworking of the principle of separation. Abraham had taken the way of separation while Lot had chosen the way of compromise with the world. Abraham grew spiritually and was in the position of acting as an intercessor in the time of crisis. Lot was becoming more and more a victim of his poor choice. He was too dull spiritually to recognize God's dealings with him. He and his family instead of taking their capture as a warning, went back and continued to live in Sodom. Finally, God's cup of wrath filled up and spilled over the brim. The cries of those suffering from sinners carried upward to heaven. After an on-site investigation, the Lord rained judgment on the cities of the plain in the form of fire and brimstone. The cities were totally destroyed. Only by the mercy of God and the prayers of Abraham did Lot escape that awful judgment.

A Divine Visitation

18:1-5 *And the Lord appeared unto him in the plains of Mamre: and he sat in the tent door in the heat of the day;*

And he lift up his eyes and looked, and, lo, three men stood by him: and when he saw them, he ran to meet them from the tent door, and bowed himself toward the ground,

And said, My Lord, if now I have found favour in thy sight, pass not away, I pray thee, from thy servant:

Let a little water, I pray you, be fetched, and wash your feet, and rest yourselves under the tree:

And I will fetch a morsel of bread, and comfort ye your hearts; after that ye shall pass on: for therefore are ye

*come to your servant. And they said, So do, as thou hast
said.*

Abraham and his household pitched their tents beneath
a grove of oak trees on a plain near Hebron in the hill
country of southern Canaan. Abraham followed the
custom of a rest period when the sun was high. One day
while Abraham was resting in his tent door he saw three
"men" standing at a distance and rose to meet them. The
patriarch immediately set about to show the proper
courtesy to these strangers. He may not have realized at
first just who they were, but it was soon apparent to him
that they were not ordinary men. The spokesman for the
three is consistently called Lord in this passage (vv. 1, 13,
17, 20, 22, 26, 33). The Hebrew word translated Lord is
literally Jehovah. This divine name is usually associated
with redemption. This was evidently a pre-incarnate
appearance of Christ. It was to this occasion that Jesus
makes reference in John 8:56. That the other two were
angels seems obvious from Hebrews 13:2.

Abraham's bowing may have been only a formal
courtesy or it may have been Abraham's recognition of
their supernatural origin. Addressing his remarks to the
leader, Abraham offered these travelers water to wash
and cool their dusty feet and bread to strengthen them.
They readily agreed to accept his hospitality.

> 18:6-8 *And Abraham hastened into the tent unto
> Sarah, and said, Make ready quickly three measures of
> fine meal, knead it, and make cakes upon the hearth.*
>
> *And Abraham ran unto the herd, and fetcht a calf
> tender and good, and gave it unto a young man; and he
> hasted to dress it.*
>
> *And he took butter, and milk, and the calf which he
> had dressed, and set it before them; and he stood by
> them under the tree, and they did eat.*

Abraham was certainly energetic for a man a century
old, but he was scheduled to live seventy-five years more
(Gen. 25:7). Sarah was put to work making flat cakes of
bread typical of that time and place, using her finest flour.
Abraham hurried to select a fat calf from his herd and

ordered a young servant to butcher it. By serving a calf rather than goat meat or mutton Abraham demonstrated his high regard for these visitors. Abraham personally served them and stood by while they ate. The patriarch by this gesture was showing that he considered these visitors very important people. Though they were supernatural beings, these three ate as ordinary men. This was probably an accommodation to Abraham. For it is evident they had come to him as messengers from heaven.

> 18:9-10a   *And they said unto him Where is Sarah thy wife? And he said, Behold, in the tent.*
> *And he said, I will certainly return unto thee according to the time of life; and, lo, Sarah thy wife shall have a son.*

After the meal the guests asked Abraham where Sarah, his wife, was. That these strangers knew his wife's name must have startled Abraham and made him realize that he was in the presence of God. He meekly replied that she was inside the tent. The Lord announced to Abraham that in about nine months, Sarah would bear a son. After waiting for twenty-five years for God to fulfill His promise to make of Abraham a great nation, it was soon to happen. No response by Abraham is recorded here.

> 18:10b-12   *And Sarah heard it in the tent door, which was behind him.*
> *Now Abraham and Sarah were old and well stricken in age; and it ceased to be with Sarah after the manner of women.*
> *Therefore Sarah laughed within herself, saying, After I am waxed old shall I have pleasure, my lord being old also?*

Sarah had been listening discreetly out of sight to what the guests were saying. When she heard the remark made by the leader about her becoming a mother, she laughed silently (or quietly to herself). This sounded incredible to her, for she and Abraham were past the years for bearing children as far as she was concerned. Her menstrual periods had probably stopped long before this. She thought that her husband was incapable of fathering children.

18:13-15 *And the Lord said unto Abraham, Wherefore did Sarah laugh, saying, Shall I of a surety bear a child, which am old?*

Is any thing too hard for the Lord? At the time appointed I will return unto thee, according to the time of life, and Sarah shall have a son.

Then Sarah denied, saying, I laughed not; for she was afraid. And he said, Nay; but thou didst laugh.

Sarah's laugh did not pass unnoticed by the heavenly stranger. Sarah, filled with fear, denied that she had laughed at His announcement. But the Lord was gentle in His dealings with Abraham and Sarah. He gave them a great truth on which to rest their faith. He said, "Is anything too hard for the Lord?" The heavenly messenger pointed this aged couple to the nature of God. God is almighty. There are no natural or supernatural limits to His power. The Lord once again assured Abraham and Sarah that in a year they would have a son. Abraham's faith had matured to a level where he now could place all his hopes on the promises of God. This time he would not seek some device of his own to fulfill the promise of God.

18:16-19 *And the men rose up from thence, and looked toward Sodom: and Abraham went with them to bring them on the way.*

And the Lord said, Shall I hide from Abraham that thing which I do;

Seeing that Abraham shall surely become a great and mighty nation, and all the nations of the earth shall be blessed in him?

For I know him, that he will command his children and his household after him, and they shall keep the way of the Lord, to do justice and judgment; that the Lord may bring upon Abraham that which he hath spoken of him.

The three strangers after their meal and time of rest started to walk in the direction of Sodom. Abraham went

120

with his three guests for part of the journey as an act of courtesy. They came to a place where the cities of the plain located at the lower part of the Dead Sea could be viewed from the hills. The Lord had determined that Abraham should know of the impending judgment on these cities. The reason for this decision is given in verses 18 and 19. It contains a basic principle. God reveals to those who walk in His ways insights about which others know nothing. All of Bible prophecy has been given to believers so they may have a God-given perspective on history and current affairs. The advanced information the Lord gave Abraham exercised his soul in one of the greatest examples of intercessory prayer of all time. What was about to happen to the sinners in the Dead Sea Valley would stand out in sharp contrast to God's blessing on Abraham.

A Lesson in Intercession

18:20-22 *And the Lord said, Because the cry of Sodom and Gomorrah is great, and because their sin is very grievous;*

I will go down now, and see whether they have done altogether according to the cry of it, which is come unto me; and if not, I will know.

And the men turned their faces from thence, and went toward Sodom: but Abraham stood yet before the Lord.

God had determined that doom was imminent for Sodom and Gomorrah, if investigation proved that they were as sinful as the complaints rising to heaven indicated them to be. Evidently many victims of evil had been crying out to God from these places. The expression "going down" to examine the situation may also be found in the account about Babel (Gen. 11:7). This has reference to a manifestation of God at a given time and place. God is omniscient and sees all that goes on in the world from His throne in heaven but He at times elects to manifest His presence to deal with a given situation.

The two other "men" (angels) started down the road toward Sodom, but Abraham and the Lord tarried for a while. As the horror of the impending destruction planned for Sodom and Gomorrah broke in upon Abraham's con-

121

sciousness, he felt that he had to do something to save Lot and his family and any other righteous people that might still be in those wicked cities.

18:23-26 *And Abraham drew near and said, Wilt thou also destroy the righteous with the wicked?*

Peradventure there be fifty righteous within the city: wilt thou also destroy and not spare the place for the fifty righteous that are therein?

That be far from thee to do after this manner, to slay the righteous with the wicked: and that the righteous should be as the wicked, that be far from thee: Shall not the Judge of all the earth do right?

And the Lord said, If I find in Sodom fifty righteous within the city, then I will spare all the place for their sakes.

There is much to be learned about intercession in this incident. First, Abraham did not question God's right to destroy Sodom, but he argued that those who were righteous ought not to be slain along with those who were sinful. Second, he argued that it was inconceivable for God who is perfectly just to act in injustice. Abraham's approach was based entirely on revealed truth. The Lord was evidently pleased with his efforts and assured him that if fifty righteous were found the city would be spared. It would be interesting to speculate as to how many modern cities are spared divine judgment because of the intercession of the righteous residing in them.

18:27-33 *And Abraham answered and said, Behold now, I have taken upon me to speak unto the Lord, which am but dust and ashes:*

Peradventure there shall lack five of the fifty righteous: wilt thou destroy all the city for lack of five? And he said, If I find there forty and five, I will not destroy it.

And he spake unto him yet again, and said, Peradventure there shall be forty found there. And he said, I will not do it for forty's sake.

And he said unto him, Oh let not the Lord be angry, and I will speak: Peradventure there shall thirty be found there. And he said, I will not do it, if I find thirty there.

And he said, Behold now, I have taken upon me to speak unto the Lord: Peradventure there shall be twenty found there. And he said, I will not destroy it for twenty's sake.

And he said, Oh let not the Lord be angry, and I will speak yet but this once: Peradventure ten shall be found there. And he said, I will not destroy it for ten's sake.

And the Lord went his way, as soon as he had left communing with Abraham: and Abraham returned unto his place.

Abraham may have found it difficult to believe that only fifty righteous people lived in those cities. But as he pondered the Lord's description of the extent of wickedness in that place he lowers his plea to forty-five. Painfully Abraham continued to lower the number until it reached ten. Abraham's prayers did not save Sodom but they had a place in the deliverance of Lot and his family. Abraham's prayer of intercession is a model of the kind of care and concern that should characterize the godly. The theme of judgment ought always to move God's people to prayer. Intercessory prayer is pleasing to God. It is unselfish and reflects a burden for the needs of others.

The Angels Visit Sodom

19:1-3 And there came two angels to Sodom at even: and Lot sat in the gate of Sodom: and Lot seeing them rose up to meet them; and he bowed himself with his face toward the ground;

And he said, Behold now, my lords, turn in, I pray you, into your servant's house, and tarry all night, and wash your feet, and ye shall rise up early, and go on your ways. And they said, Nay; but we will abide in the street all night.

And he pressed upon them greatly; and they turned in unto him, and entered into his house; and he made them a feast, and did bake unleavened bread, and they did eat.

Only the two angels were seen entering Sodom. The Scripture does not say where the Lord went after the conversation with Abraham.

Lot was sitting at the city gate when the angels arrived. The fact that he sat in the gate of the city suggests that he was one of its leading citizens. Knowing the overt wickedness of the city's population, Lot knew these strangers would not be safe in the streets at night. He persisted in an offer of hospitality until the angels consented. Little did Lot know that before the night was over they would save him rather than he saving them from difficulty.

19:4-5 *But before they lay down, the men of the city, even the men of Sodom, compassed the house round, both old and young, all the people from every quarter:*

And they called unto Lot, and said unto him, Where are the men which came in to thee this night? bring them out unto us, that we may know them.

The attack of the homosexuals on Lot's house illustrates the irrational behavior of people who are given over to physical lust. A kind of insanity drove these men to forget all decency and propriety. When the moral order instituted by God is forsaken by a culture that culture in a sense self-destructs. Reasonable men behave like animals.

19:6-8 *And Lot went out at the door unto them, and shut the door after him,*

And said, I pray you, brethren, do not so wickedly.

Behold now, I have two daughters which have not known man; let me, I pray you, bring them out unto you, and do ye to them as is good in your eyes: only unto these men do nothing; for therefore came they under the shadow of my roof.

The "moment of truth" had finally come for Lot. He must have suspected that sooner or later he would have to pay a high price for living in a community as vile as Sodom was, even if it did offer him material advantages. It is almost unbelievable to us today that he would call these men "brethren" and that he would offer to bring out his two virgin daughters to be humiliated by a degraded mob. However, he felt such a sense of responsibility for the two visiting strangers that he was willing to sink to this depth.

19:9 *And they said, Stand back. And they said again, This one fellow came in to sojourn, and he will needs be a judge: now will we deal worse with thee, than with them. And they pressed sore upon the man, even Lot, and came near to break the door.*

It was in this crisis that Lot first tasted the bitter fruit of his spiritual compromise. However, often during Lot's years of residence in Sodom he had rationalized that his presence in the city was a force for good; he now knew better. In so serious a matter as the Sodomites proposed, rape of these two strangers, they wanted nothing of Lot's moralizing. Lot had not been a credible witness to the way of righteousness.

19:10-14 *But the men put forth their hand, and pulled Lot into the house to them, and shut to the door.*
And they smote the men that were at the door of the house with blindness, both small and great: so that they wearied themselves to find the door.
And the men said unto Lot, Hast thou here any besides? son in law, and thy sons, and thy daughters, and whatsoever thou hast in the city, bring them out of this place:
For we will destroy this place, because the cry of them is waxen great before the face of the Lord; and the Lord hath sent us to destroy it.
And Lot went out, and spake unto his sons in law, which married his daughters, and said, Up, get you out of this place; for the Lord will destroy this city. But he seemed as one that mocked unto his sons in law.

Only the supernatural intervention of the angels saved Lot's household from the madness of that mob. After the trauma was over Lot no doubt sensed that the coming of his guests had some special significance. The angels lost no time in revealing the divine plan for the immediate

125

judgment of the city.

Lot was urged to contact all members of his family in Sodom and warn them to get out before the city was destroyed. Apparently Lot had many sons living in Sodom. Most versions translate "sons in law" in verse 14 as meaning men engaged to marry his two daughters, but the Authorized Version calls them actual sons-in-law. In that case, Lot may have had to go out to the homes of married daughters and try to persuade them to leave Sodom. The sons-in-law did not take him seriously. They thought that he was joking. If they were members of the mob which was at his house earlier that night, then they may have thought that he was trying to mock them by saying that they faced harm, even as they had threatened him with harm earlier that night. If Lot did have other daughters living in Sodom, they evidently chose not to leave their husbands and thus died in the general destruction. Lot's spiritual compromise had not only cost him his testimony in Sodom, it cost him his influence for God on his family.

> 19:15-17 *And when the morning arose, then the angels hastened Lot, saying, Arise, take thy wife, and thy two daughters, which are here; lest thou be consumed in the iniquity of the city.*
>
> *And while he lingered, the men laid hold upon his hand, and upon the hand of his wife, and upon the hand of his two daughters; the Lord being merciful unto him: and they brought him forth, and set him without the city.*
>
> *And it came to pass, when they had brought them forth abroad, that he said, Escape for thy life; look not behind thee, neither stay thou in all the plain; escape to the mountain, lest thou be consumed.*

Though faced with the message of God announcing Sodom's doom, Lot and his family were still reluctant to leave. The angels had to take all four members of his immediate family by the hand and drag them out of the city. Surely the mercy of God is greater than the heavens are high above the earth. Since the entire region would be engulfed in this judgment they were told to flee to the hills, probably to the west of the Dead Sea Valley and not to look back.

19:18-23 *And Lot said unto them, Oh, not so, my Lord:*

Behold now, thy servant hath found grace in thy sight, and thou hast magnified thy mercy, which thou hast shewed unto me in saving my life; and I cannot escape to the mountain, lest some evil take me, and I die:

Behold now, this city is near to flee unto, and it is a little one: Oh, let me escape thither, (is it not a little one?) and my soul shall live.

And he said unto him, See, I have accepted thee concerning this thing also, that I will not overthrow this city, for the which thou hast spoken.

Haste thee, escape thither; for I cannot do any thing till thou be come thither. Therefore the name of the city was called Zoar.

The sun was risen upon the earth when Lot entered into Zoar.

Lot was reluctant to go to the mountain as the angel had instructed him. The many years of luxury and spiritual decline had weakened Lot. The long trip to the mountain seemed too strenuous. What a strange state of mind for a man who was running for his life. Weakness left him unprepared for the time of testing. Mercy was again extended Lot and he was given leave to go to Zoar. How much better might have been the plight of Lot and his descendants had he obeyed the angels and gone to the hills. There he could have enjoyed the spiritual uplift of fellowship with Abraham.

19:24-26 *Then the Lord rained upon Sodom and upon Gomorrah brimstone and fire from the Lord out of heaven;*

And he overthrew those cities, and all the plain, and all the inhabitants of the cities, and that which grew upon the ground.

But his wife looked back from behind him, and she became a pillar of salt.

We do not know if this was a rain of fire and burning petroleum ashes from some kind of volcanic eruption, or if it was something miraculously created and sent down by the Lord, but the effect was the same. All of the people, buildings, animals, and vegetation on the whole plain were burned, including those in the cities named Admah and Zeboiim (Deut. 29:23). Lot's wife stands as a tragic warning to every generation against the foolhardiness of disobedience. Her heart was really in Sodom no matter what religious pretense she made. Jesus used the example of Lot's wife to explain to His disciples the danger of hesitation in the light of coming judgment (Luke 17:32).

19:27-29 *And Abraham gat up early in the morning to the place where he stood before the Lord:*

And he looked toward Sodom and Gomorrah, and toward all the land of the plain, and beheld, and, lo, the smoke of the country went up as the smoke of a furnace.

And it came to pass, when God destroyed the cities of the plain, that God remembered Abraham, and sent Lot out of the midst of the overthrow, when he overthrew the cities in the which Lot dwelt.

That same morning Abraham went from his tent on the plain of Mamre near Hebron to the spot where he and the Lord had talked the day before. From that vantage point he could see the whole Dead Sea Valley smoking like a huge furnace. The judgment had come on those cesspools of iniquity. Abraham's only consolation was God's remembrance of his prayer for the righteous in those cities. Here the divine record clearly states that Lot was delivered by Abraham's prayers.

19:30-36 *And Lot went up out of Zoar, and dwelt in the mountain, and his two daughters with him; for he feared to dwell in Zoar: and he dwelt in a cave, he and his two daughters.*

And the firstborn said unto the younger, Our father is old, and there is not a man in the earth to come in unto us after the manner of all the earth:

Come, let us make our father drink wine, and we will lie with him, that we may preserve seed of our father.

And they made their father drink wine that night: and the firstborn went in, and lay with her father; and he perceived not when she lay down, nor when she arose.

And it came to pass on the morrow, that the firstborn said unto the younger, Behold, I lay yesternight with my father: let us make him drink wine this night also; and go thou in, and lie with him, that we may preserve the seed of our father.

And they made their father drink wine that night also: and the younger arose, and lay with him; and he perceived not when she lay down, nor when she arose.

Thus were both the daughters of Lot with child by their father.

Lot, defeated and confused, made a home for himself and his daughters in a cave near the village of Zoar. It would be in that cave that Lot would suffer his deepest humiliation and shame. The seed of his compromise brought forth its fruit in fullness. The daughters of Lot felt the despair of their situation and decided on the deplorable act of incest as a solution to their problem. The morals of Lot's daughters had probably been twisted by their exposure to the wickedness of Sodom. If the home is to influence the children for righteousness parents must demonstrate that righteousness by a consistent walk with God and true separation from the world.

19:37-38 *And the firstborn bare a son, and called his name Moab: the same is the father of the Moabites unto this day.*

And the younger, she also bare a son, and called his name Benammi: the same is the father of the children of Ammon unto this day.

Moab means "from my father." Benammi means "son of my relative." These two sons became the fathers of the Moabites and the Ammonites, two nations which later became the enemies of Israel and ultimately fell under the judgment of Jehovah.

We can learn much from the contrast between the lives of Abraham and Lot. The patriarch Abraham had fearlessly lived a separated life and followed the Lord with his whole heart. God was pleased with Abraham's way and manifested Himself to His servant. He could intercede boldly before the Lord when he learned of Sodom's doom. Lot, on the other hand, had mingled with the wicked to the detriment of his soul. When the judgment day came Lot was powerless to act and was saved as by fire. Abraham died rich, blest, rewarded and full of hope. Lot died destitute, for all his fortune perished in Sodom, and broken in spirit by the conduct of his daughters.

10

Abraham in the Philistine Country

Genesis 20:1—21:34

Abraham decided to end his long stay on the plains of Mamre and move south toward the Negev. This was to be his fourth resting place in the land Jehovah promised him. Philistines had infiltrated that area and a powerful warlord by the name of Abimelech ruled in the valley of Gerar.

The problem Abraham had faced earlier during his stay in Egypt confronted him again, and again Abraham failed to handle the problem in God's way. The Lord was merciful and restored His servant Abraham.

> 20:1-2 *And Abraham journeyed from thence toward the south country, and dwelled between Kadesh and Shur, and sojourned in Gerar.*
> *And Abraham said of Sarah his wife, She is my sister: and Abimelech, king of Gerar sent, and took Sarah.*

Abraham and his household left the plain of Mamre near Hebron and went southward. They stayed for a while in the area between Kadesh and Shur before going to Gerar, located a few miles south of Gaza in Philistia near the Mediterranean Sea. The sacred record does not give any reason for Abraham's move to Gerar. It may have been the need for pasture and water for his growing flocks of sheep and herds of cattle. It could have also been a desire to live in every part of the land he was claiming by faith for his descendants. As he had earlier done in Egypt, Abraham called Sarah his sister and did not mention that she was also his wife. Abimelech, the local king, exercised his prerogative and took Sarah into his harem.

> 20:3-7 *But God came to Abimelech in a dream by night, and said to him, Behold, thou art but a dead man,*

for the woman which thou hast taken; for she is a man's wife.

But Abimelech had not come near her: and he said, Lord, wilt thou slay also a righteous nation?

Said he not unto me, She is my sister? and she, even she herself said, He is my brother: in the integrity of my heart and innocency of my hands have I done this.

And God said unto him in a dream, Yea, I know that thou didst this in the integrity of thy heart; for I also withheld thee from sinning against me: therefore suffered I thee not to touch her.

Now therefore restore the man his wife; for he is a prophet, and he shall pray for thee, and thou shalt live: and if thou restore her not, know thou that thou shalt surely die, thou, and all that are thine.

There are some interesting theological points to be gleaned from this passage. God himself in a sovereign way took the initiative by speaking to Abimelech and revealing the true status of Sarah. Abimelech appeared to possess some knowledge of God and His ways. He seemed to show an enlightened conscience and was repulsed at the thought of an immoral act. He had taken Sarah on the testimony of both she and Abraham that they were merely brother and sister.

Note that God would have held Abimelech guilty of sinning against *Himself*, if he had taken Sarah as his wife. The doctrinal implications of this are great. Sins are not committed just against people; they are committed against the Lord! Support for this is found in the way David prayed after manipulating things so that Uriah was slain in battle in order that David might have his wife, Bathsheba (2 Sam. 11). In his confessional prayer, David said to the Lord, "Against thee, thee only, have I sinned, and done this evil in thy sight" (Ps. 51:4). In other words, to mistreat people who are governed by God's moral laws is to offend Him most of all. In this case the Lord kept Abimelech from sinning out of ignorance. If the king persisted in keeping Sarah, he would then fall under God's condemnation, and it would mean that he and his people (or perhaps just his household) would face certain death.

20:8-10 *Therefore Abimelech rose early in the morning, and called all his servants, and told all these things in their ears: and the men were sore afraid.*

Then Abimelech called Abraham, and said unto him, What hast thou done unto us? and what have I offended thee, that thou hast brought on me and on my kingdom a great sin? thou hast done deeds unto me that ought not to be done.

And Abimelech said unto Abraham, What sawest thou, that thou hast done this thing?

Abimelech called Abraham the next morning after receiving the divine visitation and confronted the patriarch with the evidence of his duplicity. The outraged ruler pressed Abraham for an explanation of his behavior. God used Abimelech to awaken Abraham's consciousness as to the seriousness of his sin.

20:11-13 *And Abraham said, Because I thought, Surely the fear of God is not in this place; and they will slay me for my wife's sake.*

And yet indeed she is my sister; she is the daughter of my father, but not the daughter of my mother; and she became my wife.

And it came to pass, when God caused me to wander from my father's house, that I said unto her, This is thy kindness which thou shalt shew unto me; at every place whither we shall come, say of me, He is my brother.

Abraham endured the withering rebuke of Abimelech, and then explained his reasons for this course of action. The Bible always reveals the weaknesses of the saints as well as their strengths. Abraham's explanation shows that he had leaned on human wisdom rather than on divine protection. He had been afraid for his life and had assumed that he would be slain so that Sarah might become part of the king's harem. Sarah though ninety years of age was an attractive woman. She and Abraham rationalized that they were not actually lying, because Sarah was his half-sister. Nothing about the scheme was right. Abraham under most embarrassing circumstances had to admit his guilt.

The record of the deception of Abraham and Sarah has been preserved for the instruction of believers in every age. It is the telling of half-truths or the withholding of essential truths which creates deception. God will never bless deception. He expects His people to walk in truth. Abraham had to tell Abimelech the truth before he could minister to him.

20:14-16 *And Abimelech took sheep, and oxen, and menservants, and womenservants, and gave them unto Abraham, and restored him Sarah his wife.*

And Abimelech said, Behold, my land is before thee: dwell where it pleaseth thee.

And unto Sarah he said, Behold, I have given thy brother a thousand pieces of silver: behold, he is to thee a covering of the eyes, unto all that are with thee, and with all other: thus she was reproved.

Abimelech's integrity is demonstrated by his immediate actions to restore Sarah to Abraham. He did not retaliate against Abraham but rather lavished gifts upon him and publicly stated that the patriarch was free to dwell anywhere he liked in his kingdom. He showed moral courage in rebuking Sarah for her part in the deception and he took public steps to let Abraham's household and the people of his kingdom know that he had not consummated a marriage relationship with Sarah.

20:17-18 *So Abraham prayed unto God: and God healed Abimelech, and his wife, and his maidservants; and they bare children.*

For the Lord had fast closed up all the wombs of the house of Abimelech, because of Sarah Abraham's wife.

In verse 7 the Lord revealed to Abimelech that Abraham was a prophet and that Abraham's prayers would deliver him. God had made Abimelech's entire household barren. God instructed Abraham to pray for the healing of Abimelech's wife and all the other women of his household. This is the first recorded physical healing in answer to prayer. Healing is always an appropriate subject for prayer. It is a theme for intercessory prayer. James taught the believers to confess their faults one to another and then to pray for one another that they might be healed (James 5:16). This is the second time that God used Abraham as an intercessor. When Abraham confessed the sin of deception, God forgave him and restored his spiritual prerogatives. The very man who had been injured by his sin now was blessed by his prayers.

The Birth of an Heir

21:1-3 *And, the Lord visited Sarah as he had said, and the Lord did unto Sarah as he had spoken.*
For Sarah conceived, and bare Abraham a son in his old age, at the set time of which God had spoken to him.
And Abraham called the name of his son that was born unto him, whom Sarah bare to him, Isaac.

Abraham and Sarah had been waiting twenty-five years for the birth of the covenant son whom God had promised to them. The promise given by one of the three visiting strangers the previous year (Gen. 18:10, 14) was literally fulfilled in the birth of Isaac. The Lord quickened Sarah according to His word and she was able to conceive and bear the promised heir. There is no indication that Jehovah appeared to her in any visible form again. In a quiet and wonderful way this miracle took place. The Lord so worked in the aged bodies of this couple that the child could be born. It is one of many scriptural examples of God's life-giving touch on the bodies of His people. He is the Lord for the body as well as the soul. Abraham named his son Isaac, meaning "one laughs" (v. 6). It was a time of great rejoicing!

The long wait of twenty-five years was over and Abraham and Sarah were enjoying the fruit of their tested faith. God works according to His own mysterious timetable, and any attempts on man's part to speed up the process will fail. Abraham and Sarah had learned the patience of faith. Their testimony is the legacy of all who walk the way of faith even today.

21:4 *And Abraham circumcised his son Isaac being eight days old, as God had commanded him.*

135

Abraham obediently performed the rite of circumcision on Isaac on the eighth day after his birth according to the divine directive (Gen. 17:9-14). He understood the importance of this ordinance as a physical sign of the special relationship which he and his descendants had with Jehovah (Gen. 17:9-14). Though Abraham's son Ishmael was circumcised, the covenant promises were to be fulfilled only in Isaac and in his descendants (Israelites, Jews).

> 21:5-7 *And Abraham was an hundred years old, when his son Isaac was born unto him.*
> *And Sarah said, God hath made me to laugh, so that all that hear will laugh with me.*
> *And she said, Who would have said unto Abraham, that Sarah should have given children suck? for I have born him a son in his old age.*

It may seem ironic that Sarah, who had previously laughed at the idea of having a child at the age of ninety, now had a son named Isaac (meaning "one laughs"). The Lord himself had picked that name (Gen. 17:19). Now Sarah entered into the festive spirit of the occasion. Her brief remarks seemed to take on the quality of a hymn of praise to the Lord. She wanted to share her joy with others around her. She wanted to thank God for the miracle which had made her a mother for the first and only time.

A Cloud of Sorrow

> 21:8 *And the child grew, and was weaned: and Abraham made a great feast the same day that Isaac was weaned.*

According to the custom of that day the mother nursed her child for two or three years. Some evidence indicates that weaning was at times delayed until the child's fifth birthday. The weaning of the child was always an occasion for special celebration. The child would be given a special robe to wear and come into the midst of the celebrants to partake of solid food. Abraham was a rich man, so he sponsored an elaborate feast to be enjoyed by all of his household and invited friends.

> 21:9-11 *And Sarah saw the son of Hagar the Egyptian, which she had born unto Abraham, mocking.*
>
> *Wherefore she said unto Abraham, Cast out this bondwoman and her son: for the son of this bondwoman shall not be heir with my son, even with Isaac.*
>
> *And the thing was very grievous in Abraham's sight because of his son.*

What started out to be one of the happiest days of Abraham's life was to end in days of sorrow. Ishmael was a teen-ager now. He was already beginning to show the antagonistic spirit which would alienate him from other people when he grew to maturity (Gen. 16:12). According to Galatians 4:29, Ishmael actually persecuted little Isaac. He ridiculed or made fun of him. It is not difficult to know who his teacher was, for his mother had been guilty of mocking before (Gen. 16:4-5). There seems to have been more here than the usual teasing typical of youngsters. When Sarah saw Ishmael's behavior, she insisted that Abraham drive Hagar and Ishmael away. She could not bear the thought that Ishmael would share the inheritance with Isaac. Abraham was grieved over this, for he truly loved Ishmael and did not want to be guilty of mistreating him or his mother.

> 21:12-14 *And God said unto Abraham, Let it not be grievous in thy sight because of the lad, and because of thy bondwoman; in all that Sarah hath said unto thee, hearken unto her voice; for in Isaac shall thy seed be called.*
>
> *And also of the son of the bondwoman will I make a nation, because he is thy seed.*
>
> *And Abraham rose up early in the morning, and took bread, and a bottle of water, and gave it unto Hagar, putting it on her shoulder, and the child, and sent her away: and she departed, and wandered in the wilderness of Beer-sheba.*

As Abraham agonized over what to do, the Lord spoke

to him and let him know that Sarah was right about Hagar and Ishmael. They had to go. If they stayed, there would continue to be trouble. In order to make the separation more acceptable to Abraham, God said that He would fulfill His previous promise to make of Ishmael a great nation (Gen. 17:20). It was to be through Isaac alone that the covenant promises would be fulfilled (Gen. 17:19, 21).

Abraham had learned that prompt obedience brought the blessing of God. Early the next morning he sent Hagar and Ishmael on their way. We do not know where Abraham's household was living at this time, but it was probably at Beer-sheba (Gen. 21:33), which was located at the southern extremity of Canaan. Ishmael must have been at least fifteen or sixteen years old at this time, and so he was capable of carrying some of the provisions they would need. Hagar was given a supply of bread and a pitcher or goatskin of water to carry on her shoulder according to the custom of the time. Mother and son headed off into the wilderness near Beer-sheba. We can only imagine the strain which this put upon Abraham, but he had to commit them to the Lord's care and have faith in God's promise to sustain them in their new life.

21:15-16 *And the water was spent in the bottle, and she cast the child under one of the shrubs.*

And she went, and sat her down over against him a good way off, as it were a bowshot: for she said, Let me not see the death of the child. And she sat over against him, and lift up her voice, and wept.

Beer-sheba was the last outpost before entering the Negev Desert. Hagar and Ishmael apparently lost their way and wandered aimlessly about. When the water was all gone, the dry heat did its worst. Completely worn out, they stopped. Hagar helped Ishmael to get a little shade under a bush or shrub. She could not bear to watch Ishmael die, so she moved about a hundred yards away and collapsed. She lay there weeping for her son and her own fate. All hope seemed to be gone.

21:17-19 *And God heard the voice of the lad; and the angel of God called to Hagar out of heaven, and said unto her, What aileth thee, Hagar? fear not; for God hath heard the voice of the lad where he is.*

Arise, lift up the lad, and hold him in thine hand; for I will make him a great nation.

And God opened her eyes, and she saw a well of water; and she went, and filled the bottle with water, and gave the lad drink.

Did Hagar and Ishmael pray to the Lord as they lay in their respective spots? They may well have done that. The Lord saw their plight and the angel of God spoke from heaven to encourage them. Hagar was reminded of the previous promise that Ishmael would survive and grow to manhood (Gen. 16:11-12). God opened her eyes and she discovered a well close by. She and Ishmael were revived by God's intervention. Hagar's experience is a beautiful picture of the grace of God. Twice in her life this slave woman had been saved from despair and death by the goodness of God.

21:20-21 *And God was with the lad; and he grew, and dwelt in the wilderness, and became an archer.*

And he dwelt in the wilderness of Paran: and his mother took him a wife out of the land of Egypt.

Jehovah was faithful to the promise he made to Abraham regarding Ishmael. "God was with the lad" describes the providential care He gave to Ishmael. It is likely that both Hagar and Ishmael served the God of heaven all of their days. Ishmael's descendants did not. No doubt Hagar's unwise choice of an Egyptian wife for her son introduced the family to paganism.

Abraham's Treaty with Abimelech

21:22-24 *And it came to pass at that time, that Abimelech and Phichol the chief captain of his host spake unto Abraham, saying, God is with thee in all that thou doest:*

Now therefore swear unto me here by God that thou wilt not deal falsely with me, nor with my son, nor with my son's son: but according to the kindness that I have

done unto thee, thou shalt do unto me, and to the land
wherein thou hast sojourned.
And Abraham said, I will swear.

Abimelech's request for a covenant arrangement with
Abraham is indicative of the high status the patriarch
now enjoyed in the land. The issue was the water, for in
the Negev region all of life was dependent on the available water supply. The growth of Abraham's household
made Abimelech realize the threat either Abraham or his
descendants might pose to the welfare of his tribe.
Abimelech had come to respect Abraham and he knew
that God blessed him.

21:25-26 *And Abraham reproved Abimelech be-*
cause of a well of water, which Abimelech's servants
had violently taken away.
And Abimelech said, I wot not who hath done this
thing: neither didst thou tell me, neither yet heard I of it,
but to day.

Having confirmed the treaty with each other, Abraham
now brought up a point of contention. He had acquired a
well, either by having it newly dug or having an old one
unclogged, but Abimelech's servants had taken it
forcibly. Abimelech claimed to have had no knowledge of
this until informed of it by Abraham. It is obvious that he
was upset by the incident and wanted it to be resolved
peacefully.

21:27-33 *And Abraham took sheep and oxen, and*
gave them unto Abimelech; and both of them made a
covenant.
And Abraham set seven ewe lambs of the flock by
themselves.
And Abimelech said unto Abraham, What mean
these seven ewe lambs which thou hast set by them-
selves?
And he said, For these seven ewe lambs shalt thou
take of my hand, that they may be a witness unto me,
that I have digged this well.
Wherefore he called that place Beer-sheba; because

there they swear both of them.

Thus they made a covenant at Beer-sheba: then Abimelech rose up, and Phichol the chief captain of his host, and they returned into the land of the Philistines.

And Abraham planted a grove in Beer-sheba, and called there on the name of the Lord, the everlasting God.

The covenant negotiations show Abimelech to be a most conciliatory man. According to custom Abraham gave the sacrifice animals offered in the covenant ritual as described in verse 27. Abimelech noticed seven ewes more than the number prescribed by the ritual. When he inquired as to the reason for the extra animals Abraham answered that they were a witness that he had digged the well.

The animals given to Abimelech by Abraham were to be accepted as a sign that the well really did belong to Abraham. The well was called Beer (well)-sheba (oath), or "well of the oath." The negotiations completed, the king and his commander left for home in Gerar. Abraham planted a grove of tamarisks (some say just one of them) by the well at Beer-sheba and worshiped God. He called on the eternal Jehovah, probably in thankfulness and also in petition that peace would prevail for him and his descendants. By faith Abraham was claiming the land for his seed.

21:34 *And Abraham sojourned in the Philistines' land many days.*

It is uncertain just what this means. It could mean that he literally left Beer-sheba and moved his household about in the land of Philistia in search of sufficient pasturage for his huge flocks and herds and then came back. Abraham found the southern part of the land most desirable for his nomadic life. We later find him living in Hebron farther to the north (Gen. 23:2). It was apparently common for him to move to new locations periodically.

This is the last of five chapters on the life of Abraham before Isaac's role in this remarkable saga begins. Abraham has come a long way by faith. Twenty-five years of waiting for the son of promise had matured Abraham. He had learned from both his failures and his triumphs how to walk with God. Neither his great wealth or his prestige in the land of the Philistines turned his heart from following God. When he had failed God through yielding to his own way he was quick to confess it and obey God. As his history unfolds there is a pattern of immediate response to the will of God in Abraham's life.

11

Abraham's Supreme Test

Genesis 22:1—23:20

Abraham's entire life was a journey of faith and it was not an easy way. The hand of God led Abraham through repeated seasons of testing until he learned to trust completely in the revealed will of God. As Abraham looked with joy on his teen-age son, Isaac, he perhaps thought the testings of his faith were at last over. Just the opposite proved to be true for Abraham was at that time brought to the greatest test of his entire life.

22:1-2 *And it came to pass after these things, that God did tempt Abraham, and said unto him, Abraham: and he said, Behold, here I am.*
And he said, Take now thy son, thine only son Isaac, whom thou lovest, and get thee into the land of Moriah; and offer him there for a burnt offering upon one of the mountains which I will tell thee of.

Abraham was still living at Beer-sheba when the Lord tested his faith again. The King James Version says "God did tempt Abraham." The word "tempt" is usually thought of by us as an enticement to do evil, but it can also mean to test a person. James in his letter distinguishes between the two meanings of tempt. He concluded that God never entices man to evil. "Let no man say when he is tempted, I am tempted of God: for God cannot be tempted with evil, neither tempteth he any man: But every man is tempted, when he is drawn away of his own lust, and enticed [by Satan to do evil]" (James 1:13-14). James also lays down a principle regarding the blessing of being tested. Standing joyfully in the hour of testing brings forth the fruit of patience and maturity. "My brethren, count it all joy when ye fall into divers temptations [different kinds of testings of your faith]; knowing this, that the trying of your faith worketh patience [produces endurance]. But let patience have her perfect work, that ye may be perfect and entire [mature and complete in character], wanting [or lacking] nothing" (James 1:2-4).

This scriptural teaching should be kept in mind, as we look at the test which God had for Abraham's faith. When Abraham heard God calling to him, he readily responded and waited for the divine instruction. What Abraham heard must have horrified him. He was told to take Isaac to the land of Moriah and offer him up as a sacrifice to the Lord. The Lord described Isaac as Abraham's "only son." He was an "only son" in that he was the son of promise born by the direct intervention of God. After waiting for twenty-five years for the covenant son to appear, and after the miracle of Isaac's conception and birth in Abraham's and Sarah's old age, how disturbing this word must have been to the patriarch. It is difficult to imagine the struggle through which Abraham passed as he considered the Lord's command. He could have reasoned that since Isaac was the son through which the covenant promises were to be fulfilled God really did not mean that he should be sacrificed.

Abraham knew that his pagan neighbors offered their children as human sacrifices to the demons. How could Jehovah require him to offer up Isaac? But Abraham had walked long enough with God to completely trust Him and he, therefore, made preparation to go to Moriah. The land of Moriah was a region located to the north of Abraham's camp near Salem (later to be called Jerusalem). In that same area some nineteen centuries later God himself was to offer up His own Son as an atonement for the sins of the world. Thus Abraham and Isaac serve as types of God and His Son in this particular incident.

The Journey of Obedience

22:3-5 *And Abraham rose up early in the morning, and saddled his ass, and took two of his young men with him, and Isaac his son, and clave the wood for the burnt offering, and rose up, and went unto the place of which God had told him.*

Then on the third day Abraham lifted up his eyes, and saw the place afar off.

And Abraham said unto his young men, Abide ye here with the ass; and I and the lad will go yonder and worship, and come again to you.

As Abraham, Isaac, and the two servants set out to the land of Moriah, it is unlikely that anyone other than Abraham knew the purpose of this trip. Isaac and the servants may have thought that he was simply going for the purpose of making a sacrifice.

One cannot help but wonder how Abraham could be so calm as he was at this time. The answer is found in Hebrews 11:17-19. Abraham's faith rested on God's promise to give him many descendants through Isaac. He, therefore, was confident that his son would be resurrected from the dead to fulfill God's promise!

If Abraham and his party averaged twenty-five miles a day, they were able to see the hills of Moriah early on the third day. The distance from Beer-sheba to Moriah was about fifty miles.

22:6-8 *And Abraham took the wood of the burnt offering, and laid it upon Isaac his son; and he took the fire in his hand, and a knife; and they went both of them together.*

And Isaac spake unto Abraham his father, and said, My father: and he said, Here am I, my son. And he said, Behold the fire and the wood: but where is the lamb for a burnt offering?

And Abraham said, My son, God will provide himself a lamb for a burnt offering: so they went both of them together.

Even as Christ was later to carry His own cross on the road to Calvary, so Isaac here was required to carry the wood for his own sacrifice. The use of the word "lad" usually infers a child but Isaac was probably a strong teen-ager of about seventeen. Abraham carried the fire-box, a container which probably had ashes and embers in it from the previous night's campfire. He also took a sharp knife for slaying the sacrifice.

As the two of them walked along, Isaac realized that something important was missing. The fuel and fire were

145

there, but where was the animal to sacrifice? He evidently had no idea that *he* was to be the sacrifice.

Abraham's response to Isaac's inquiry regarding the lamb is one of the highlights of the Old Testament. It was a brilliant confession of faith, "God will provide himself a lamb." Isaac failed to understand his father's statement but raised no further questions. Perhaps something of the mystery of this event was now becoming obvious to Isaac.

> 22:9-12 *And they came to the place which God had told him of; and Abraham built an altar there, and laid the wood in order, and bound Isaac his son, and laid him on the altar upon the wood.*
>
> *And Abraham stretched forth his hand, and took the knife to slay his son.*
>
> *And the angel of the Lord called unto him out of heaven, and said, Abraham, Abraham: and he said, Here am I.*
>
> *And he said, Lay not thine hand upon the lad, neither do thou any thing unto him: for now I know that thou fearest God, seeing thou hast not withheld thy son, thine only son from me.*

Abraham as the head of his household was responsible for constructing the altar and arranging the wood for the sacrifice. Isaac had watched his father perform this ritual of worship on other occasions and probably knew no apprehension until Abraham began to bind him with the cords intended for the sacrifice. It is a testimony to Abraham's spiritual integrity that Isaac offered no resistance. He had come to trust his father. Even as Jesus was later to go to the cross in obedience to His Father's will, so now Isaac submitted to his father. In a very real sense, this young man offered up himself at that moment.

God knew that Abraham had sincerely sacrificed Isaac to the Lord *in his heart.* At the dramatic moment when he was about to lift the sacrifice knife, the voice of the angel of Jehovah called and stopped him. God tested Abraham to know the state of his heart. Abraham's complete submission pleased God.

> 22:13-14 *And Abraham lifted up his eyes, and*

146

looked, and behold behind him a ram caught in a thicket by his horns: and Abraham went and took the ram, and offered him up for a burnt offering in the stead of his son.

And Abraham called the name of that place Jehovah-jireh: as it is said to this day, In the mount of the Lord it shall be seen.

On the way to Mount Moriah, Abraham had told Isaac that the Lord would provide a lamb for the sacrifice. In a sense he spoke prophetically on that occasion for as yet Abraham had no idea how God would deliver him from this testing. The presence of the ram caught in the thicket could not have been considered providential had there not been the voice of the angel of the Lord. The sacrifice was not called off. God gave a substitute for Isaac. No more complete type of the substitutionary death of Christ can be found than this. The father and son worshiped the Lord with new understanding that day. Abraham called the place Jehovah-jireh. This compound name of God is rich in meaning. Jehovah is the covenant name of God and means the "eternal I Am." The compound name means "The eternally sufficient One provides." The biblical doctrine of redemption rests upon the principle of substitution and the divine provision of the substitute. Christ in His death and resurrection is the perfect fulfillment of that provision.

Every animal sacrifice made in Old Testament times looked ahead to the one perfect sacrifice of Christ himself. His was the final sacrifice and the fulfillment of every type and shadow of Old Testament order.

The Renewal of the Covenant

22:15-19 *And the angel of the Lord called unto Abraham out of heaven the second time,*

And said, By myself have I sworn, saith the Lord, for because thou hast done this thing, and hast not withheld thy son, thine only son:

That in blessing I will bless thee, and in multiplying I will multiply thy seed as the stars of the heaven, and as the sand which is upon the sea shore; and thy seed shall

147

possess the gate of his enemies;
And in thy seed shall all the nations of the earth be blessed; because thou hast obeyed my voice.
So Abraham returned unto his young men, and they rose up and went together to Beer-sheba; and Abraham dwelt at Beer-sheba.

Abraham heard the voice of the angel a second time while he and Isaac were on the mount in Moriah. The angel of the Lord reiterated the promises God had made Abraham. There seems to be a pattern that with every crisis of faith came a fresh affirmation of God's covenant with Abraham. Obedience is the pathway to understanding and assurance. Abraham had learned that total commitment meant the surrender of the dearest treasure of his heart to the will of God.

22:20-24   *And it came to pass after these things, that it was told Abraham, saying, Behold, Milcah, she hath also born children unto thy brother Nahor;*
Huz his firstborn, and Buz his brother, and Kemuel the father of Aram.
And Chesed, and Hazo, and Pildash, and Jidlaph, and Bethuel.
And Bethuel begat Rebekah: these eight Milcah did bear to Nahor, Abraham's brother.
And his concubine, whose name was Reumah, she bare also Tebah, and Gaham, and Thahash, and Maachah.

Abraham through the years of his residence in Canaan had lost all contact with his family in Mesopotamia. One day a traveler brought to the patriarch news of his brother Nahor. He knew the family well enough to give Abraham the names of Nahor's children. The narrator had a purpose in making a record of this information. Rebekah, Nahor's daughter, was to become the wife of Isaac.

The Death of Sarah

23:1-2   *And Sarah was an hundred and seven and*

twenty years old: these were the years of the life of Sarah.

And Sarah died in Kirjath-arba; the same is Hebron in the land of Canaan: and Abraham came to mourn for Sarah, and to weep for her.

The age, death, and burial of many men are recorded in the Bible, but Sarah is the only woman honored in this way. Sarah is also honored in the New Testament. Peter distinguished her as a holy woman, rich in faith and spiritually attractive (1 Pet. 3:4-6). Her life and testimony is a model for godly women to emulate in every age. She was the mother of the Hebrew race through her son Isaac. Abraham had apparently moved back to Mamre near Hebron, where Sarah died. Moses accurately uses both the ancient name Hebron and the name Kirjath-arba commonly used at the time he was writing Genesis. Sarah was one hundred and twenty-seven years old at the time of her death. Abraham was one hundred and thirty-seven. Isaac was thirty-seven. Abraham was to live thirty-eight more years (Gen. 25:7). Isaac was to live one hundred and forty-three more years (Gen. 35:28).

23:3-6 *And Abraham stood up from before his dead, and spake unto the sons of Heth, saying,*

I am a stranger and a sojourner with you: give me a possession of a buryingplace with you, that I may bury my dead out of my sight.

And the children of Heth answered Abraham, saying unto him,

Hear us, my lord: thou art a mighty prince among us: in the choice of our sepulchres bury thy dead; none of us shall withhold from thee his sepulchre, but that thou mayest bury thy dead.

When the word was sent from Sarah's tent that she was dead Abraham came to mourn and weep for her. He felt all the anguish any man would experience at the loss of one so dear to him. He wept unashamedly and mourned for Sarah. At the same time Abraham was the head of his house and he realized the necessity of making proper arrangements for the burial. He turned to his neighbors the sons of Heth (Hittites) and expressed a desire to acquire a proper burying ground for his wife. It was customary in those days for each family to have its own burial plot on their private property. But Abraham was a stranger in the land and had no legal property. Sarah's death was for Abraham a time of deeper understanding of his calling. He was a pilgrim in a strange land.

The Hittites had a high regard for Abraham as a "prince of God." They were sympathetic to his desire to have a permanent burying place. The negotiations for the property were typical of the Middle East. While the children of Heth appear willing to give him land, in reality they expected a payment for it. Abraham had every intention of buying the land and proceeded to bargain with the Hittites.

> 23:7-9   *And Abraham stood up, and bowed himself to the people of the land, even to the children of Heth.*
>
> *And he communed with them, saying, If it be your mind that I should bury my dead out of my sight; hear me, and intreat for me to Ephron the son of Zohar,*
>
> *That he may give me the cave of Machpelah, which he hath, which is in the end of his field; for as much money as it is worth he shall give it me for a possession of a buryingplace amongst you.*

Abraham had already selected a desirable site for his family's burial plot. It was the cave of Machpelah located at the end of a field owned by Ephron. The transaction described here probably took place at the gate to the city of Hebron. Abraham offered to pay whatever the cave was worth.

> 23:10-20   *And Ephron dwelt among the children of Heth: and Ephron the Hittite answered Abraham in the audience of the children of Heth, even of all that went in at the gate of his city, saying,*
>
> *Nay, my lord, hear me: the field give I thee, and the cave that is therein, I give it thee; in the presence of the sons of my people give I it thee: bury thy dead.*
>
> *And Abraham bowed down himself before the people of the land.*

And he spake unto Ephron in the audience of the people of the land, saying, But if thou wilt give it, I pray thee, hear me: I will give thee money for the field; take it of me, and I will bury my dead there.

And Ephron answered Abraham, saying unto him,

My lord, hearken unto me: the land is worth four hundred shekels of silver; what is that betwixt me and thee? bury therefore thy dead.

And Abraham hearkened unto Ephron; and Abraham weighed to Ephron the silver, which he had named in the audience of the sons of Heth, four hundred shekels of silver, current money with the merchant.

And the field of Ephron, which was in Machpelah, which was before Mamre, the field, and the cave which was therein, and all the trees that were in the field, that were in all the borders round about, were made sure

Unto Abraham for a possession in the presence of the children of Heth, before all that went in at the gate of his city.

And after this, Abraham buried Sarah his wife in the cave of the field of Machpelah before Mamre: the same is Hebron in the land of Canaan.

And the field, and the cave that is therein, were made sure unto Abraham for a possession of a buryingplace by the sons of Heth.

Abraham observed the usual courtesies involved in the bargaining situation. A crowd had gathered to observe the business transaction between their own townsman and Abraham. Little did Ephron know that the sale of Machpelah was a part of the plan of God. Canaan would someday belong to Abraham's descendants. This property was not only a burial place for Sarah and other family members, it was an earnest of their coming inheritance. The deal was closed and Abraham acquired a deed to the field, the trees surrounding it, and the double cave. This was probably oral, but a document may have been written for evidence of the transfer.

The cave of Machpelah later became the sepulchre for not only Sarah, but also Abraham, Isaac, Rebekah, Leah, and Jacob (Gen. 25:9; 35:27-29; 49:30-31; 50:13).

12

Isaac, a Man of Peace

Genesis 24:1—26:35

The years had taken their toll on Abraham and he was concerned that every preparation be made in the behalf of Isaac the heir of his covenant. Isaac was by this time almost forty years of age. The Bible narrative places Isaac as a central figure beginning with chapter 24 of Genesis. Abraham was wise in spiritual matters and realized that Isaac must not marry a pagan woman if he is to remain true to the covenant. The son of promise must take his wife from among believers. Abraham wanted Isaac's marriage settled before his death.

The Mission of Eliezer

24:1-4 *And Abraham was old, and well stricken in age: and the Lord had blessed Abraham in all things.*
And Abraham said unto his eldest servant of his house, that ruled over all that he had, Put, I pray thee, thy hand under my thigh:
And I will make thee swear by the Lord, the God of heaven, and the God of the earth, that thou shalt not take a wife unto my son of the daughters of the Canaanites, among whom I dwell:
But thou shalt go unto my country, and to my kindred, and take a wife unto my son Isaac.

The paternal role in the selection of a wife was not uncommon in Abraham's time. In many parts of the world it is still practiced. Perhaps the old patriarch remembered the visitor who some years before had advised him of the welfare of his brother Nahor's family. Abraham realized that someone must go to Haran and seek a bride for Isaac from Nahor's household. Abraham selected his most trusted servant for this mission. There is more than romance in the story of Isaac and Rebekah. The line of the promised Messiah had to be kept pure. The "eldest servant" mentioned here is generally thought to be Eliezer of Damascus (Gen. 15:2), so he will be called by that name in our study of chapter 24.

Some think that in this passage Abraham is a type of God seeking a bride for His Son; Isaac is a type of Christ; Rebekah is a type of the Church; and Eliezer is a type of the Holy Spirit sent to bring the Church to Christ. The oath taken by Eliezer was sacred and cannot be compared with oaths practiced by the pagans. The same oath is found in Genesis 47:29 when Jacob asked Joseph to swear that he would not bury him in Egypt. To break an oath accompanied by this solemn act was to put oneself in jeopardy. Eliezer promised to abide strictly by his master's wish in the securing of a suitable wife for Isaac.

24:5-9 *And the servant said unto him, Peradventure the woman will not be willing to follow me unto this land: must I needs bring thy son again unto the land from whence thou camest?*

And Abraham said unto him, Beware thou that thou bring not my son thither again.

The Lord God of heaven, which took me from my father's house, and from the land of my kindred, and which spake unto me, and that sware unto me, saying, Unto thy seed will I give this land; he shall send his angel before thee, and thou shalt take a wife unto my son from thence.

And if the woman will not be willing to follow thee, then thou shalt be clear from this my oath: only bring not my son thither again.

And the servant put his hand under the thigh of Abraham his master, and sware to him concerning that matter.

Once again the faith of Abraham rises to the occasion. Abraham spoke prophetically as he assured Eliezer that a woman could be found in Haran to be Isaac's wife. He knew that God would send an angel to prepare the way for Eliezer to accomplish his mission. He was adamant about Isaac staying in Canaan, where the covenant promises were eventually to be fulfilled for his descendants.

24:10-14 *And the servant took ten camels of the camels of his master, and departed; for all the goods of his master were in his hand: and he arose, and went to Mesopotamia, unto the city of Nahor.*

And he made his camels to kneel down without the city by a well of water at the time of the evening, even the time that women go out to draw water.

And he said, O Lord God of my master Abraham, I pray thee, send me good speed this day, and shew kindness unto my master Abraham.

Behold, I stand here by the well of water; and the daughters of the men of the city come out to draw water:

And let it come to pass, that the damsel to whom I shall say, Let down thy pitcher, I pray thee, that I may drink; and she shall say, Drink, and I will give thy camels drink also: let the same be she that thou hast appointed for thy servant Isaac; and thereby shall I know that thou hast shewed kindness unto my master.

The account moves swiftly to the time of Eliezer's arrival in Haran. When he and his party came to the city of Nahor, Eliezer stopped by the community well outside of the city and there submitted the matter to the Lord in prayer. The wise old servant asked God to confirm the divine choice by a sign. The sign was not selected at random but summarized Eliezer's conception of the kind of woman that would make Isaac a good wife. She must be hospitable, generous, and ready to serve others. Eliezer would know by the sign if she possessed these qualities.

24:15-21 *And it came to pass, before he had done speaking, that, behold, Rebekah came out, who was born to Bethuel, son of Milcah, the wife of Nahor, Abraham's brother, with her pitcher upon her shoulder.*

And the damsel was very fair to look upon, a virgin, neither had any man known her: and she went down to the well, and filled her pitcher, and came up.

And the servant ran to meet her, and said, Let me, I pray thee, drink a little water of thy pitcher.

And she said, Drink, my lord: and she hasted, and let down her pitcher upon her hand, and gave him drink.

And when she had done giving him drink, she said, I

*will draw water for thy camels also, until they have
done drinking.*

*And she hasted, and emptied her pitcher into the
trough, and ran again unto the well to draw water, and
drew for all his camels.*

*And the man wondering at her held his peace, to wit
whether the Lord had made his journey prosperous or
not.*

Before Eliezer could finish his prayer, a girl came to the
well. She was Rebekah the daughter of Bethuel and the
granddaughter of Milcah and Nahor, Abraham's brother.
Eliezer seemed to have an intuition that this girl was the
divine choice for Isaac. He applied the sign to test her and
was not disappointed. Eliezer's heart filled with joy at the
beauty and personality of Rebekah.

24:22-28 *And it came to pass, as the camels had done
drinking, that the man took a golden earring of half a
shekel weight, and two bracelets for her hands of ten
shekels weight of gold;*

*And said, Whose daughter art thou? tell me, I pray
thee: is there room in thy father's house for us to lodge
in?*

*And she said, I am the daughter of Bethuel the son of
Milcah, which she bare unto Nahor.*

*She said moreover unto him, We have both straw and
provender enough, and room to lodge in.*

*And the man bowed down his head, and worshipped
the Lord.*

*And he said, Blessed be the Lord God of my master
Abraham, who hath not left destitute my master of his
mercy and his truth: I being in the way, the Lord led me
to the house of my master's brethren.*

*And the damsel ran, and told them of her mother's
house these things.*

Since Eliezer was only a servant he needed some means
of establishing his integrity and his identity with the
family of Nahor. The ten camels loaded with wealth were
all the witness he needed. The gifts given Rebekah may be
compared to the grace that we receive when the Holy

Spirit brings the life of Christ to us. It was an earnest of what was yet to come. Rebekah would soon enjoy all the riches of Abraham's household.

24:29-33 *And Rebekah had a brother, and his name was Laban: and Laban ran out unto the man, unto the well.*

And it came to pass, when he saw the earring and bracelets upon his sister's hands, and when he heard the words of Rebekah his sister, saying, Thus spake the man unto me; that he came unto the man; and, behold, he stood by the camels at the well.

And he said, Come in, thou blessed of the Lord; wherefore standest thou without? for I have prepared the house, and room for the camels.

And the man came into the house: and he ungirded his camels, and gave straw and provender for the camels, and water to wash his feet, and the men's feet that were with him.

And there was set meat before him to eat: but he said, I will not eat, until I have told mine errand. And he said, Speak on.

Laban, Rebekah's brother, was the spokesman for the family and gave Eliezer a lavish welcome. To hear from Abraham after all of these years must have caused great excitement in Nahor's home. The display of wealth Eliezer carried with him also made an impression. Laban in particular was attracted by the gold and jewelry Eliezer had given Rebekah. Laban proves to be a very greedy man as subsequent chapters of Genesis will show.

24:34-36 *And he said, I am Abraham's servant.*

And the Lord hath blessed my master greatly; and he is become great: and he hath given him flocks, and herds, and silver, and gold, and menservants, and maidservants, and camels, and asses.

And Sarah my master's wife bare a son to my master when she was old: and unto him hath he given all that he hath.

Eliezer immediately presented the facts of his case.

Eliezer's introduction of himself and his mission was in the form of a testimony. The old servant reported that the Lord had blessed Abraham. That alone accounted for his prosperity and his son. Nahor's family may have been skeptical of Abraham's decision to leave Haran and become a pilgrim. Now they were to learn that his venture of faith was not a mistake.

(The information in verses 37-48 is repetitious and therefore omitted.)

24:49 And now if ye will deal kindly and truly with my master, tell me: and if not, tell me; that I may turn to the right hand, or to the left.

Eliezer pressed for an immediate decision as to whether or not Rebekah would be given in marriage to Isaac by her family. Abraham's servant was a man with a mission so urgent he dare not be delayed by anything—even the ordinary civilities of such an occasion. One feels that Eliezer, so long in Abraham's household, had come to sense the importance of the God covenant with his master. This marriage was essential to God's plan for forming Israel, the covenant nation. He also knew that God was working in the circumstances of this journey and he wanted to see it through as soon as possible.

24:50-54 Then Laban and Bethuel answered and said, The thing proceedeth from the Lord: we cannot speak unto thee bad or good.

Behold, Rebekah is before thee, take her, and go, and let her be thy master's son's wife, as the Lord hath spoken.

And it came to pass, that, when Abraham's servant heard their words, he worshipped the Lord, bowing himself to the earth.

And the servant brought forth jewels of silver, and jewels of gold, and raiment, and gave them to Rebekah: he gave also to her brother and to her mother precious things.

And they did eat and drink, he and the men that were with him, and tarried all night; And they rose up in the morning, and he said, Send me away unto my master.

Bethuel and Laban agreed that God had spoken and they, therefore, gave their consent for Rebekah to marry Isaac. Eliezer distributed the gifts sent from Abraham's wealth. This probably served as a dowry payment for the bride. The dedication of Eliezer comes through in every phase of this narrative. He would not eat until his master's business had been carried out. Abraham's mandate was Eliezer's first priority.

24:55-61 *And her brother and mother said, Let the damsel abide with us a few days, at the least ten; after that she shall go.*

And he said unto them, Hinder me not, seeing the Lord hath prospered my way; send me away that I may go to my master.

And they said, We will call the damsel, and enquire at her mouth.

And they called Rebekah, and said unto her, Wilt thou go with this man? And she said, I will go.

And they sent away Rebekah their sister, and her nurse, and Abraham's servant, and his men.

And they blessed Rebekah, and said unto her, Thou art our sister, be thou the mother of thousands of millions, and let thy seed possess the gate of those which hate them.

And Rebekah arose, and her damsels, and they rode upon the camels, and followed the man: and the servant took Rebekah, and went his way.

There is always a tension between the way of faith and the way of the secular world. While a celebration for Rebekah's engagement was appropriate the urgency of Eliezer's mission had to take priority over custom. Eliezer's faith was being tested by the sentiment of Rebekah's family who found it difficult to comply with the request that Rebekah leave immediately.

24:62-67 *And Isaac came from the way of the well Lahairoi; for he dwelt in the south country.*

And Isaac went out to meditate in the field at the eventide: and he lifted up his eyes, and saw, and, behold, the camels were coming.

And Rebekah lifted up her eyes, and when she saw Isaac, she lighted off the camel.

For she had said unto the servant, What man is this that walketh in the field to meet us? And the servant had said, It is my master: therefore she took a vail, and covered herself.

And the servant told Isaac all things that he had done.

And Isaac brought her into his mother Sarah's tent, and took Rebekah, and she became his wife; and he loved her: and Isaac was comforted after his mother's death.

Isaac was evidently living down in the Negev area near the well named earlier by Hagar (Gen. 16:13-14). When Eliezer and his camel caravan arrived in that area Isaac was walking in the field meditating. This passage gives the first indication of what Isaac was like as an adult. He differed from his father in personality and that difference was to be reflected in his leadership of the covenant family. Isaac was a quiet and peaceful man.

25:1-6 *Then again Abraham took a wife, and her name was Keturah.*

And she bare him Zimran, and Jokshan, and Medan, and Midian, and Ishbak, and Shuah.

And Jokshan begat Sheba, and Dedan. And the sons of Dedan were Asshurim, and Letushim, and Leummim.

And the sons of Midian; Ephah, and Epher, and Hanoch, and Abidah, and Eldaah. All these were the children of Keturah.

And Abraham gave all that he had unto Isaac.

But unto the sons of the concubines, which Abraham had, Abraham gave gifts, and sent them away from Isaac his son, while he yet lived, eastward, unto the east country.

God had promised to make Abraham the father of many nations. It was through the children born to Abraham and Keturah that this promise was fulfilled. These sons became the fathers of Arab tribes scattered across the

Middle East. Some of these nations became the enemies of Israel even during Old Testament times. In 1 Chronicles 1:32, 33 the same table of names is given. In that passage Keturah is said to be Abraham's concubine. Some scholars have contended that Abraham had Keturah during Sarah's lifetime but this seems inconsistent with Abraham's stand on monogamous marriage.

Abraham realized that to protect the covenant Isaac alone could be his heir. He, therefore, prior to his death generously endowed his other sons and sent them away from Canaan.

The Death of Abraham

25:7-11 *And these are the days of the years of Abraham's life which he lived, an hundred threescore and fifteen years.*

Then Abraham gave up the ghost, and died in a good old age, an old man, and full of years; and was gathered to his people.

And his sons Isaac and Ishmael buried him in the cave of Machpelah, in the field of Ephron the son of Zohar the Hittite, which is before Mamre:

The field which Abraham purchased of the sons of Heth: there was Abraham buried, and Sarah his wife.

And it came to pass after the death of Abraham, that God blessed his son Isaac; and Isaac dwelt by the well Lahairoi.

The patriarch Abraham had a full, rich life and evidently died with great peace and confidence in Jehovah. The Bible says that he "was gathered to his people." What a beautiful description of the hope of the faithful. Abraham's body was buried by Sarah in the cave of Machpelah many miles from their own people. But the soul of Abraham was gathered in conscious blessing to the bosom of God and the fellowship of those who died in the faith. This is a clear testimony to the biblical doctrine of life after death.

Isaac at the death of Abraham becomes the patriarch, or the leader of the covenant family. He made his home in the area where many years before Hagar had been rescued by the angel of the Lord. The Lord blessed Isaac as he dwelt by the well of Beer-lahai-roi. Rather than wandering over Canaan as Abraham had done Isaac was more settled. As we study Isaac's life it becomes evident that it lacked the excitement characteristic of Abraham's career.

25:12-18 *Now these are the generations of Ishmael, Abraham's son, whom Hagar the Egyptian, Sarah's handmaid, bare unto Abraham:*

And these are the names of the sons of Ishmael, by their names, according to their generations: the first-born of Ishmael, Nebajoth; and Kedar, and Adbeel, and Mibsam,

And Mishma, and Dumah, and Massa,

Hadar, and Tema, Jetur, Naphish, and Kedemah:

These are the sons of Ishmael, and these are their names, by their towns, and by their castles; twelve princes according to their nations.

And these are the years of the life of Ishmael, an hundred and thirty and seven years: and he gave up the ghost and died; and was gathered unto his people.

And they dwelt from Havilah unto Shur, that is before Egypt, as thou goest toward Assyria: and he died in the presence of all his brethren.

The short history of Ishmael and his descendants was given to demonstrate God's faithfulness to His promises. Ishmael was to father twelve sons from which nations would descend.

The Birth of Isaac's Heir

25:19-26 *And these are the generations of Isaac, Abraham's son: Abraham begat Isaac:*

And Isaac was forty years old when he took Rebekah to wife, the daughter of Bethuel the Syrian of Padan-aram, the sister to Laban the Syrian.

And Isaac intreated the Lord for his wife, because she was barren: and the Lord was intreated of him, and Rebekah his wife conceived.

And the children struggled together within her; and

161

she said, If it be so, why am I thus? And she went to enquire of the Lord.

And the Lord said unto her, Two nations are in thy womb, and two manner of people shall be separated from thy bowels; and the one people shall be stronger than the other people; and the elder shall serve the younger.

And when her days to be delivered were fulfilled, behold, there were twins in her womb.

And the first came out red, all over like an hairy garment: and they called his name Esau.

And after that came his brother out, and his hand took hold on Esau's heel; and his name was called Jacob: and Isaac was threescore years old when she bare them.

Isaac like his father before him had to face the test of patiently waiting God's intervention to give him an heir. For twenty years Rebekah was childless. God healed Rebekah's barrenness in answer to her husband's intercession. This is the second recorded healing given in answer to believing prayer. The birth of twins introduced the possibility of conflict in Isaac's household. Which of these sons would receive the birthright?

25:27-34 *And the boys grew: and Esau was a cunning hunter, a man of the field; and Jacob was a plain man, dwelling in tents.*

And Isaac loved Esau, because he did eat of his venison: but Rebekah loved Jacob.

And Jacob sod pottage: and Esau came from the field, and he was faint:

And Esau said to Jacob, Feed me, I pray thee, with that same red pottage; for I am faint: therefore was his name called Edom.

And Jacob said, Sell me this day thy birthright.

And Esau said, Behold, I am at the point to die: and what profit shall this birthright do to me?

And Jacob said, Swear to me this day; and he sware unto him: and he sold his birthright unto Jacob.

Then Jacob gave Esau bread and pottage of lentiles; and he did eat and drink, and rose up, and went his way:

thus Esau despised his birthright.

While the life of Isaac was one of relative quiet and peace he did suffer tension in his family. Isaac and Rebekah unwisely practiced paternal favoritism. Isaac liked Esau because he was a man's man and Rebekah preferred Jacob because of his cleverness. This domestic conflict came to a head one day when Jacob succeeded in deceiving Esau out of his birthright.

The birthright was spiritual in nature. It was not just an inheritance of land, cattle, and gold. The birthright was the divine covenant. The trickery of Jacob betrayed his lack of faith in God who could have overruled Isaac's portion to Esau and given Jacob the covenant. What sorrow he brought on himself and others by yielding to the way of the flesh.

26:1-5 *And there was famine in the land, beside the first famine that was in the days of Abraham. And Isaac went unto Abimelech king of the Philistines unto Gerar.*

And the Lord appeared unto him, and said, Go not down into Egypt; dwell in the land which I shall tell thee of:

Sojourn in this land, and I will be with thee, and will bless thee; for unto thee, and unto thy seed, I will give all these countries, and I will perform the oath which I sware unto Abraham thy father;

And I will make thy seed to multiply as the stars of heaven, and will give unto thy seed all these countries; and in thy seed shall all the nations of the earth be blessed;

Because that Abraham obeyed my voice, and kept my charge, my commandments, my statutes, and my laws.

The Abimelech mentioned in this passage was apparently a different man from the one whom Abraham had earlier known. Abimelech was probably a Philistine title for a ruler, much as the term Pharaoh was in Egypt. Isaac must have been about to leave for Egypt, when God warned him against leaving the land. Jehovah at that time reconfirmed the covenant given to Isaac's father and assured him that he and his seed would possess the land of Canaan. Abraham's obedience to divine revelation was the reason Jehovah was confirming the covenant to Isaac. Isaac was to walk in this same path of trust and obedience. Verse 5 indicates that some collection of divine principles of conduct existed before the Mosaic code was revealed. The revelation of truth was progressive in Old Testament times. From Adam on the known truth was transmitted either in written form or by word of mouth.

Isaac's Lapse of Faith

26:6-11 *And Isaac dwelt in Gerar:*
And the men of the place asked him of his wife; and he said, She is my sister: for he feared to say, She is my wife; lest, said he, the men of the place should kill me for Rebekah; because she was fair to look upon.

And it came to pass, when he had been there a long time, that Abimelech king of the Philistines looked out at a window, and saw, and, behold, Isaac was sporting with Rebekah his wife.

And Abimelech called Isaac, and said, Behold, of a surety she is thy wife: and how saidst thou, She is my sister? And Isaac said unto him, Because I said, Lest I die for her.

And Abimelech said, What is this thou hast done unto us? one of the people might lightly have lien with thy wife, and thou shouldest have brought guiltiness upon us.

And Abimelech charged all his people, saying, He that toucheth this man or his wife shall surely be put to death.

Isaac had obeyed the Lord in that he did not go to Egypt during the famine but remained in the land of promise. It was in the land that his faith was tested by the presence of the Philistines. Like his father Abraham, Isaac foolishly attempted to deceive Abimelech regarding his relationship to Rebekah. The moral integrity of Abimelech saved Isaac from the results of his folly.

There is a lesson to be drawn from Isaac's repetition of Abraham's sin. Those who are heads of families are responsible to set a right example for their children. Though Abraham's life was one of maturity in the way of faith, his weaknesses as well as his strengths were repeated in his son.

God so worked that Abimelech who had posed such a threat to Isaac became kindly disposed to him and became Isaac's protector. God's mercy continued even when Isaac's faith had failed.

Isaac in the Place of Blessing

26:12-22 *Then Isaac sowed in that land, and received in the same year an hundredfold: and the Lord blessed him.*

And the man waxed great, and went forward, and grew until he became very great:

For he had possession of flocks, and possession of herds, and great store of servants: and the Philistines envied him.

For all the wells which his father's servants had digged in the days of Abraham his father, the Philistines had stopped them, and filled them with earth.

And Abimelech said unto Isaac, Go from us; for thou art much mightier than we.

And Isaac departed thence, and pitched his tent in the valley of Gerar, and dwelt there.

And Isaac digged again the wells of water, which they had digged in the days of Abraham his father; for the Philistines had stopped them after the death of Abraham: and he called their names after the names by which his father had called them.

And Isaac's servants digged in the valley, and found there a well of springing water.

And the herdmen of Gerar did strive with Isaac's herdmen, saying, The water is our's: and he called the name of the well Esek; because they strove with him.

And they digged another well, and strove for that also: and he called the name of it Sitnah.

And he removed from thence, and digged another well; and for that they strove not: and he called the name of it Rehoboth; and he said, For now the Lord hath

165

made room for us, and we shall be fruitful in the land.

These were the best years of Isaac's life. The blessing of God had given him both prosperity and peace. He became so mighty in wealth and influence that the Philistines feared him and asked him to leave.

Isaac was a man of peace and offered no resistance to Abimelech's request. He moved on to the valley of Gerar and the familiar campsites of Abraham's day.

While the Philistines feared Isaac and his powerful household they continued to harass him by filling up the wells of water so essential to Isaac's great herds of livestock. He patiently reopened the wells and dug new ones.

Over a period of time Isaac opened two new wells. The digging of each well prompted a confrontation with the Philistines. Isaac moved on each time without resisting the Philistines until he dug a third well which he named Rehoboth, meaning "wide places." The strife was brought to an end. Isaac's policy of peace had yielded its benefits. The third well was symbolic of the fullness of blessing the patriarch had come to enjoy in his covenant relationship to Jehovah.

26:23-33 *And he went up from thence to Beer-sheba.*
And the Lord appeared unto him the same night, and said, I am the God of Abraham thy father: fear not, for I am with thee, and will bless thee, and multiply thy seed for my servant Abraham's sake.

And he builded an altar there, and called upon the name of the Lord, and pitched his tent there: and there Isaac's servants digged a well.

Then Abimelech went to him from Gerar, and Ahuzzath one of his friends, and Phichol the chief captain of his army.

And Isaac said unto them, Wherefore come ye to me, seeing ye hate me, and have sent me away from you?

And they said, We saw certainly that the Lord was with thee: and we said, Let there be now an oath betwixt us, even betwixt us and thee, and let us make a covenant with thee;

That thou wilt do us no hurt, as we have not touched thee, and as we have done unto thee nothing but good, and have sent thee away in peace: thou art now the blessed of the Lord.

And he made them a feast, and they did eat and drink.

And they rose up betimes in the morning, and sware one to another: and Isaac sent them away, and they departed from him in peace.

And it came to pass the same day, that Isaac's servants came, and told him concerning the well which they had digged, and said unto him, We have found water.

And he called it Sheba: therefore the name of the city is Beer-sheba unto this day.

The movements of Isaac in the land follow a pattern similar to those of Abraham. Once back from the valley of Gerar, Isaac built an altar and worshiped the Lord there, just as Abraham had done at Bethel after his return from Egypt (Gen. 13:1-4). The history of Isaac can be traced in the well he opened. The well he named Beer-sheba had a special significance. It meant an oath. Beer-sheba was the "well of an oath." Here Isaac's hecklers had come to express their high regard for him and to ask a covenant of peace with him. Isaac had won the victory by the patience and peace of the walk of faith.

26:34-35 *And Esau was forty years old when he took to wife Judith the daughter of Beeri the Hittite, and Bashemath the daughter of Elon the Hittite:*

Which were a grief of mind unto Isaac and to Rebekah.

At the pinnacle of blessing in Isaac's life a dark cloud came on the horizon. The self-willed, fleshly Esau married a pagan. Isaac and Rebekah went through bitter suffering as they watched the spiritual erosion of Esau's life. While Isaac had many great and noble qualities, the breakdown in his family life leaves a blot on his spiritual biography.

167

13

Isaac's Sorrow

Genesis 27:1—28:9

The closing years of Isaac's life were filled with sorrow. Though Isaac was a man of great patience and a man who always sought peace, he lacked discernment and that weakness brought spiritual blight to him and his family. Isaac did not sense that the heir of the covenant would be determined by divine election (Rom. 9:8-13). It would not be his prerogative to determine which of his twin sons received the birthright. God had made that decision.

At the birth of Jacob and Esau, God revealed to Rebekah that Jacob would be the heir (Gen. 25:23). Isaac never took seriously this word from the Lord.

> 27:1-4 *And it came to pass, that when Isaac was old, and his eyes were dim, so that he could not see, he called Esau his eldest son, and said unto him, My son: and he said unto him, Behold, here am I.*
>
> *And he said, Behold now, I am old, I know not the day of my death:*
>
> *Now therefore take, I pray thee, thy weapons, thy quiver and thy bow, and go out to the field, and take me some venison;*
>
> *And make me savoury meat, such as I love, and bring it to me, that I may eat; that my soul may bless thee before I die.*

Isaac is a clear example of a saint whose life was limited by condoned weaknesses. Forty years before his death the patriarch was a semi-invalid and thought himself about to die. His physical powers were evidently weakened and his eyesight had grown dim. It may have been his preoccupation with death that distorted his perception of a choice of the heir to carry on the covenant with Jehovah to the next generation.

There is evidence in this passage that Isaac had allowed

his personal pleasure to interfere with his spiritual judgments. He liked Esau better than he liked Jacob. Isaac had learned to love the wild game Esau got in the hunt. That unbridled taste became a snare to this man of God. With no consideration of the word of the Lord on the matter, Isaac on the basis of personal preference decided to give Esau the birthright.

The Deception of Jacob

27:5-13 *And Rebekah heard when Isaac spake to Esau his son. And Esau went to the field to hunt for venison, and to bring it.*

And Rebekah spake unto Jacob her son, saying, Behold, I heard thy father speak unto Esau thy brother, saying,

Bring me venison, and make me savoury meat, that I may eat, and bless thee before the Lord before my death.

Now therefore, my son, obey my voice according to that which I command thee.

Go now to the flock, and fetch me from thence two good kids of the goats; and I will make them savoury meat for thy father, such as he loveth:

And thou shalt bring it to thy father, that he may eat, and that he may bless thee before his death.

And Jacob said to Rebekah his mother, Behold, Esau my brother is a hairy man, and I am a smooth man:

My father peradventure will feel me, and I shall seem to him as a deceiver; and I shall bring a curse upon me, and not a blessing.

And his mother said unto him, Upon me be thy curse, my son: only obey my voice, and go fetch me them.

The seeds of a divided home were now bearing their fruit. Rebekah like Isaac had developed a personal preference. Jacob was her favorite. She also remembered God's word to her at the birth of her sons. She knew that Jacob was the destined heir. But Rebekah's faith failed as much as did her husband's. She sought by the deceptive methods of the flesh to assure Jacob the birthright.

Jacob joined her in the scheme of deception when he had been reassured that Isaac would not discover him.

169

Something of the duplicity of Jacob's heart comes through in this scene. It was to take years of divine chastening before Jacob would yield fully to the will of God.

27:14-24 *And he went, and fetched, and brought them to his mother: and his mother made savoury meat, such as his father loved.*

And Rebekah took goodly raiment of her eldest son Esau, which were with her in the house, and put them upon Jacob her younger son:

And she put the skins of the kids of the goats upon his hands, and upon the smooth of his neck:

And she gave the savoury meat and the bread, which she had prepared, into the hand of her son Jacob.

And he came unto his father, and said, My father: and he said, Here am I; who art thou, my son?

And Jacob said unto his father, I am Esau thy first-born; I have done according as thou badest me: arise, I pray thee, sit and eat of my venison, that thy soul may bless me.

And Isaac said unto his son, How is it that thou hast found it so quickly, my son? And he said, Because the Lord thy God brought it to me.

And Isaac said unto Jacob, Come near, I pray thee, that I may feel thee, my son, whether thou be my very son Esau or not.

And Jacob went near unto Isaac his father; and he felt him, and said, The voice is Jacob's voice, but the hands are the hands of Esau.

And he discerned him not, because his hands were hairy, as his brother Esau's hands: so he blessed him.

And he said, Art thou my very son Esau? And he said, I am.

Little did Isaac realize the tragedy that would come out of his willful plan to give Esau the birthright. Every member of the family became involved in this affair. One sin led to another. Jacob, so determined to have Esau's blessing, stood before his father and told one lie after another. Like most deceived people he even invoked God's blessing to make his lies sound plausible.

Poor Isaac used every one of his physical senses to discover the identity of the man in his room. Was it really Esau? But never once did he resort to his spiritual senses. Had Isaac's spiritual senses been more developed than his physical senses, he may well have discerned Jacob's and Rebekah's scheme and the years of subsequent sorrow might have been avoided.

27:25-27 And he said, Bring it near to me, and I will eat of my son's venison, that my soul may bless thee. And he brought it near to him, and he did eat: and he brought him wine, and he drank.

And his father Isaac said unto him, Come near now, and kiss me, my son.

And he came near, and kissed him: and he smelled the smell of his raiment, and blessed him, and said, See, the smell of my son is as the smell of a field which the Lord hath blessed:

By the time Isaac had eaten the meal his insight had not improved. He asked Jacob to come near and kiss him. How tragic that Jacob was willing to use an expression of affection to complete his deception. The sin that impelled Jacob that day would drive another man centuries later to betray the Lord of glory with a kiss. Still moved by his physical senses Isaac smelled Jacob's garments and it reminded him of the field that the Lord blessed. Without further thought he began to bless Jacob with the birthright.

27:28-29 Therefore God give thee of the dew of heaven, and the fatness of the earth, and plenty of corn and wine:

Let people serve thee, and nations bow down to thee: be lord over thy brethren, and let thy mother's sons bow down to thee: cursed be every one that curseth thee, and blessed be he that blesseth thee.

The blessing Isaac bestowed upon Jacob, was irrevocable. Since Abraham's descendants were an earthly people, the divine blessing took that into consideration. The blessing Isaac spoke over Jacob was related to the covenant God had made with Abraham. The blessing was given in the form of poetry. Isaac by this time was deeply moved in his heart and spoke in exalted language the benediction that would affect the history of Israel through all of time. The first benefit was the promise of material prosperity as a result of the fruitfulness of the land of promise.

The second benefit was political in nature and assured Jacob that his seed would enjoy political ascendancy as a nation.

The third benefit revealed the spiritual blessing that would come to the world through the sons of Jacob. The Messianic promise is inherent in this blessing.

Esau's Bitter Cry

27:30-40 *And it came to pass, as soon as Isaac had made an end of blessing Jacob, and Jacob was yet scarce gone out from the presence of Isaac his father, that Esau his brother came in from his hunting.*

And he also had made savoury meat, and brought it unto his father, and said unto his father, Let my father arise, and eat of his son's venison, that thy soul may bless me.

And Isaac his father said unto him, Who art thou? And he said, I am thy son, thy firstborn Esau.

And Isaac trembled very exceedingly, and said, Who? where is he that hath taken venison, and brought it to me, and I have eaten of all before thou camest, and have blessed him? yea, and he shall be blessed.

And when Esau heard the words of his father, he cried with a great and exceeding bitter cry, and said to his father, Bless me, even me also, O my father.

And he said, Thy brother came with subtilty and hath taken away thy blessing.

And he said, Is not he rightly named Jacob? for he hath supplanted me these two times: he took away my birthright; and, behold, now he hath taken away my blessing. And he said, Hast thou not reserved a blessing for me?

And Isaac answered and said unto Esau, Behold, I have made him thy lord, and all his brethren have I given to him for servants; and with corn and wine have I sustained him: and what shall I do now unto thee, my son?

And Esau said unto his father, Hast thou but one blessing, my father? bless me, even me also, O my father. And Esau lifted up his voice, and wept.

And Isaac his father answered and said unto him, Behold, thy dwelling shall be the fatness of the earth, and of the dew of heaven from above;

And by thy sword shalt thou live, and shalt serve thy brother; and it shall come to pass when thou shalt have the dominion, that thou shalt break his yoke from off thy neck.

Jacob was gone from his father but a short time when Esau entered the chamber with Isaac's favorite game dish. What was to have been the high moment of joy in Esau's life turned into a tragedy. His profane heart reaped what it had sown. The birthright he had treated so lightly was forever gone. Esau wept and cried out in the bitterness of his soul but to no avail. Isaac could not retract the blessing given to Jacob. Poor Esau received only the blessing of the profane, a measure of material blessing without spiritual blessing. Esau's repentance came too late (Heb. 12:17). His cry of despair stands as a warning to all succeeding generations. Esau himself was never subjected to Jacob's rule but Isaac's prediction did come true when Esau's descendants were brought under Israel's dominion in the reign of Joram (2 Kings 8:20-21; 2 Chron. 21:8).

Jacob Flees

27:41—28:5 And Esau hated Jacob because of the blessing wherewith his father blessed him: and Esau said in his heart, The days of mourning for my father are at hand; then will I slay my brother Jacob.

And these words of Esau her elder son were told to Rebekah: and she sent and called Jacob her younger son, and said unto him, Behold, thy brother Esau, as touching thee, doth comfort himself, purposing to kill thee.

173

*Now therefore, my son, obey my voice; and arise, flee
thou to Laban my brother to Haran;*

*And tarry with him a few days, until thy brother's
fury turn away;*

*Until thy brother's anger turn away from thee, and he
forget that which thou hast done to him: then I will
send, and fetch thee from thence: why should I be de-
prived also of you both in one day?*

*And Rebekah said to Isaac, I am weary of my life be-
cause of the daughters of Heth: if Jacob take a wife of
the daughters of Heth, such as these which are of the
daughters of the land, what good shall my life do me?*

*And Isaac called Jacob, and blessed him, and
charged him, and said unto him, Thou shalt not take a
wife of the daughters of Canaan.*

*Arise, go to Padan-aram, to the house of Bethuel, thy
mother's father; and take thee a wife from thence of the
daughters of Laban thy mother's brother.*

*And God Almighty bless thee, and make thee fruitful,
and multiply thee, that thou mayest be a multitude of
people;*

*And give thee the blessing of Abraham, to thee, and
to thy seed with thee; that thou mayest inherit the land
wherein thou art a stranger, which God gave unto Abraham.*

*And Isaac sent away Jacob: and he went to Padan-
aram unto Laban, son of Bethuel the Syrian, the brother
of Rebekah, Jacob's and Esau's mother.*

Rebekah heard of Esau's anger and realized that
Jacob's life was in jeopardy. Again she resorted to a
scheme to get Isaac's approval for her plan to send Jacob
away to safety. She reasoned with Isaac that their home
had known enough strife as a result of Esau's pagan
wives. How much more difficult it would be if Jacob also
married a pagan wife. She urged that Jacob be sent to
Mesopotamia for a wife from Laban's family. Isaac
agreed and Jacob was on his way to Padan-aram.

28:6-9 *When Esau saw that Isaac had blessed Jacob,
and sent him away to Padan-aram, to take him a wife
from thence; and that as he blessed him he gave him a*

charge, saying, Thou shalt not take a wife of the daughters of Canaan;

And that Jacob obeyed his father and his mother, and was gone to Padan-aram;

And Esau seeing that the daughters of Canaan pleased not Isaac his father;

Then went Esau unto Ishmael, and took unto the wives which he had Mahalath the daughter of Ishmael, Abraham's son, the sister of Nebajoth, to be his wife.

Some scholars believe that Esau married Mahalath, daughter of Ishmael, in an attempt to mollify his parents. His previous marriages to pagan Canaanites brought the displeasure of Isaac and Rebekah. But whatever Esau's motive was in marrying Mahalath it did not improve the situation. She evidently did no more to encourage walking with Jehovah in His covenant than did Esau's other wives. Esau never learned that obedience to God was the only way to blessing. This marriage was only a fleshly effort to achieve some degree of domestic peace and it failed. Isaac and Rebekah in the golden years, when their family should have been bringing them joy, had to suffer loneliness and the disappointment of Esau's waywardness. The years of family strife bore its bitter fruit. The great patriarch of peace had to die in the midst of domestic turmoil.

14

The Years of Testing

Genesis 28:10—30:24

The patriarchal leadership of the covenant family was about to pass to the third generation. Abraham, the father of the covenant family, had been a man of faith. His son Isaac had been a man of peace. Jacob, the grandson, was destined to be the most complex and controversial of the patriarchs. The writer of Genesis selected the incident of Jacob's deceptive seizure of the birthright to move him into the place of preeminence in the biblical narrative. Though Jacob's life was to be characterized by conflict and struggle, the sovereign hand of Jehovah kept working to bring him to a place of full blessing.

Jacob Meets God

28:10-15 *And Jacob went out from Beer-sheba, and went toward Haran.*

And he lighted upon a certain place, and tarried there all night, because the sun was set; and he took of the stones of that place, and put them for his pillows, and lay down in that place to sleep.

And he dreamed, and behold a ladder set up on the earth, and the top of it reached to heaven: and behold the angels of God ascending and descending on it.

And, behold, the Lord stood above it, and said, I am the Lord God of Abraham thy father, and the God of Isaac: the land whereon thou liest, to thee will I give it, and to thy seed;

And thy seed shall be as the dust of the earth, and thou shalt spread abroad to the west, and to the east, and to the north, and to the south: and in thee and in thy seed shall all the families of the earth be blessed.

And, behold, I am with thee, and will keep thee in all places whither thou goest, and will bring thee again into this land; for I will not leave thee, until I have done that which I have spoken to thee of.

In that lonely vigil at Bethel, Jacob had his first personal experience with God. The impressions of that encounter were deep and lasting. There was much to be done in Jacob's life before he reached spiritual maturity, but at Bethel he had a new beginning.

Jehovah witnessed to Jacob that he was the heir of the covenant. The provisions of the covenant Jehovah gave Jacob were exactly the same as those originally given to Abraham (Gen. 12:1-3, 7). Canaan would be the possession of his descendants. The nation that would come from his seed would bless the world.

Jehovah added to the covenant provisions a personal word of encouragement for Jacob. The Lord promised He would go with Jacob and protect him. He assured the patriarch that he would some day return to the land of promise. While he lived in Haran, Jacob could be sure of the presence of the Lord with him. God's word to Jacob that memorable night all proved to be true. Twenty years later Jacob returned to Bethel and praised God for fulfilling His promises (Gen. 35:1-15).

We might wonder why the Lord was so gracious to Jacob who had much to learn about moral and spiritual values. We have to realize that His sovereign will is worked out, even in the face of perverse spiritual and character qualities in the people involved. Before Jacob was born, God intended him to be the covenant son (Gen. 25:23), and He was going to make this happen. The Lord was able to see Jacob for the kind of person he would later become.

28:16-22 *And Jacob awaked out of his sleep, and he said, Surely the Lord is in this place; and I knew it not.*

And he was afraid, and said, How dreadful is this place! this is none other but the house of God, and this is the gate of heaven.

And Jacob rose up early in the morning, and took the stone that he had put for his pillows, and set it up for a pillar, and poured oil upon the top of it.

And he called the name of that place Beth-el: but the name of that city was called Luz at the first.

177

And Jacob vowed a vow, saying, If God will be with me, and will keep me in this way that I go, and will give me bread to eat, and raiment to put on,

So that I come again to my father's house in peace; then shall the Lord be my God:

And this stone, which I have set for a pillar, shall be God's house: and of all that thou shalt give me I will surely give the tenth unto thee.

The dream had such a deep impression on Jacob that he awakened with the awareness that he was on holy ground. He had experienced a spiritual dimension beyond the range of the normal senses. Heaven had opened up to Jacob. With all his defects and carnal struggles, he would never be able to forget the reality of that moment at the gate of heaven. Though he did not fully understand the realm of spiritual blessing at this point in his life, Jacob had a new perspective on the birthright he had received.

His response to the divine visitation was as complete as his level of spiritual maturity would permit. Jacob's first impulse upon awakening from the dream was to worship God by making a definite commitment. The anointing of the stone was symbolic of his consecration. The name he gave the place of this encounter had a special significance. Bethel means the "house of God." This concept was to be developed as the nation grew and the unfolding of the covenant truth continued. The house of God would come to mean the place where God's people meet with Him.

This is the second mention of the tithe in the Book of Genesis. Abraham had passed this practice on to his descendants. The tithe had a long history before it was made a part of the Levitical system. The principle of proportionate giving transcends the ages.

Jacob's Arrival in Haran

29:1-8 Then Jacob went on his journey, and came into the land of the people of the east.

And he looked, and behold a well in the field, and, lo, there were three flocks of sheep lying by it; for out of that well they watered the flocks: and a great stone was upon

178

the well's mouth.

And thither were all the flocks gathered: and they rolled the stone from the well's mouth, and watered the sheep, and put the stone again upon the well's mouth in his place.

And Jacob said unto them, My brethren, whence be ye? And they said, Of Haran are we.

And he said unto them, Know ye Laban the son of Nahor? And they said, We know him.

And he said unto them, Is he well? And they said, He is well: and, behold, Rachel his daughter cometh with the sheep.

And he said, Lo, it is yet high day, neither is it time that the cattle should be gathered together: water ye the sheep, and go and feed them.

And they said, We cannot, until all the flocks be gathered together, and till they roll the stone from the well's mouth; then we water the sheep.

Jacob traveled northward and eastward for about four hundred miles to reach Padan-aram, the land of the east. He came to a well in a field and there learned that he had arrived in the area of Haran. The shepherds gathered at the well knew his kinsman.

29:9-12 *And while he yet spake with them, Rachel came with her father's sheep: for she kept them.*

And it came to pass, when Jacob saw Rachel the daughter of Laban his mother's brother, and the sheep of Laban his mother's brother, that Jacob went near, and rolled the stone from the well's mouth, and watered the flock of Laban his mother's brother.

And Jacob kissed Rachel, and lifted up his voice, and wept.

And Jacob told Rachel that he was her father's brother, and that he was Rebekah's son: and she ran and told her father.

Before Jacob had finished questioning the shepherds, Rachel, the daughter of Laban, brought her flock to the well. The story of Jacob's meeting with Rachel reflects both the elements of humor and tenderness. He became so excited that he lifted the lid of the well without anyone's assistance, an unusual demonstration of strength. The sight of his cousin moved Jacob deeply. It was love at first sight.

> 29:13-19 *And it came to pass, when Laban heard the tidings of Jacob his sister's son, that he ran to meet him, and embraced him, and kissed him, and brought him to his house. And he told Laban all these things.*
>
> *And Laban said to him, Surely thou art my bone and my flesh. And he abode with him the space of a month.*
>
> *And Laban said unto Jacob, Because thou art my brother, shouldest thou therefore serve me for nought? tell me, what shall thy wages be?*
>
> *And Laban had two daughters: the name of the elder was Leah, and the name of the younger was Rachel.*
>
> *Leah was tender eyed; but Rachel was beautiful and well favoured.*
>
> *And Jacob loved Rachel; and said, I will serve thee seven years for Rachel thy younger daughter.*
>
> *And Laban said, It is better that I give her to thee, than that I should give her to another man: abide with me.*

After the formalities of greeting were over the two men agreed on the terms by which Jacob would live in Laban's household. Jacob evidently fled without any financial resources. If he was to take a bride some dowry had to be provided.

Since Jacob had neither gifts nor cattle his only recourse was to work out his dowry, so he arranged to work seven years for Laban as a dowry for Rachel. Laban accepted the offer. Little did Jacob realize that he had met his match at duplicity. Laban was to deceive him many times during the years Jacob worked for him. Men reap what they sow. Many times Jacob suffered under Laban and must have regretted his own duplicity.

Jacob's Double Marriage

> 29:20-35 *And Jacob served seven years for Rachel; and they seemed unto him but a few days, for the love he*

180

had to her.

And Jacob said unto Laban, Give me my wife, for my days are fulfilled, that I may go in unto her.

And Laban gathered together all the men of the place, and made a feast.

And it came to pass in the evening, that he took Leah his daughter, and brought her to him; and he went in unto her.

And Laban gave unto his daughter Leah Zilpah his maid for an handmaid.

And it came to pass, that in the morning, behold, it was Leah: and he said to Laban, What is this thou hast done unto me? did not I serve with thee for Rachel? wherefore then hast thou beguiled me?

And Laban said, It must not be so done in our country, to give the younger before the firstborn.

Fulfil her week, and we will give thee this also for the service which thou shalt serve with me yet seven other years.

And Jacob did so, and fulfilled her week: and he gave him Rachel his daughter to wife also.

And Laban gave to Rachel his daughter Bilhah his handmaid to be her maid.

And he went in also unto Rachel, and he loved also Rachel more than Leah, and served with him yet seven other years.

And when the Lord saw that Leah was hated, he opened her womb: but Rachel was barren.

And Leah conceived, and bare a son, and she called his name Reuben: for she said, Surely the Lord hath looked upon my affliction; now therefore my husband will love me.

And she conceived again, and bare a son; and said, Because the Lord hath heard that I was hated, he hath therefore given me this son also: and she called his name Simeon.

And she conceived again, and bare a son; and said, Now this time will my husband be joined unto me, because I have born him three sons: therefore was his name called Levi.

And she conceived again, and bare a son: and she said, Now will I praise the Lord: therefore she called his name Judah; and left bearing.

As the seven-year indenture came to an end Jacob anticipated the joy of marrying Rachel. Little did he know that the happiness of that union was to be forever marred by the deception of Laban. The trickery of Laban's maneuver required a second seven years of servitude for Jacob.

Years of unhappy home life were to follow the double marriage. The loveless relationship with Leah produced strife. Rachel's barrenness added another cross for Jacob to bear. The Lord chastens those whom He loves. God had a plan for Jacob that called for the perfecting of his spiritual life. The hard years of labor under the unfair hand of Laban along with the heartbreak of his family situation, were a part of the divine plan for Jacob's spiritual growth.

The domestic weaknesses of Isaac and Rebekah's household seemed now to be repeated in their son's experience. The trials of the covenant family through those two generations give some helpful insight into the very forces that are destroying the family in today's culture.

The Evils of Polygamy

30:1-21 *And when Rachel saw that she bare Jacob no children, Rachel envied her sister; and said unto Jacob, Give me children, or else I die.*

And Jacob's anger was kindled against Rachel: and he said, Am I in God's stead, who hath withheld from thee the fruit of the womb?

And she said, Behold my maid Bilhah, go in unto her; and she shall bear upon my knees, that I may also have children by her.

And she gave him Bilhah her handmaid to wife: and Jacob went in unto her.

And Bilhah conceived, and bare Jacob a son.

And Rachel said, God hath judged me, and hath also heard my voice, and hath given me a son: therefore called she his name Dan.

And Bilhah Rachel's maid conceived again, and bare Jacob a second son.

And Rachel said, With great wrestlings have I

wrestled with my sister, and I have prevailed: and she called his name Naphtali.

When Leah saw that she had left bearing, she took Zilpah her maid, and gave her Jacob to wife.

And Zilpah Leah's maid bare Jacob a son.

And Leah said, A troop cometh: and she called his name Gad.

And Zilpah Leah's maid bare Jacob a second son.

And Leah said, Happy am I, for the daughters will call me blessed: and she called his name Asher.

And Reuben went in the days of wheat harvest, and found mandrakes in the field, and brought them unto his mother Leah. Then Rachel said to Leah, Give me, I pray thee, of thy son's mandrakes.

And she said unto her, Is it a small matter that thou hast taken my husband? and wouldest thou take away my son's mandrakes also? And Rachel said, Therefore he shall lie with thee to night for thy son's mandrakes.

And Jacob came out of the field in the evening, and Leah went out to meet him, and said, Thou must come in unto me; for surely I have hired thee with my son's mandrakes. And he lay with her that night.

And God hearkened unto Leah, and she conceived, and bare Jacob the fifth son.

And Leah said, God hath given me my hire, because I have given my maiden to my husband: and she called his name Issachar.

And Leah conceived again, and bare Jacob the sixth son.

And Leah said, God hath endued me with a good dowry; now will my husband dwell with me, because I have born him six sons: and she called his name Zebulun.

And afterwards she bare a daughter, and called her name Dinah.

God's will for the family is a monogamous marriage. The practice of polygamy though tolerated by God in patriarchal times was never His will. Leah and Rachel were caught up in rivalry that promoted hatred and jealousy between them. Polygamy never allowed for a truly happy home.

Leah could not win Jacob's love even after giving him

six sons and a daughter. Rachel, frustrated by her inability to have a child, was peevish and unreasonable. Only Jacob's great love for her kept him patient with her tactics.

While polygamy is not a problem in Western culture, the breakdown in the family is fast producing the same kind of problem. Homes fractured by repeated divorces and remarriages leave their victims with the same frustrations Leah, Rachel, and Jacob suffered.

> 30:22-24 *And God remembered Rachel, and God hearkened to her, and opened her womb.*
>
> *And she conceived, and bare a son; and said, God hath taken away my reproach:*
>
> *And she called his name Joseph; and said, The Lord shall add to me another son.*

Rachel was the third wife of a patriarch to suffer barrenness. Sarah could only bear Isaac when God intervened supernaturally. Rebekah was barren until God healed her of it in answer to Isaac's prayers. Rachel prevailed in prayer for her condition. God enabled her to bear Joseph. The promise made to Adam and Eve in the garden that the seed of the woman would be man's Savior and destroy Satan's power was challenged throughout the Old Testament. In every instance God intervened to assure the continuation of the line from which Christ was to be born.

15

Jacob's Years of Prosperity

Genesis 30:25—31:16

Jacob had worked fourteen years for Laban and wanted to go back to Canaan. Laban had discovered that Jacob's presence in his household had brought him blessing and he, therefore, wanted to detain Jacob longer. A new working agreement was made between Laban and Jacob which under the hand of God proved a blessing to Jacob. The six years Jacob cared for Laban's livestock made him enormously rich. Laban grew more resentful of Jacob's growing wealth with the passing of the years. It was this unhappy relationship that became the occasion for the patriarch's departure from Haran.

30:25-33 *And it came to pass, when Rachel had born Joseph, that Jacob said unto Laban, Send me away, that I may go unto mine own place, and to my country.*

Give me my wives and my children, for whom I have served thee, and let me go: for thou knowest my service which I have done thee.

And Laban said unto him, I pray thee, if I have found favour in thine eyes, tarry: for I have learned by experience that the Lord hath blessed me for thy sake.

And he said, Appoint me thy wages, and I will give it.

And he said unto him, Thou knowest how I have served thee, and how thy cattle was with me.

For it was little which thou hadst before I came, and it is now increased unto a multitude; and the Lord hath blessed thee since my coming: and now when shall I provide for mine own house also?

And he said, What shall I give thee? And Jacob said, Thou shalt not give me any thing: if thou wilt do this thing for me, I will again feed and keep thy flock.

I will pass through all thy flock to day, removing from thence all the speckled and spotted cattle, and all the brown cattle among the sheep, and the spotted and

speckled among the goats: and of such shall be my hire.
So shall my righteousness answer for me in time to come, when it shall come for my hire before thy face: every one that is not speckled and spotted among the goats, and brown among the sheep, that shall be counted stolen with me.

Laban evidently worshiped the God of the Hebrews and had some understanding of moral truth, yet he was carnal and measured blessing in terms of material prosperity. He seemed to lack sensitivity as to Jacob's spiritual destiny as an heir of Abraham's covenant. Laban's greedy heart could not bear the thought of Jacob leaving to return to Canaan. What did Laban care for Jacob's heritage? He must find a way to keep Jacob near.

Once again Laban proposed a business deal with Jacob that put the younger man at a disadvantage. But Jacob had been learning of the devious nature of his father-in-law and made a counter proposal that seemed to place Jacob at an even greater disadvantage. Laban agreed little realizing that the husbandry skills of Jacob and the blessing of Jehovah would give Jacob the advantage.

Jacob's offer to take the less acceptable livestock for his wages was not so pious an act as it appears on the surface. The years of service Jacob had already given had developed his skill in selective breeding of cattle and goats. Jacob felt justified in using this knowledge to increase his own herds.

30:34-43 *And Laban said, Behold, I would it might be according to thy word.*
And he removed that day the he goats that were ringstraked and spotted, and all the she goats that were speckled and spotted, and every one that had some white in it, and all the brown among the sheep, and gave them into the hand of his sons.
And he set three days' journey betwixt himself and Jacob: and Jacob fed the rest of Laban's flocks.
And Jacob took him rods of green poplar, and of the hazel and chestnut tree; and pilled white strakes in them, and made the white appear which was in the rods.
And he set the rods which he had pilled before the

flocks in the gutters in the watering troughs when the flocks came to drink, that they should conceive when they came to drink.

And the flocks conceived before the rods, and brought forth cattle ringstraked, speckled, and spotted.

And Jacob did separate the lambs, and set the faces of the flocks toward the ringstraked, and all the brown in the flock of Laban; and he put his own flocks by themselves, and put them not into Laban's cattle.

And it came to pass, whensoever the stronger cattle did conceive, that Jacob laid the rods before the eyes of the cattle in the gutters, that they might conceive among the rods.

But when the cattle were feeble, he put them not in: so the feebler were Laban's, and the stronger Jacob's.

And the man increased exceedingly, and had much cattle, and maidservants, and menservants, and camels, and asses.

Laban did not trust Jacob and separated the off-colored animals himself to prevent any dishonesty. He judiciously placed his own flocks a three day's journey away from the flocks of Jacob. Laban was to learn that no scheming or trickery on his part could defeat Jacob. He was slow to see the hand of the Lord in the life and circumstances of Jacob. A total of ten times in twenty years he changed Jacob's wages but nothing deterred the steady increase of Jacob's wealth.

Jacob had either learned from some human source or from the Lord Himself that prenatal influence could affect the coloring of animals when they are conceived and then born. He took branches of the green poplar (or green branches of the poplar), hazel (or almond), and chestnut (or plane) trees and peeled off strips of bark to reveal white streaks underneath. These he placed in the gutters by the watering troughs where the sheep and goats came to drink. This was the place where the animals mated, so the varied-colored rods influenced them to conceive marked and off-colored offspring. Scholars differ in their interpretation of this practice but the possibility that God used it to enrich Jacob ought not to be ruled out.

Jacob used selective breeding to improve his own

animals. He separated his marked and off-colored animals and did not allow them to breed with Laban's single-colored animals. He bred the stronger animals to produce higher-quality offspring for his own collection and left the weaker ones for Laban's collection.

As the years passed by Jacob's methods of animal husbandry paid off handsomely. As his wealth accumulated he traded for male and female servants, camels, and asses. No doubt he also acquired precious metals, fine raiment, and the other things which people of that time considered valuable. Since the pagan mentality associated wealth with the power of one's god, Jacob had opportunity through his prosperity to honor Jehovah God in the eyes of the people of Haran. The promise God made to Jacob at Bethel was not forgotten.

31:1-3 *And he heard the words of Laban's sons, saying, Jacob hath taken away all that was our father's; and of that which was our father's hath he gotten all this glory.*

And Jacob beheld the countenance of Laban, and, behold, it was not toward him as before.

And the Lord said unto Jacob, Return unto the land of thy fathers, and to thy kindred; and I will be with thee.

As Jacob's wealth increased Laban viewed him with suspicion. He felt that not only was Jacob prospering but that he was doing it at his employer's expense. Laban's sons shared their father's convictions. Greed and jealousy worked in Laban's heart until his attitude toward his nephew became hostile. Jacob sensed the change in Laban and became apprehensive. The patriarch did not yet understand that this crisis was to be used of the Lord to send him back to the land of promise.

Like his grandfather Abraham and his father, Isaac, Jacob experienced the visitation of God in the hour of his need. Jehovah gave him a clear directive to return to Canaan.

31:4-16 *And Jacob sent and called Rachel and Leah to the field unto his flock,*

And said unto them, I see your father's countenance,

that it is not toward me as before; but the God of my father hath been with me.

And ye know that with all my power I have served your father.

And your father hath deceived me, and changed my wages ten times; but God suffered him not to hurt me.

If he said thus, The speckled shall be thy wages; then all the cattle bare speckled: and if he said thus, The ringstraked shall be thy hire; then bare all the cattle ringstraked.

Thus God hath taken away the cattle of your father, and given them to me.

And it came to pass at the time that the cattle conceived, that I lifted up mine eyes, and saw in a dream, and, behold, the rams which leaped upon the cattle were ringstraked, speckled, and grisled.

And the angel of God spake unto me in a dream, saying, Jacob: And I said, Here am I.

And he said, Lift up now thine eyes, and see, all the rams which leap upon the cattle are ringstraked, speckled, and grisled: for I have seen all that Laban doeth unto thee.

I am the God of Bethel, where thou anointedst the pillar, and where thou vowedst a vow unto me: now arise, get thee out from this land, and return unto the land of thy kindred.

And Rachel and Leah answered and said unto him, Is there yet any portion or inheritance for us in our father's house?

Are we not counted of him strangers? for he hath sold us, and hath quite devoured also our money.

For all the riches which God hath taken from our father, that is our's, and our children's: now then, whatsoever God hath said unto thee, do.

Jacob sensed the potential danger in Laban's displeasure and decided to share his concern with Leah and Rachel. The testimony recorded in verse 9 indicated Jacob realized that his new prosperity was largely a matter of divine intervention. The hard years in Laban's employment had heightened Jacob's spiritual understanding. He was beginning to see the futility of the flesh.

It became evident that Jacob's prosperity was not due entirely to his own ingenuity. The crisis with Laban was to be another test of Jacob's faith. He shared with his wives the word of instruction he had received from the Lord. God told Jacob to return to Bethel. Jacob's perspective was changing from the low level of accumulating wealth to the high level of pursuing the covenant blessing God had promised him and his descendants.

Leah and Rachel could see the duplicity of their father. They were also ready to confess that God had been helping Jacob to prosper in spite of his mistreatment by Laban. The concurrence of Leah and Rachel made the departure for Canaan much easier for Jacob. There could be no question but that it was God's time for Jacob to go back to Bethel and renew the covenant.

God reminded Jacob of the vow he made twenty years earlier (Gen. 28:20-22). Jacob had said that if God protected him and prospered him then he would serve the Lord and give him a tenth of all that he acquired. The anointed pillar at Bethel stood as a memorial to that promise. The time had come to fulfill that vow.

The family agreed that they should take their possessions and leave. Both wives also agreed that Jacob should follow the directive given to him by Jehovah. This was an indication that the women were devoted to the Lord as well as Jacob. Though their faith was imperfect they were ready to obey God and follow their husband to the land of promise.

16

A Prince with God

Jacob's caravan set out for the land of promise under a dark cloud of distrust. Rachel and Leah were disappointed in their father. Jacob was weary from the struggle with Laban and wanted release from the servitude that had filled his life with difficulties for twenty years. Jacob knew that leaving Haran and moving to Canaan would not resolve all of his problems. He had no idea what would happen if he were to meet Esau whom he deceived so many years before. The family's suspicion of Laban prompted a secret departure in the hope of avoiding a confrontation.

31:17-24 *Then Jacob rose up, and set his sons and his wives upon camels;*
And he carried away all his cattle, and all his goods which he had gotten, the cattle of his getting, which he had gotten in Padan-aram, for to go to Isaac his father in the land of Canaan.
And Laban went to shear his sheep: and Rachel had stolen the images that were her father's.
And Jacob stole away unawares to Laban the Syrian, in that he told him not that he fled.
So he fled with all that he had; and he rose up, and passed over the river, and set his face toward the mount Gilead.
And it was told Laban on the third day that Jacob was fled.
And he took his brethren with him, and pursued after him seven days' journey; and they overtook him in the mount Gilead.
And God came to Laban the Syrian in a dream by night, and said unto him, Take heed that thou speak not to Jacob either good or bad.

In the excitement of getting underway Jacob did not learn of Rachel's theft of Laban's household idols. Though Laban and his daughters recognized the Creator God, the God of Abraham, they were still infected with the superstitions of paganism. Rachel's purpose in stealing the idols was probably unrelated to worship. Possession of the idols automatically gave her special power in the clan. It enhanced her inheritance. This may have been Rachel's way of getting even with Laban for prostituting her dowry. Whatever the reason Rachel took a risk in stealing the idols.

Laban received word of Jacob's flight and immediately set out to overtake him. The Scripture does not state Laban's intentions but they seem to infer that he pursued Jacob to make him return to Haran or he may even have intended to take some measure of revenge. Jacob was to learn again that his own cleverness could not save him. The danger was averted only because of God's intervention. God spoke to Laban in a dream and warned him not to do harm to Jacob. Laban was with all his faults a God-fearing man and he heeded the divine warning.

Laban Finds Jacob

31:25-35 *Then Laban overtook Jacob. Now Jacob had pitched his tent in the mount: and Laban with his brethren pitched in the mount of Gilead.*

And Laban said to Jacob, What hast thou done, that thou hast stolen away unawares to me, and carried away my daughters, as captives taken with the sword?

Wherefore didst thou flee away secretly, and steal away from me; and didst not tell me, that I might have sent thee away with mirth, and with songs, with tabret, and with harp?

And hast not suffered me to kiss my sons and my daughters? thou hast now done foolishly in so doing.

It is in the power of my hand to do you hurt: but the God of your father spake unto me yesternight, saying, Take thou heed that thou speak not to Jacob either good or bad.

And now, though thou wouldest needs be gone, because thou sore longedst after thy father's house, yet wherefore hast thou stolen my gods?

And Jacob answered and said to Laban, Because I was afraid: for I said, Peradventure thou wouldest take by force thy daughters from me.

With whomsoever thou findest thy gods, let him not live: before our brethren discern thou what is thine with me, and take it to thee. For Jacob knew not that Rachel had stolen them.

And Laban went into Jacob's tent, and into Leah's tent, and into the two maidservants' tents; but he found them not. Then went he out of Leah's tent, and entered into Rachel's tent.

Now Rachel had taken the images, and put them in the camel's furniture, and sat upon them. And Laban searched all the tent, but found them not.

And she said to her father, Let it not displease my lord that I cannot rise up before thee; for the custom of women is upon me. And he searched, but found not the images.

By the time Laban reached Jacob's camp in Mount Gilead his anger had subsided. The warning from God made him realize that he could not resist Jacob's return to Canaan. He was forthright with Jacob and told him that only God's word had spared him hurt. Laban's complaint that Jacob's unannounced departure had not allowed for a proper celebration of the event may have been a facade to hide Laban's real feelings about the loss of his two daughters. He was frustrated and hurt by their compliance with Jacob.

The burning issue with Laban was the matter of the household idols. He was angry at this act of crime and perhaps realized the complications the loss of them might bring to him as the family leader. He was never to recover them. The duplicity that characterized his life brought forth its fruit. Rachel deceived her father and carried his treasured idols away with her. The irony is that the instrument of retribution for Laban's duplicity was his own daughter.

Jacob Rebukes Laban

31:36-42 And Jacob was wroth, and chode with Laban: and Jacob answered and said to Laban, What is my trespass? what is my sin, that thou hast so hotly pursued after me?

Whereas thou hast searched all my stuff, what hast thou found of all thy household stuff? set it here before my brethren and thy brethren, that they may judge betwixt us both.

This twenty years have I been with thee; thy ewes and thy she goats have not cast their young, and the rams of thy flock have I not eaten.

That which was torn of beasts I brought not unto thee; I bare the loss of it; of my hand didst thou require it, whether stolen by day, or stolen by night.

Thus I was; in the day the drought consumed me, and the frost by night; and my sleep departed from mine eyes.

Thus have I been twenty years in thy house; I served thee fourteen years for thy two daughters, and six years for thy cattle: and thou hast changed my wages ten times.

Except the God of my father, the God of Abraham, and the fear of Isaac, had been with me, surely thou hadst sent me away now empty. God hath seen mine affliction and the labour of my hands, and rebuked thee yesternight.

When Laban was unable to find the household idols Jacob could hold his peace no longer. Moved with anger at the many injustices he had suffered, Jacob pointed out the hardships he had endured to serve Laban and meet his demands. He boldly confronted his uncle with the many instances of unfair treatment he had suffered at his hands.

Jacob's description of the life of a shepherd in the days of the patriarchs is unequaled in biblical literature. It dispels the false notion that the shepherd's life was relaxed and trouble-free. The analogy of the pastor to a shepherd has often left the false impression that shepherding is easy. Nothing could be further from the truth. The man who considers the high calling of the pastorate does well to read these verses for they are an accurate account of the shepherd's experience. As Jacob suffered to care for the flocks of Laban so the man of God suffers to care for the flock of God.

The testimony Jacob gave to Laban evidences the patriarch's enlarged spiritual understanding. Jacob gave God the glory for his success in Haran. Everything had been against him but God made the difference.

The Covenant of Nonviolence

31:43-55 *And Laban answered and said unto Jacob, These daughters are my daughters, and these children are my children, and these cattle are my cattle, and all that thou seest is mine: and what can I do this day unto these my daughters, or unto their children which they have born?*

Now therefore come thou, let us make a covenant, I and thou; and let it be for a witness between me and thee.

And Jacob took a stone, and set it up for a pillar.

And Jacob said unto his brethren, Gather stones; and they took stones, and made an heap: and they did eat there upon the heap.

And Laban called it Jegar-sahadutha: but Jacob called it Galeed.

And Laban said, This heap is a witness between me and thee this day. Therefore was the name of it called Galeed;

And Mizpah; for he said, The Lord watch between me and thee, when we are absent one from another.

If thou shalt afflict my daughters, or if thou shalt take other wives beside my daughters, no man is with us; see, God is witness betwixt me and thee.

And Laban said to Jacob, Behold this heap, and behold this pillar, which I have cast betwixt me and thee;

This heap be witness, and this pillar be witness that I will not pass over this heap to thee, and that thou shalt not pass over this heap and this pillar unto me, for harm.

The God of Abraham, and the God of Nahor, the God of their father, judge betwixt me. And Jacob sware by

195

the fear of his father Isaac.

Then Jacob offered sacrifice upon the mount, and called his brethren to eat bread: and they did eat bread, and tarried all night in the mount.

And early in the morning Laban rose up, and kissed his sons and his daughters, and blessed them: and Laban departed, and returned unto his place.

The impassioned words of Jacob moved Laban deeply. He felt enough remorse at his wrongdoing to want to terminate his relationship with Jacob on some level of reconciliation. Laban was still superior in strength and could have by sheer force overpowered his nephew, but Laban was ready to recognize the hand of God in Jacob's life. Something of compassion for his own flesh and blood took hold of him, and he proposed to Jacob a covenant to assure they would not face a confrontation in the future. This passage gives a different side of Laban than was previously reflected. Jacob sensed the sincerity of Laban's words and agreed to the covenant.

This scene is not entirely free of tension for the erection of the stone of witness was to establish a boundary between their families. This narrative is sometimes used to illustrate Christian unity but that interpretation hardly fits the context. It was an agreement to recognize their great differences and not to use violence to deal with them.

It is remarkable that Jacob offered the sacrifice on the occasion of this covenant. Ordinarily the senior household member would have administrated in making such an offering. Both Laban and Jacob knew intuitively that Jacob had a special place of spiritual leadership. The communal meal was eaten at the close of the sacrifice to confirm the covenant.

Laban seems to behave as a different man when he takes leave of his daughters and grandchildren the next morning. It is a scene marked with affection and loving concern.

The Presence of Angels

32:1-12 *And Jacob went on his way, and the angels of God met him.*

And when Jacob saw them, he said, This is God's host; and he called the name of that place Mahanaim.

And Jacob sent messengers before him to Esau his brother unto the land of Seir, the country of Edom.

And he commanded them, saying, Thus shall ye speak unto my lord Esau; Thy servant Jacob saith thus, I have sojourned with Laban, and stayed there until now:

And I have oxen, and asses, flocks, and menservants, and womenservants: and I have sent to tell my lord, that I may find grace in thy sight.

And the messengers returned to Jacob, saying, We came to thy brother Esau, and also he cometh to meet thee, and four hundred men with him.

Then Jacob was greatly afraid and distressed: and he divided the people that was with him, and the flocks, and herds, and the camels, into two bands;

And said, If Esau come to the one company, and smite it, then the other company which is left shall escape.

And Jacob said, O God of my father Abraham, and God of my father Isaac, the Lord which saidst unto me, Return unto thy country, and to thy kindred, and I will deal well with thee:

I am not worthy of the least of all the mercies, and of all the truth, which thou hast shewed unto thy servant; for with my staff I passed over this Jordan; and now I am become two bands.

Deliver me, I pray thee, from the hand of my brother, from the hand of Esau: for I fear him, lest he will come and smite me, and the mother with the children.

And thou saidst, I will surely do thee good, and make thy seed as the sand of the sea, which cannot be numbered for multitude.

Jacob and his caravan moved from Mount Gilead to the Jabbok River where the angels of God met him. When Jacob fled to Haran the angels of God ministered to him at Bethel and now upon his return to the promised land the angels once again minister to him. God was teaching Jacob the way of dependence. It was not until Jacob was "on his way" that God sent the angels to help. The place of blessing is always found by those who walk in God's way.

The patriarch called the place of this divine visitation Mahanaim which means two camps. Jacob knew that beside his camp was a strong camp of angels concerned with his welfare.

Jacob soon turned from his preoccupation with the

197

angels to the formidable threat of Esau. The divine visitation had not erased the fear Jacob had of possible retaliation from his brother.

Representatives were dispatched to Edom to give Esau a message. Jacob wanted his brother to know the events of the past twenty years and that he now returned enormously rich in domesticated animals and servants. Jacob wanted to ask Esau's forgiveness for the way he had treated him in the past.

Guilt promotes fear. Jacob felt remorse for his deception of Isaac and the stolen birthright. He had by this time learned that God would have given him the birthright had he been willing to trust Him. The manifestation of angels and Jacob's best reasoning could not deliver him from the anxiety he felt at meeting his offended brother.

Finally, Jacob turns to God in prayer. Stripped of pride, Jacob throws himself upon the mercies of God. This is the first recorded prayer in the Bible. Jacob earnestly sought God's help in his predicament. He identified Jehovah as the God of his grandfather Abraham and of his father Isaac. He reminded the Lord that it was at His instruction that he came back to Canaan. He pressed the promises God had made to him. This prayer more than anything else in Jacob's life reveals the maturity that came as a result of his years of chastening in Haran. His petition was for deliverance from Esau.

32:13-23 *And he lodged there that same night; and took of that which came to his hand a present for Esau his brother;*

Two hundred she goats, and twenty he goats, two hundred ewes and twenty rams,

Thirty milch camels with their colts, forty kine, and ten bulls, twenty she asses, and ten foals.

And he delivered them into the hand of his servants, every drove by themselves; and said unto his servants, Pass over before me, and put a space betwixt drove and drove.

And he commanded the foremost, saying, When Esau my brother meeteth thee, and asketh thee, saying, Whose art thou? and whither goest thou? and whose are these before thee?

Then thou shalt say, They be thy servant Jacob's; it is a present sent unto my lord Esau: and, behold, also he is behind us.

And so commanded he the second, and the third, and all that followed the droves, saying, On this matter shall ye speak unto Esau, when ye find him.

And say ye moreover, Behold, thy servant Jacob is behind us. For he said, I will appease him with the present that goeth before me, and afterward I will see his face; peradventure he will accept of me.

So went the present over before him: and himself lodged that night in the company.

And he rose up that night, and took his two wives, and his two womenservants, and his eleven sons, and passed over the ford Jabbok.

And he took them, and sent them over the brook, and sent over that he had.

The season of prayer Jacob had with God did not remove the anxiety of his heart. Still determined to use his own ingenuity to solve the problem he devised a way to at least retrieve himself, his family, and a part of his possessions if Esau did prove to be hostile toward him. How blind the fleshly mind can be. God had already revealed an attendant camp of angels near him and he recognized them by calling the place "two camps." Not willing to trust God's provision of two camps Jacob created two camps of his own.

He responded to his own natural inclination to bargain and sent an extravagant gift of livestock to Esau. Jacob systematically selected his very best breeding stock with the hope that this generous gift would appease Esau's anger.

As a last precaution, Jacob took his family to a place of safety. He had done all that human wisdom could do to meet the crisis.

No More Jacob

32:24-32 *And Jacob was left alone; and there wrestled a man with him until the breaking of the day.*

And when he saw that he prevailed not against him, he touched the hollow of his thigh; and the hollow of Jacob's thigh was out of joint, as he wrestled with him.

199

And he said, Let me go, for the day breaketh. And he said, I will not let thee go, except thou bless me.

And he said unto him, What is thy name? And he said, Jacob.

And he said, thy name shall be called no more Jacob, but Israel: for as a prince hast thou power with God and with men, and hast prevailed.

And Jacob asked him, and said, Tell me, I pray thee, thy name. And he said, Wherefore is it that thou dost ask after my name? And he blessed him there.

And Jacob called the name of the place Peniel: for I have seen God face to face, and my life is preserved.

And as he passed over Penuel the sun rose upon him, and he halted upon his thigh.

Therefore the children of Israel eat not of the sinew which shrank, which is upon the hollow of the thigh, unto this day: because he touched the hollow of Jacob's thigh in the sinew that shrank.

The "man" who wrestled with Jacob that night is not identified by Scripture. Some think that it was an angel, while others think it may have been a pre-incarnate appearance of Christ himself. This was both a literal wrestling match and a spiritual one. As dawn began to break, the stranger wanted to go, but Jacob held onto him tenaciously. The stranger struck a blow to Jacob's leg and dislocated it at the hip. He must have been in great pain from this, but he was determined not to let the heavenly messenger go until he received a blessing from him. Jacob had been a strong man in body, mind, and will. He had feverishly worked at helping God make him a patriarch in the covenant family. All his years of chastening had not taught him the danger of the self-life. The time had come for Jacob, the supplanter, to die. This was a spiritual death and not a physical one. The angel of the Lord weakened him physically to show the futility of the flesh.

Jacob probably limped the rest of his life. It was a constant reminder that he must not lean on the arm of the flesh. When Jacob was weak and broken the Lord blessed him. The angel changed his name to symbolize the spiritual transformation in Jacob's life. His name was changed to Israel, which meant "prince with God" or "one who prevails or perseveres with God." Jacob called the place Peniel or Penuel, meaning "face of God." He was convinced that he had been in a struggle with God himself, and he was grateful that he had not only survived but that he was a changed man. From now on he was to be a God-dominated man.

It became a tradition among the Israelites to extract the sciatic muscle from animals' hips and not eat it along with the rest of the meat. This reminded them of the glorious encounter their illustrious ancestor had with God that night.

17

Jacob Returns to Canaan

Genesis 33:1—34:31

The return of Jacob to the land of promise was essential to the plan of God. When he left Canaan, God revealed to him at Bethel that he must return to the land (Gen. 28:15). The covenant God made with Abraham, Isaac, and Jacob was related to the land. Since Jacob would take up the covenant family leadership at the death of Isaac, his return to the land was urgent. Isaac was now advanced in years and near death.

It was a wiser and more mature Jacob who moved his caravan to the banks of Jabbok than had left for Haran twenty years before. The testings of his faith had taught him the faithfulness of Jehovah. Jacob was learning the truth that spiritual blessings were superior to material blessings. But God was not through with Jacob. There would be other testings of his faith as he came back home. He had to meet Esau and work out a reconciliation. This was to be Jacob's first test after his encounter with Jehovah at Peniel.

The Reconciliation of Jacob and Esau

33:1-15 *And Jacob lifted up his eyes, and looked, and, behold, Esau came, and with him four hundred men. And he divided the children unto Leah, and unto Rachel, and unto the two handmaids.*

And he put the handmaids and their children foremost, and Leah and her children after, and Rachel and Joseph hindermost.

And he passed over before them, and bowed himself to the ground seven times, until he came near to his brother.

And Esau ran to meet him, and embraced him, and fell on his neck, and kissed him: and they wept.

And he lifted up his eyes, and saw the women and the

children; and said, Who are those with thee? And he said, The children which God hath graciously given thy servant.

Then the handmaidens came near, they and their children, and they bowed themselves.

And Leah also with her children came near, and bowed themselves: and after came Joseph near and Rachel, and they bowed themselves.

And he said, What meanest thou by all this drove which I met? And he said, These are to find grace in the sight of my lord.

And Esau said, I have enough, my brother; keep that thou hast unto thyself.

And Jacob said, Nay, I pray thee, if now I have found grace in thy sight, then receive my present at my hand: for therefore I have seen thy face, as though I had seen the face of God, and thou wast pleased with me.

Take, I pray thee, my blessing that is brought to thee; because God hath dealt graciously with me, and because I have enough. And he urged him, and he took it.

And he said, Let us take our journey, and let us go, and I will go before thee.

And he said unto him, My lord knoweth that the children are tender, and the flocks and herds with young are with me: and if men should overdrive them one day, all the flock will die.

Let my lord, I pray thee, pass over before his servant: and I will lead on softly, according as the cattle that goeth before me and the children be able to endure, until I come unto my lord unto Seir.

And Esau said, Let me now leave with thee some of the folk that are with me. And he said, What needeth it? let me find grace in the sight of my lord.

The anxiety that kept Jacob's heart in a turmoil had been subdued by his meeting with God by the brook side. Though free of anxiety, Jacob was deeply moved emotionally upon meeting his brother after all those unhappy years of separation. Twenty years had changed both men. Each was independently wealthy and wiser. The anger and bitterness of the past had subsided. Jacob showed humility by treating Esau as the elder and more honored person. He bowed before him in the custom of the Oriental. The depth of the bow indicated his great respect for Esau. Esau in turn had mellowed through the years and when he saw Jacob he ran to embrace him. It was a happy reconciliation.

Jacob introduced his family to Esau and again the elder brother was impressed with dignity and respect with which he was treated. For the first time in his adult life Jacob is acting without pretense. The whole scene with Esau is marked with sincerity.

The gift of livestock Jacob presented to Esau had a special significance. Jacob wanted to overtly demonstrate his deep desire for reconciliation with his brother. Esau really did not want Jacob's cattle, but Jacob insisted that Esau accept them. The acceptance of the gift proved that Esau also wanted to be reconciled to Jacob. Esau's gracious acceptance told Jacob that all was forgiven and they could have fellowship again. Jacob gave testimony to God's faithfulness in the years he had been away. He was humbled by the realization that only by the goodness of God had he acquired his possessions and was now back in the land of promise.

The only dark shadow on the meeting with Esau was Jacob's failure to tell Esau that God had sent him back to Bethel. When Esau proposed that Jacob come to Seir and live with him, Jacob said nothing of this divine directive. When Esau and his party started back to Mount Seir, Jacob turned toward Succoth rather than Bethel.

Jacob Moves to Succoth

33:16-20 *So Esau returned that day on his way unto Seir.*

And Jacob journeyed to Succoth, and built him an house, and made booths for his cattle: therefore the name of the place is called Succoth.

And Jacob came to Shalem, a city of Shechem, which is in the land of Canaan, when he came from Padan-aram; and pitched his tent before the city.

And he bought a parcel of a field, where he had spread his tent, at the hand of the children of Hamor,

204

Shechem's father, for an hundred pieces of money.

And he erected there an altar, and called it El-elohe-Israel.

After the meeting with Esau, Jacob moved to the east of the Jordan River and located at Succoth. The Scripture is silent as to why Jacob did not go to Bethel as God had directed him. Whatever the reason for this move, God in His sovereign way used the situation to deal with the patriarch. Jacob seemed to lose sight of his pilgrim calling and settled with a house and cattle stalls. It may have been an inner dissatisfaction that prompted his move from Succoth to Shechem. He was now near Bethel but not in the place where God wanted him.

The move to Shechem indicated something of Jacob's inner struggle. Even his show of piety in the erection of an altar did not fully satisfy his heart. Jacob called the altar El-elohe-Israel which means God is the God of Israel. One hears in this name an echo of his vow to God at Bethel before going to Haran. Jacob was to learn that worship could not take the place of complete obedience to God.

Tragedy Comes to Jacob's Household

34:1-19 *And Dinah the daughter of Leah, which she bare unto Jacob, went out to see the daughters of the land.*

And when Shechem the son of Hamor the Hivite, prince of the country, saw her, he took her, and lay with her, and defiled her.

And his soul clave unto Dinah the daughter of Jacob, and he loved the damsel, and spake kindly unto the damsel.

And Shechem spake unto his father Hamor, saying, Get me this damsel to wife.

And Jacob heard that he had defiled Dinah his daughter: now his sons were with his cattle in the field: and Jacob held his peace until they were come.

And Hamor the father of Shechem went out unto Jacob to commune with him.

And the sons of Jacob came out of the field when they heard it: and the men were grieved, and they were very wroth, because he had wrought folly in Israel in lying with Jacob's daughter; which thing ought not to be done.

And Hamor communed with them, saying, The soul of my son Shechem longeth for your daughter: I pray you give her him to wife.

And make ye marriages with us, and give your daughters unto us, and take our daughters unto you.

And ye shall dwell with us: and the land shall be before you; dwell and trade ye therein, and get you possessions therein.

And Shechem said unto her father and unto her brethren, Let me find grace in your eyes, and what ye shall say unto me I will give.

Ask me never so much dowry and gift, and I will give according as ye shall say unto me: but give me the damsel to wife.

And the sons of Jacob answered Shechem and Hamor his father deceitfully, and said, because he hath defiled Dinah their sister:

And they said unto them, We cannot do this thing, to give our sister to one that is uncircumcised; for that were a reproach unto us:

But in this will we consent unto you: If ye will be as we be, that every male of you be circumcised;

Then will we give our daughters unto you, and we will take your daughters to us, and we will dwell with you, and we will become one people.

But if ye will not hearken unto us, to be circumcised; then will we take our daughter, and we will be gone.

And their words pleased Hamor, and Shechem Hamor's son.

And the young man deferred not to do the thing, because he had delight in Jacob's daughter: and he was more honourable than all the house of his father.

During his stay at Shechem, Jacob suffered one of the greatest heartbreaks of his life. His lovely teen-age daughter, Dinah, was raped by a pagan chieftain's son. Some of Jacob's remorse over this tragedy may have been a regret for having compromised himself and his family by moving to Shechem. Jacob had learned from his fathers that the covenant required a separated walk with God. Abraham's children were only sojourners in a land dominated by immoral spirit worshipers. Every precaution had to be taken to prevent mingling with the ungodly. One must ask why Dinah was seeking her circle of friends among the daughters of Shalem. Some level of compromise had taken over in the family of Jacob.

Hamor, the father of the young man guilty of this assault, came immediately to Jacob to arrange a marriage. His understanding of the affair was from the perspective of a pagan. Shechem loved Dinah, so the immorality of Shechem was incidental from Hamor's view of the matter. A legal marriage would resolve the whole problem. Jacob and his sons saw the situation in a different light. The law of God had been violated. Inherent in the covenant was the principle of separation; a daughter of Jacob could not marry a pagan man.

Jacob's sons like their father before them resorted to deceit. They pretended to accept Hamor's terms for an ongoing policy of marriage agreements between Jacob's family and the Shechemites. The sons of Jacob very cleverly requested that all the males of Shechem be circumcised as ratification of their agreement.

34:20-31 *And Hamor and Shechem his son came unto the gate of their city, and communed with the men of their city, saying,*

These men are peaceable with us; therefore let them dwell in the land, and trade therein; for the land, behold, it is large enough for them; let us take their daughters to us for wives, and let us give them our daughters.

Only herein will the men consent unto us for to dwell with us, to be one people, if every male among us be circumcised, as they are circumcised.

Shall not their cattle and their substance and every beast of their's be our's? only let us consent unto them, and they will dwell with us.

And unto Hamor and unto Shechem his son hearkened all that went out of the gate of his city; and every male was circumcised, all that went out of the gate of his city.

And it came to pass on the third day, when they were

sore, that two of the sons of Jacob, Simeon and Levi, Dinah's brethren, took each man his sword, and came upon the city boldly, and slew all the males.

And they slew Hamor and Shechem his son with the edge of the sword, and took Dinah out of Shechem's house, and went out.

The sons of Jacob came upon the slain, and spoiled the city, because they had defiled their sister.

They took their sheep, and their oxen, and their asses, and that which was in the city, and that which was in the field.

And all their wealth, and all their little ones, and their wives took they captive, and spoiled even all that was in the house.

And Jacob said to Simeon and Levi, Ye have troubled me to make me to stink among the inhabitants of the land, among the Canaanites and the Perizzites: and I being few in number, they shall gather themselves together against me, and slay me; and I shall be destroyed, I and my house.

And they said, Should he deal with our sister as with an harlot?

Hamor returned from Jacob's home to the gate of the city and discussed the agreement for intermarriage with the men of the city. They were willing to accept the agreement even with the requirement for circumcision.

When the men of Shalem were physically incapacitated by the circumcision, Jacob's sons killed all the males, and plundered the whole community. This turn of events grieved Jacob's heart. He would never forget the rash acts of his sons and on his deathbed he meted out retribution on some of them for their part in the massacre of Shalem.

The flesh had its way in this tragedy. The sons of Jacob had forgotten that vengeance is the Lord's. To avenge oneself is to bring spiritual disaster. How much different the record would have been had they committed this matter to the Lord. Their own tempers blinded them to the alternatives other than violence. Jacob's family had suffered a great injustice, but God knew that and would have dealt with the matter had they trusted Him. The lives of the patriarchs are a running commentary on the struggle between the way of the flesh and the way of faith. The irrational vengeance of Jacob's sons on the innocent as well as the guilty cannot be justified.

The whole countryside became alarmed at the atrocity committed by this alien shepherd and his family. Jacob's position as a stranger in the land of promise was threatened. This crisis may have been what was needed to move Jacob to Bethel for a much needed encounter with God.

Reports evidently began to drift in to Jacob that the people in outlying areas were appalled at what his sons had done at Shalem. He was distressed at this, for he was afraid that the pagans might band together and come to attack him and his clan. Since he would be numerically at a disadvantage, he feared annihilation. Then what would happen to the Abrahamic Covenant?

18

Revival in the Covenant Family

Genesis 35:1—36:43

The spiritual journey of Jacob moved through one crisis after another until he returned to Bethel. His reluctance to go there immediately upon returning to Canaan cost him years of difficulty. God was faithful to Jacob and brought him through every trial with a new understanding of what it meant to walk with God. Those who walk the way of faith may falter and at times deviate from it, but God's mercy continues to minister to them. The sovereignty of God overrules the weaknesses and builds into that life the way of victory. Jacob had experienced a great spiritual crisis at Peniel but he was not yet completely mature. The need for revival in the heart of Jacob and his family was evident.

Back to Bethel

35:1-8 *And God said unto Jacob, Arise, go up to Bethel, and dwell there: and make there an altar unto God, that appeared unto thee when thou fleddest from the face of Esau thy brother.*

Then Jacob said unto his household, and to all that were with him, Put away the strange gods that are among you, and be clean, and change your garments:

And let us arise, and go up to Bethel; and I will make there an altar unto God, who answered me in the day of my distress, and was with me in the way which I went.

And they gave unto Jacob all the strange gods which were in their hand, and all their earrings which were in their ears; and Jacob hid them under the oak which was by Shechem.

And they journeyed: and the terror of God was upon the cities that were round about them, and they did not pursue after the sons of Jacob.

So Jacob came to Luz, which is in the land of Canaan,

that is, Bethel, he and all the people that were with him.

And he built there an altar, and called the place El-bethel: because there God appeared unto him, when he fled from the face of his brother.

But Deborah Rebekah's nurse died, and she was buried beneath Bethel under an oak: and the name of it was called Allon-bachuth.

Jacob had been back in Palestine for at least ten years and had not gone to Bethel as God had wanted him to do. The fear that the massacre at Shalem might provoke an attack upon his family prompted Jacob to heed God's summons to Bethel. There was a specific reason for which the Lord called Jacob back to Bethel. Jacob had made a vow to the Lord at that sacred place and God was holding Jacob to it. The Lord's blessing had rested on Jacob the whole twenty years he spent in Haran. Everything Jacob had asked was fulfilled. But Jacob was slow to fulfill his promise to God. There could be no sense of spiritual fulfillment until Jacob obeyed God by paying his vow at Bethel.

Inherent in this account are some of the basic laws of spiritual revival. First, revival does not come from some new spiritual experience but from the renewal of an old experience. Jacob had to go back to the house of God and renew the covenant made with Him there. The blessing at Peniel was not sufficient. The unchanging truth Jacob learned at Bethel had to be reviewed. He had to face up to any deviation from God's word to him there.

The second revival principle evident in Jacob's return to Bethel was cleansing. He requested his household to put away all of their idols. By this time he was aware that Rachel had stolen Laban's household idols. The presence of idols had hindered the covenant family in their walk with God. That Jacob requested them to give up their earrings is significant. In that culture earrings were worn as fetishes to ward off evil spirits. This pagan practice was displeasing to the Lord and had to be stopped before Jacob came to Bethel. The patriarch instructed the family to bathe and change to clean garments. The intent of this ritual was to symbolize the cleansing of the heart. Jacob knew that Bethel was holy ground and only the sanctified heart could go there.

The third revival principle is found in verse 7. Jacob built an altar at Bethel. The altar was a place of worship. The sacrifice placed upon it symbolized the devotion of the heart. True worship is always essential to spiritual renewal.

The sacred meeting with God at Bethel was interrupted by the death of Deborah, the aged maid of Rebekah. Her long service to the family had brought her to a place of respect and love. There is a lesson to be learned from the scriptural record of Deborah's burial. When the people of God are seeking Him with their whole heart the interruptions of daily responsibilities and routines do not necessarily impede their spiritual progress.

Jacob continued his meeting with God after Deborah's funeral without any loss of spiritual momentum.

35:9-15 *And God appeared unto Jacob again, when he came out of Padan-aram, and blessed him.*

And God said unto him, Thy name is Jacob: thy name shall not be called any more Jacob, but Israel shall be thy name: and he called his name Israel.

And God said unto him, I am God Almighty: be fruitful and multiply; a nation and a company of nations shall be of thee, and kings shall come out of thy loins;

And the land which I gave Abraham and Isaac, to thee I will give it, and to thy seed after thee will I give the land.

And God went up from him in the place where he talked with him.

And Jacob set up a pillar in the place where he talked with him, even a pillar of stone: and he poured a drink offering thereon, and he poured oil thereon.

And Jacob called the name of the place where God spake with him, Bethel.

The Lord evidently came down from heaven in some visible form to talk with Jacob. His words brought reassurance to His servant. No new truth was introduced here. The Lord reaffirmed Jacob's new name given to him at Peniel. Israel meant a prince with God. It conveyed the idea of power and authority. Jacob would exercise that spiritual authority in prayer. The name Israel was to become the title of the covenant nation formed from Abraham's seed. It indicated something of the character that special nation would have in the world.

Once again as had been the case with the patriarchs before Jacob, the provisions of the Abrahamic Covenant were reconfirmed to him. The central emphasis of the covenant was the land. Jacob, like his fathers, would not live to see the day when Israel possessed Canaan but he was assured that Jehovah would keep this promise. Like Abraham and Isaac, Jacob would continue to live as a pilgrim of faith.

Verse 11 enlarges upon Jehovah's plan for Israel. Jacob was to confidently believe that Israel would become a glorious nation with mighty kings. To reinforce this promise, God spoke again His name El Shaddai, "Almighty God." The outcome of the covenant was not Jacob's strength or ability but the omnipotence of El Shaddai.

After the theophany Jacob erected a pillar much as he had done thirty years before. On this occasion Jacob was not alone. Before his family he publicly acknowledged this remarkable visitation from heaven and his commitment to walk with the Lord in a covenant relationship.

The Death of Rachel

35:16-20 *And they journeyed from Bethel; and there was but a little way to come to Ephrath: and Rachel travailed, and she had hard labour.*

And it came to pass, when she was in hard labour, that the midwife said unto her, Fear not; thou shalt have this son also.

And it came to pass, as her soul was in departing, (for she died) that she called his name Ben-oni: but his father called him Benjamin.

And Rachel died, and was buried in the way to Ephrath, which is Bethlehem.

And Jacob set a pillar upon her grave: this is the pillar of Rachel's grave unto this day.

Not many days after Jacob's mountaintop experience at Bethel he was to be plunged into great sorrow. Rachel,

213

whom he dearly loved, was with child again and this brought immeasurable happiness to both Rachel and Jacob. The caravan arrived at Ephrath, about six miles south of Jerusalem when Rachel went into labor. She died giving birth to her second son. Something of Jacob's spiritual maturity can be seen in the way he handled this situation of deep grief. Rachel was overcome by grief and named her baby "son of my sorrow." Jacob renamed the child "son of my right hand." He trusted the Lord in this trial and received the needed strength to go through it with victory.

Jacob's Sons

35:21-26 *And Israel journeyed, and spread his tent beyond the tower of Edar. And it came to pass, when Israel dwelt in that land, that Reuben went and lay with Bilhah his father's concubine: and Israel heard it. Now the sons of Jacob were twelve:*

The sons of Leah; Reuben, Jacob's firstborn, and Simeon, and Levi, and Judah, and Issachar, and Zebulun:

The sons of Rachel; Joseph, and Benjamin:

And the sons of Bilhah, Rachel's handmaid; Dan, and Naphtali:

And the sons of Zilpah, Leah's handmaid; Gad, and Asher: these are the sons of Jacob, which were born to him in Padan-aram.

The sorrow of Rachel's death was compounded for Jacob by the discovery that Reuben his eldest son, had committed immorality with Jacob's concubine. The biblical account uses Jacob's new name, Israel, in relating this incident. That he was a prince with God seemed to accentuate the wickedness of Reuben. From this point in the narrative Jacob is treated as Israel, although God often calls him Jacob to remind him of what he was in the flesh.

For the first time the twelve sons of Jacob are listed. From them would come the twelve tribes that make up the whole house of Israel.

The Death of Isaac

35:27-29 *And Jacob came unto Isaac his father unto Mamre, unto the city of Arbah, which is Hebron, where Abraham and Isaac sojourned.*

And the days of Isaac were an hundred and fourscore years.

And Isaac gave up the ghost, and died, and was gathered unto his people, being old and full of days: and his sons Esau and Jacob buried him.

Isaac had thought that he was about to die before Jacob left for Haran but God preserved him to the ripe old age of one hundred and eighty years. He had moved back to Mamre near Hebron in the Judean hill country. The death of Isaac brought Jacob and Esau together again. Peace prevailed between them and the old hurts were forgotten. Esau seems never to have questioned Jacob's right to the covenant birthright at the death of Isaac. Jacob became the leader of the covenant family.

The Generations of Esau

36:1-8 *Now these are the generations of Esau, who is Edom.*

Esau took his wives of the daughters of Canaan; Adah the daughter of Elon the Hittite, and Aholibamah the daughter of Anah the daughter of Zibeon the Hivite;

And Bashemath Ishmael's daughter, sister of Nebajoth.

And Adah bare to Esau Eliphaz; and Bashemath bare Reuel;

And Aholibamah bare Jeush, and Jaalem, and Korah: these are the sons of Esau, which were born unto him in the land of Canaan.

And Esau took his wives, and his sons, and his daughters, and all the persons of his house, and his cattle, and all his beasts, and all his substance, which he had got in the land of Canaan; and went into the country from the face of his brother Jacob.

For their riches were more than that they might dwell

215

together; and the land wherein they were strangers
could not bear them because of their cattle.
Thus dwelt Esau in mount Seir: Esau is Edom.

The writer of Genesis digresses from the story of the
patriarch Jacob to give a brief history of Esau and the
nation formed from his descendants. The Edomites
emerge at several times in the course of Old Testament
history. It is difficult to determine whether Esau had three
wives or four wives. Judith, the daughter of Beeri the
Hittite is not mentioned in chapter 36. It could be that she
died without producing any children. He settled with his
family in Seir. Deuteronomy 2:1-5 gives Esau's descendants the right to the land of Seir. God was faithful to Esau
and every aspect of the blessing he received from Jacob
was fulfilled.

36:9-19 *And these are the generations of Esau the*
father of the Edomites in mount Seir:
These are the names of Esau's sons; Eliphaz the son
of Adah the wife of Esau, Reuel the son of Bashemath
the wife of Esau.
And the sons of Eliphaz were Teman, Omar, Zepho,
and Gatam, and Kenaz.
And Timna was concubine to Eliphaz Esau's son; and
she bare to Eliphaz Amalek: these were the sons of
Adah Esau's wife.
And these are the sons of Reuel; Nahath, and Zerah,
Shammah, and Mizzah: these were the sons of Bashe-
math Esau's wife.
And these were the sons of Aholibamah, the daughter
of Anah the daughter of Zibeon, Esau's wife: and she
bare to Esau Jeush, and Jaalam, and Korah.
These were dukes of the sons of Esau: the sons of
Eliphaz the firstborn son of Esau; duke Teman, duke
Omar, duke Zepho, duke Kenaz.
Duke Korah, duke Gatam, and duke Amalek: these
are the dukes that came of Eliphaz in the land of Edom;
these were the sons of Adah.
And these are the sons of Reuel Esau's son; duke
Nahath, duke Zerah, duke Shammah, duke Mizzah:
these are the dukes that came of Reuel in the land of

Edom; these are the sons of Bashemath Esau's wife.

And these are the sons of Aholibamah Esau's wife: duke Jeush, duke Jaalam, duke Korah: these were the dukes that came of Aholibamah the daughter of Anah, Esau's wife.

These are the sons of Esau, who is Edom, and these are their dukes.

Esau. . .

. . .and Adah, daughter of Elon the Hittite	. . .and Aholibamah, daughter of Anah and granddaughter of Zibeon the Hivite	. . .and Bashemath, daughter of Ishmael and sister of Nebajoth
Eliphaz and unnamed wife	Duke Jeush Duke Jaalem Duke Korah	Reuel and unnamed wife
Duke Teman Duke Omar Duke Zepho Duke Gatam Duke Kenaz		Duke Nahath Duke Zerah Duke Shammah Duke Mizzah
Eliphaz and concubine named Timna		
Duke Amalek		
Duke Korah, son of Adah listed in verse 16		

The fourteen "dukes" of Edom were probably sheiks or chieftains who headed up clans descending from Esau. Korah, the son of Adah, was not listed in verse 11 as a son of Eliphaz, so perhaps he was Adah's son by a husband other than Esau. Do not confuse him with Korah, son of Esau and his wife Aholibamah.

217

36:20-30 *These are the sons of Seir the Horite, who inhabitated the land; Lotan, and Shobal, and Zibeon, and Anah,*

And Dishon, and Ezer, and Dishan: these are the dukes of the Horites, the children of Seir in the land of Edom.

And the children of Lotan were Hori and Hemam; and Lotan's sister was Timna.

And the children of Shobal were these; Alvan, and Manahath, and Ebal, Shepho, and Onam.

And these are the children of Zibeon; both Ajah, and Anah: this was that Anah that found the mules in the wilderness, as he fed the asses of Zibeon his father.

And the children of Anah were these; Dishon, and Aholibamah the daughter of Anah.

And these were the children of Dishon; Hemdan, and Eshban, and Ithran, and Cheran.

The children of Ezer are these; Bilhan, and Zaavan, and Akan.

The children of Dishan are these; Uz, and Aran.

These are the dukes that came of the Horites; duke Lotan, duke Shobal, duke Zibeon, duke Anah.

Duke Dishon, duke Ezer, duke Dishan: these are the dukes that came of Hori, among their dukes in the land of Seir.

Seir the Horite
and unnamed wife
or wives

Duke Lotan	Duke Shobal	Duke Zibeon	Duke Anah	Duke Dishon	Duke Ezer	Duke Dishan
Hori	Alvan	Ajah	Dishon	Hemdan	Bilhan	Uz
Hemam	Mana-hath Ebal Shepho Onam	Anah	Aholi-bamah	Eshban Ithran Cheran	Zaavan Akan	Aran

This passage lists the descendants of the pre-Edomite population of Seir. Scholars believe that the Horites lived in the many caves found in that locality. They were subjugated by Esau's descendants. Esau married into a leading family from this race and apparently the Horites as a result of this union were absorbed by Edom. There were seven dukes of Seir, just half the number given for Esau's descendants.

The Edomite Kings

36:31-39 *And these are the kings that reigned in the land of Edom, before there reigned any king over the children of Israel.*

And Bela the son of Beor reigned in Edom: and the name of his city was Dinhabah.

And Bela died, and Jobab the son of Zerah of Bozrah reigned in his stead.

And Jobab died, and Husham of the land of Temani reigned in his stead.

And Husham died, and Hadad the son of Bedad, who smote Midian in the field of Moab, reigned in his stead: and the name of his city was Avith.

And Hadad died, and Samlah of Masrekah reigned in his stead.

And Samlah died, and Saul of Rehoboth by the river reigned in his stead.

And Saul died, and Baal-hanan the son of Achbor reigned in his stead.

And Baal-hanan the son of Achbor died, and Hadar reigned in his stead: and the name of his city was Pau; and his wife's name was Mehetabel, the daughter of Matred, the daughter of Mezahab.

King	Father	City or Land	Comment
1. Bela	Beor	Dinhabah	
2. Jobab	Zerah	Bozrah	
3. Husham	?	Temani	
4. Hadad	Bedad	Avith	Smote Midian in the field of Moab
5. Samlah	?	Masrekah	
6. Saul	?	Rehoboth by the river	(The river was the Euphrates.)
7. Baal-hanan	Achbor	?	

219

8. Hadar	?	Pau	Wife was Mehetebal, daughter of Matred and granddaughter of Mezahab

Edom as a nation introduced the monarchy long before Israel called for a king. It may have been the kings of Edom along with other kings in the countries surrounding Canaan that prompted the Israelites to insist that Samuel give them a king, thus rejecting the theocracy (rule of God), 1 Samuel 8:19-20. It is interesting that the first king anointed in Israel was named Saul, similar to the early Edomite king named Saul (or Shaul). None of the kings of Edom were descendants of their predecessors. The throne apparently was not inherited but came by election or public acclamation.

God permitted the nation of Edom to reach the culmination of its political and military power long before Israel became a kingdom. Edom was not a threat to the security of the nation of Israel. Judgment came upon Edom for its blatant disregard for God's covenant people (Obad. 1—21). The spirit of Esau lived on in the nation he generated.

36:40-43 *And these are the names of the dukes that came of Esau, according to their families, after their places, by their names; duke Timnah, duke Alvah, duke Jetheth,*
Duke Aholibamah, duke Elah, duke Pinon,
Duke Kenaz, duke Teman, duke Mibzar,
Duke Magdiel, duke Iram: these be the dukes of Edom, according to their habitations in the land of their possessions: he is Esau the father of the Edomites.

These eleven men were probably sub-chiefs in Edom who came to places of leadership. The genealogy of Esau demonstrates God's faithfulness in making Esau a nation. The nation of Edom would not enjoy covenant blessing. Esau's poor choice not only changed his life, it left an imprint on the lives of generations after him. The Edomites, like Esau, tended to go the way of the flesh and were in tension with those who walked in the way of the Lord.

19

The Sons of Jacob

Genesis 37:1—38:30

At this point in the history of the covenant family Joseph becomes the central figure. Jacob is mentioned on occasion throughout the remainder of the Book of Genesis until the account of his death in chapter 50, but the patriarch gives place to his illustrious son who was destined to save Israel and his family from the great famine. The life of Joseph is a lesson in the sovereignty of God and the kind of patient faith that trusts divine sovereignty.

37:1-11 *And Jacob dwelt in the land wherein his father was a stranger, in the land of Canaan.*

These are the generations of Jacob. Joseph, being seventeen years old, was feeding the flock with his brethren; and the lad was with the sons of Bilhah, and with the sons of Zilpah, his father's wives: and Joseph brought unto his father their evil report.

Now Israel loved Joseph more than all his children, because he was the son of his old age: and he made him a coat of many colours.

And when his brethren saw that their father loved him more than all his brethren, they hated him, and could not speak peaceably unto him.

And Joseph dreamed a dream, and he told it his brethren: and they hated him yet the more.

And he said unto them, Hear, I pray you, this dream which I have dreamed:

For, behold, we were binding sheaves in the field, and, lo, my sheaf arose, and also stood upright; and, behold, your sheaves stood round about, and made obeisance to my sheaf.

And his brethren said to him, Shalt thou indeed reign over us? or shalt thou indeed have dominion over us? And they hated him yet the more for his dreams, and for his words.

And he dreamed yet another dream, and told it his brethren, and said, Behold, I have dreamed a dream more; and, behold, the sun and the moon and the eleven stars made obeisance to me.

And he told it to his father, and to his brethren: and his father rebuked him, and said unto him, What is this dream that thou hast dreamed? Shall I and thy mother and thy brethren indeed come to bow down ourselves to thee to the earth?

And his brethren envied him; but his father observed the saying.

Verse 2 marks the beginning of a new division of the Book of Genesis with the expression "the generations of Jacob." The unusual thing about this record is the exaltation of the next to the youngest son to a place of prominence. By all that was traditional in that culture the oldest son should have such a preeminent position. There is both a natural and a supernatural reason for this departure from custom. Joseph was the son of Rachel, Jacob's primary wife and it would not be unusual for such a son to be treated with special deference over other older sons born of a secondary wife or a slave concubine. Joseph was seventeen years old and had been sent to learn shepherding from his older brothers. Most scholars agree that the word translated lad infers that he was a helper. Joseph's candid reports to his father as to the behavior of his older brothers was very much resented by them. That resentment was to be deepened by Joseph's prophetic dream of his future place of leadership over the sons of Israel.

It was not uncommon in Old Testament times for God to speak directly to His servants by dreams. That which gave the dream validity was its fulfillment. Joseph's brothers had no spiritual sensitivity and interpreted his dream as one more evidence of his arrogance. They now hated him all the more.

Even Jacob questioned the boy's dreams at first but apparently Jacob discerned something of God in the matter. He had learned by many hard experiences that God works in the circumstances of His people to carry out His own will. While he did not understand the implications of Joseph's dreams, he took note of the testimony of Joseph and believed that God was at work in the life of his son. The other sons of Jacob are classic examples of the carnal mind. They thought only in terms of their own prejudices and bitter feelings.

The poor relationship between Joseph and his older brothers was to some extent promoted by Jacob's partiality toward Joseph. The special coat he gave him according to some scholars was not only a coat of many colors but a full length coat with sleeves rather than the short coat usually worn by teen-agers in that day. The full length coat was a symbol of maturity and status. Joseph's brothers were not about to give him that kind of recognition. Jacob evidently had not learned from his own unhappy experience as a youth the tragedy that comes from internal family conflicts.

Joseph's Unfortunate Journey

37:12-17 *And his brethren went to feed their father's flock in Shechem.*

And Israel said unto Joseph, Do not thy brethren feed the flock in Shechem? come, and I will send thee unto them. And he said to him, Here am I.

And he said to him, Go, I pray thee, see whether it be well with thy brethren, and well with the flocks; and bring me word again. So he sent him out of the vale of Hebron, and he came to Shechem.

And a certain man found him, and, behold, he was wandering in the field: and the man asked him, saying, What seekest thou?

And he said, I seek my brethren: tell me, I pray thee, where they feed their flocks.

And the man said, They are departed hence; for I heard them say, Let us go to Dothan. And Joseph went after his brethren, and found them in Dothan.

Pasture around Hebron evidently became scarce, so the older sons of Jacob moved the flocks northward to Shechem, about fifty miles from Hebron. After awhile, Jacob became anxious about their welfare and sent Joseph to check on them and report back to him. Neither Joseph nor his father sensed the danger in such a journey.

The country over which Joseph had to travel was sparsely populated. He was unable to find his brothers until a stranger told him of their location.

37:18-36 *And when they saw him afar off, even before he came near unto them, they conspired against him to slay him.*

And they said to one another, Behold, this dreamer cometh.

Come now therefore, and let us slay him, and cast him into some pit, and we will say, Some evil beast hath devoured him: and we shall see what will become of his dreams.

And Reuben heard it, and he delivered him out of their hands; and said, Let us not kill him.

And Reuben said unto them, Shed no blood, but cast him into this pit that is in the wilderness, and lay no hand upon him; that he might rid him out of their hands, to deliver him to his father again.

And it came to pass, when Joseph was come unto his brethren, that they stript Joseph out of his coat, his coat of many colours that was on him;

And they took him, and cast him into a pit: and the pit was empty, there was no water in it.

And they sat down to eat bread: and they lifted up their eyes and looked, and, behold, a company of Ishmeelites came from Gilead with their camels bearing spicery and balm and myrrh, going to carry it down to Egypt.

And Judah said unto his brethren, What profit is it if we slay our brother, and conceal his blood?

Come, and let us sell him to the Ishmeelites, and let not our hand be upon him; for he is our brother and our flesh. And his brethren were content.

Then there passed by Midianites merchantmen; and they drew and lifted up Joseph out of the pit, and sold Joseph to the Ishmeelites for twenty pieces of silver; and they brought Joseph into Egypt.

And Reuben returned unto the pit; and, behold, Joseph was not in the pit; and he rent his clothes.

And he returned unto his brethren, and said, The child is not; and I, whither shall I go?

And they took Joseph's coat, and killed a kid of the goats, and dipped the coat in the blood;

And they sent the coat of many colours, and they brought it to their father; and said, This have we found: know now whether it be thy son's coat or no.

And he knew it, and said, It is my son's coat; an evil beast hath devoured him; Joseph is without doubt rent in pieces.

And Jacob rent his clothes, and put sackcloth upon his loins, and mourned for his son many days.

And all his sons and all his daughters rose up to comfort him; but he refused to be comforted; and he said, For I will go down into the grave unto my son mourning. Thus his father wept for him.

And the Midianites sold him into Egypt unto Potiphar, an officer of Pharaoh's, and captain of the guard.

When the brothers saw Joseph the deep hatred in their hearts came to the surface. It was so intense that they plotted to kill him. Only Reuben had the good judgment to suggest that they not bring the guilt of his blood on themselves but rather put him in a pit in the wilderness. He hoped by their maneuver to later release Joseph and return him to his father. But while Reuben was gone the other brothers sold Joseph to a passing slave trader who took him to Egypt. It is evident that not only Reuben but Judah felt guilty murdering their own brother. He evidently saw selling Joseph into slavery as less criminal than murder. The carnal heart is always ready to justify its wickedness. They had to cover up this diabolical act with a lie. One sin always leads to another in the syndrome of disobedience.

The heartlessness of Jacob's sons is seen as they sit down to eat a meal with the cry of Joseph ringing in their ears. They knew nothing of pity or mercy. Their heartlessness is most evident in the lie they told Jacob. They watched the old man's sorrow and even pretended to be in mourning themselves. All the while they were rejoicing in their hearts that the chief contender for the leadership of Israel had been eliminated.

The Moral Failure of Judah

38:1-26 *And it came to pass at that time that Judah went down from his brethren, and turned in to a certain Adullamite, whose name was Hirah.*

And Judah saw there a daughter of a certain Canaanite, whose name was Shuah; and he took her, and went in unto her.

And she conceived, and bare a son; and he called his name Er.

And she conceived again, and bare a son; and she called his name Onan.

And she yet again conceived, and bare a son; and called his name Shelah; and he was at Chezib, when she bare him.

And Judah took a wife for Er his firstborn, whose name was Tamar.

And Er, Judah's firstborn, was wicked in the sight of the Lord; and the Lord slew him.

And Judah said unto Onan, Go in unto thy brother's wife, and marry her, and raise up seed to thy brother.

And Onan knew that the seed should not be his; and it came to pass, when he went in unto his brother's wife, that he spilled it on the ground, lest that he should give seed to his brother.

And the thing which he did displeased the Lord: wherefore he slew him also.

Then said Judah to Tamar his daughter in law, Remain a widow at thy father's house, till Shelah my son be grown: for he said, Lest peradventure he die also, as his brethren did. And Tamar went and dwelt in her father's house.

And in process of time the daughter of Shuah Judah's wife died; and Judah was comforted, and went up unto his sheepshearers to Timnath, he and his friend Hirah the Adullamite.

And it was told Tamar, saying, Behold thy father in law goeth up to Timnath to shear his sheep.

And she put her widow's garments off from her, and covered her with a vail, and wrapped herself, and sat in an open place, which is by the way to Timnath; for she saw that Shelah was grown, and she was not given unto him to wife.

When Judah saw her, he thought her to be an harlot; because she had covered her face.

And he turned unto her by the way, and said, Go to, I pray thee, let me come in unto thee; (for he knew not that she was his daughter in law.) And she said, What wilt thou give me, that thou mayest come in unto me?

And he said, I will send thee a kid from the flock. And she said, Wilt thou give me a pledge; till thou send it?

And he said, What pledge shall I give thee? And she said, Thy signet, and thy bracelets, and thy staff that is in thine hand. And he gave it to her, and came in unto her, and she conceived by him.

And she arose, and went away, and laid by her vail from her, and put on the garments of her widowhood.

And Judah sent the kid by the hand of his friend the Adullamite, to receive his pledge from the woman's hand: but he found her not.

Then he asked the men of that place, saying, Where is the harlot that was openly by the way side? And they said, There was no harlot in this place.

And he returned to Judah, and said, I cannot find her; and also the men of the place said, that there was no harlot in this place.

And Judah said, Let her take it to her, lest we be shamed: behold, I sent this kid, and thou hast not found her.

And it came to pass about three months after, that it was told Judah, saying, Tamar thy daughter in law hath played the harlot; and also, behold, she is with child by whoredom. And Judah said, Bring her forth, and let her be burnt.

When she was brought forth, she sent to her father in law, saying, By the man, whose these are, am I with child: and she said, Discern, I pray thee, whose are these, the signet, and bracelets, and staff.

And Judah acknowledged them, and said, She hath been more righteous than I; because that I gave her not to Shelah my son. And he knew her again no more.

The record of Judah's lapse and its subsequent results are more than parenthetical. They give a cross section of the trials going on in Jacob's family while Joseph was suffering in Egypt. The influence of the ungodly Canaanites brought heartache to the patriarch. Judah who should have become a leader in the covenant family disqualified himself by a shameful marriage with a pagan woman. The heart of Judah was so turned from God that he separated himself from Jacob's household and made his home with Hirah, a Canaanite. From Judah's unholy marriage came three sons.

Er, Judah's firstborn son was so wicked God put him to death before he had any children. Upon the death of Er, Judah covenanted with Tamar, Er's wife, that when his son Shelah was of marriageable age Tamar could marry him. This was an act of deception because Judah feared that Shelah might also die and so when Shelah became of age Judah did not arrange the marriage.

Tamar's revenge was a clever deception designed to publicly expose Judah. If Tamar, as some scholars believe, posed as a religious prostitute, Judah's sin was compounded. He not only committed adultery but was an idolater as well. The fear, the wickedness, the dishonesty, and the immorality of Judah brought him shame and robbed him of blessing.

Jacob must have grieved over Judah's sin as much as he grieved over the loss of Joseph. The old patriarch had met God at Bethel and been revived in his soul, but the seed of the self-life sown in his early days was producing sorrow in his family.

The Birth of Pharez and Zarah

38:27-30 *And it came to pass in the time of her travail, that, behold, twins were in her womb.*

And it came to pass, when she travailed, that the one put out his hand: and the midwife took and bound upon his hand a scarlet thread, saying, This came out first.

And it came to pass, as he drew back his hand, that, behold, his brother came out: and she said, How hast thou broken forth? this breach be upon thee: therefore his name was called Pharez.

And afterward came out his brother, that had the

scarlet thread upon his hand: and his name was called Zarah.

The struggle between the twin sons born of Judah's incestuous relationship to Tamar was a pattern of the divisions that would come in the family line of Judah. Pharez was father of the line from which David was born and ultimately the Messiah. How rich is the mercy of God and how great is the grace of God that from a family begun in such shame as this passage describes, God was pleased to bring into the world His Son.

20

Joseph in Adversity

Genesis 39:1—40:23

The life of Joseph was a constant demonstration of divine sovereignty at work in the human situation. Events that to the secular mind would have appeared to be a season of bad luck under God's hand shaped the young Joseph for his coming role of leadership. Whatever psychological and spiritual trauma he suffered under the cruel and criminal treatment of his brothers by God's grace Joseph was able to overcome. The difficult years were the making of him. His attitude was positive and his trust in the Lord unfaltering.

The key to Joseph's triumph in adversity is found in verse 2, "and the Lord was with Joseph. . . ." Lord in this instance is Jehovah, the redemptive name of God. This is the God of the covenant. God's name Jehovah speaks of His eternal resources and is always associated with His saving power.

The psalmist summarized the sanctifying process in Joseph's experience when he said, "He sent a man before them, even Joseph, who was sold a servant: Whose feet they hurt with fetters: he was laid in iron" (Ps. 105:17, 18).

Joseph Made Overseer

39:1-6 *And Joseph was brought down to Egypt; and Potiphar, an officer of Pharaoh, captain of the guard, an Egyptian, bought him of the hands of the Ishmeelites, which had brought him down thither.*

And the Lord was with Joseph, and he was a prosperous man; and he was in the house of his master the Egyptian.

And his master saw that the Lord was with him, and that the Lord made all that he did to prosper in his hand.

And Joseph found grace in his sight, and he served him: and he made him overseer over his house, and all that he had he put into his hand.

And it came to pass from the time that he had made him overseer in his house, and over all that he had, that the Lord blessed the Egyptian's house for Joseph's sake; and the blessing of the Lord was upon all that he had in the house, and in the field.

And he left all that he had in Joseph's hand; and he knew not ought he had, save the bread which he did eat. And Joseph was a goodly person, and well favoured.

Potiphar was a royal officer who enjoyed great wealth and influence. He soon realized that this young slave he had purchased from the Ishmeelites had unusual abilities. He, therefore, made Joseph the overseer (or manager) of his entire domestic operation. In this position, Joseph was learning about Egypt and developing his managerial skills not realizing that some day he would be a major ruler in that country.

The Scripture explains Joseph's expertise as an overseer to be the direct gift of God. As the Lord blessed Joseph, he in turn blessed Potiphar's household. His master took notice of this fact and enlarged the sphere of his responsibilities.

Joseph's Temptation

39:7-20 And it came to pass after these things, that his master's wife cast her eyes upon Joseph; and she said, Lie with me.

But he refused, and said unto his master's wife, Behold, my master wotteth not what is with me in the house, and he hath committed all that he hath to my hand;

There is none greater in this house than I; neither hath he kept back any thing from me but thee, because thou art his wife: how then can I do this great wickedness, and sin against God?

And it came to pass, as she spake to Joseph day by day, that he hearkened not unto her, to lie by her, or to be with her.

And it came to pass about this time, that Joseph went into the house to do his business; and there was none of

231

the men of the house there within.

And she caught him by his garment, saying, Lie with me: and he left his garment in her hand, and fled, and got him out.

And it came to pass, when she saw that he had left his garment in her hand, and was fled forth,

That she called unto the men of her house, and spake unto them, saying, See, he hath brought in an Hebrew unto us to mock us; he came in unto me to lie with me, and I cried with a loud voice:

And it came to pass, when he heard that I lifted up my voice and cried, that he left his garment with me, and fled, and got him out.

And she laid up his garment by her, until his lord came home.

And she spake unto him according to these words, saying, The Hebrew servant, which thou hast brought unto us, came in unto me to mock me:

And it came to pass, as I lifted up my voice and cried, that he left his garment with me, and fled out.

And it came to pass, when his master heard the words of his wife, which she spake unto him, saying, After this manner did thy servant to me; that his wrath was kindled.

And Joseph's master took him, and put him into the prison, a place where the king's prisoners were bound: and he was there in the prison.

Times of prosperity and blessing are often followed by seasons of temptation. Joseph was to face an incredible temptation in his new home. The environment of Joseph's servitude made him especially vulnerable. Egypt was a pagan society and lacked the moral and spiritual standards by which Joseph had been instructed in Jacob's household. It was not uncommon for unscrupulous slave owners to take advantage of their servants by exploiting them sexually.

The wicked wife of Potiphar had no understanding of the principles that governed Joseph's conduct. He refused her proposition first of all on ethical grounds. His master was good to him and Joseph would have no part in doing him wrong. When the logic of ethics failed Joseph appealed to his spiritual reason for refusing her proposition. Joseph would not knowingly sin against God. But Potiphar's wife continued to press him. When the crisis came Joseph fled from the house to avoid her temptations. Then all the fury of her spurned heart broke loose and she plotted his downfall. Before the day was out Joseph was a prisoner rather than an overseer. A victim of lies and gross injustice Joseph could do nothing but look to God for his consolation.

Joseph was to learn that the prison was just a step away from the throne. The dark days of his imprisonment would be God's way of putting "iron" in his soul. Adversity under God's hand strengthens character.

Joseph in Prison

39:21-23 *But the Lord was with Joseph, and shewed him mercy, and gave him favour in the sight of the keeper of the prison.*

And the keeper of the prison committed to Joseph's hand all the prisoners that were in the prison; and whatsoever they did there, he was the doer of it.

The keeper of the prison looked not to any thing that was under his hand; because the Lord was with him, and that which he did, the Lord made it to prosper.

Some scholars believe that Potiphar did not believe his wife's testimony regarding Joseph and that he sent Joseph to prison as an example to his other slaves. He may have encouraged the warden, who was a lesser official, to show some favor to Joseph and may have pointed out his managerial skills. Whether that supposition is true we have no way of knowing. But it was true that Joseph found the Lord to be his helper once again as he adjusted to life in the Egyptian prison. Because of the favor of God on Joseph's life he was soon elevated to a place of oversight among the prisoners. The warden of the prison noticed Joseph's many capabilities and his strength of character. Everything Joseph did while in prison was made to prosper by the goodness of God. Because Joseph was trustworthy his lot in the prison was much better than most of his fellow prisoners.

Joseph's Gift

40:1-23   *And it came to pass after these things, that
the butler of the king of Egypt and his baker had
offended their lord the king of Egypt.*

*And Pharaoh was wroth against two of his officers,
against the chief of the butlers, and against the chief of
the bakers.*

*And he put them in ward in the house of the captain of
the guard, into the prison, the place where Joseph was
bound.*

*And the captain of the guard charged Joseph with
them, and he served them: and they continued a season
in ward.*

*And they dreamed a dream both of them, each man
his dream in one night, each man according to the interpretation of his dream, the butler and the baker of the
king of Egypt, which were bound in the prison.*

*And Joseph came in unto them in the morning, and
looked upon them, and, behold, they were sad.*

*And he asked Pharaoh's officers that were with him
in the ward of his lord's house, saying, Wherefore look
ye so sadly to day?*

*And they said unto him, We have dreamed a dream,
and there is no interpreter of it. And Joseph said unto
them, Do not interpretations belong to God? tell me
them, I pray you.*

*And the chief butler told his dream to Joseph, and
said to him, In my dream, behold, a vine was before me;*

*And in the vine were three branches: and it was as
though it budded, and her blossoms shot forth; and the
clusters thereof brought forth ripe grapes:*

*And Pharaoh's cup was in my hand: and I took the
grapes, and pressed them into Pharaoh's cup, and I
gave the cup into Pharaoh's hand.*

*And Joseph said unto him, This is the interpretation
of it: The three branches are three days:*

*Yet within three days shall Pharaoh lift up thine
head, and restore thee unto thy place: and thou shalt
deliver Pharaoh's cup into his hand, after the former
manner when thou wast his butler.*

But think on me when it shall be well with thee, and

234

shew kindness, I pray thee, unto me, and make mention of me unto Pharaoh, and bring me out of this house:

For indeed I was stolen away out of the land of the Hebrews: and here also have I done nothing that they should put me into the dungeon.

When the chief baker saw that the interpretation was good, he said unto Joseph, I also was in my dream, and, behold, I had three white baskets on my head:

And in the uppermost basket there was of all manner of bakemeats for Pharaoh; and the birds did eat them out of the basket upon my head.

And Joseph answered and said, This is the interpretation thereof: The three baskets are three days:

Yet within three days shall Pharaoh lift up thy head from off thee, and shall hang thee on a tree; and the birds shall eat thy flesh from off thee.

And it came to pass the third day, which was Pharaoh's birthday, that he made a feast unto all his servants: and he lifted up the head of the chief butler and of the chief baker among his servants.

And he restored the chief butler unto his butlership again; and he gave the cup into Pharaoh's hand:

But he hanged the chief baker: as Joseph had interpreted to them.

Yet did not the chief butler remember Joseph, but forgat him.

Among Joseph's fellow prisoners were two men from the king's palace. Both had been banished to prison because the king was angry with them.

One day they came to Joseph to tell him that each of them had had an unusual dream and they shared an account of the dreams with Joseph. Among pagans in Egyptian culture dreams were considered with great seriousness. They associated dreams with divination. Ordinarily sorcerers were called to interpret the dreams. They did not have access to a sorcerer in prison and lamented this fact to Joseph.

Joseph testified to both men that it was God who gave the right interpretation of dreams. The Lord gave him the interpretation of both the butler's and the baker's dreams. The capacity to interpret dreams was a gift God gave

Joseph. Other Old Testament men of God exercised this same power of discernment. Daniel received the meaning of dreams in answer to prayer (Dan. 2:27-30). God did speak to people through dreams in Old Testament times (Num. 12:6). The law was severe with any who used dreams that were not from God (Deut. 13:1-5). When a dream came from God it was for His glory and the events it predicted would come to pass. Joseph interpreted correctly in both instances. He hoped that the butler when restored to favor with Pharaoh would remember him and speak to the king in his behalf. But this was not God's plan for Joseph's release from prison. His gift for interpreting dreams, however, would prove to be the key to his triumph over all the injustices he had suffered at the hand of his brothers and as a slave in Egypt.

God was teaching Joseph the patience he needed. His prison experience may have given him a concern for those in trouble and prepared him for the days ahead when he would be responsible to help the Egyptians and also his own family. Joseph was learning that he must put his trust in God alone.

21

Joseph Vindicated

Genesis 41:1-57

The dreams Joseph had as a teen-ager back in Canaan must have come to his mind as he waited in prison for some favorable change of his circumstances. God was not pleased to give Joseph an advance understanding of his own dream though he had power to interpret the meaning of dreams for others. But the day came when the meaning of Joseph's dream became clear. God vindicated Joseph by exalting him from a slave in prison on false charges to the most powerful ruler in all Egypt next to the Pharaoh himself. Joseph's dreams had not been the foolish thinking of a boy but a prophecy from God that he would some day become a ruler and even his own family would bow before him in respect.

Pharaoh's Dreams

41:1-13 *And it came to pass at the end of two full years, that Pharaoh dreamed: and, behold, he stood by the river.*

And, behold, there came up out of the river seven well favoured kine and fatfleshed; and they fed in a meadow.

And, behold, seven other kine came up after them out of the river, ill favoured and leanfleshed; and stood by the other kine upon the brink of the river.

And the ill favoured and leanfleshed kine did eat up the seven well favoured and fat kine. So Pharaoh awoke.

And he slept and dreamed the second time: and, behold, seven ears of corn came up upon one stalk, rank and good.

And, behold, seven thin ears and blasted with the east wind sprung up after them.

And the seven thin ears devoured the seven rank and full ears. And Pharaoh awoke, and, behold, it was a dream.

And it came to pass in the morning that his spirit was troubled; and he sent and called for all the magicians of Egypt, and all the wise men thereof; and Pharaoh told them his dream; but there was none that could interpret them unto Pharaoh.

Then spake the chief butler unto Pharaoh, saying, I do remember my faults this day:

Pharaoh was wroth with his servants, and put me in ward in the captain of the guard's house, both me and the chief baker:

And we dreamed a dream in one night, I and he; we dreamed each man according to the interpretation of his dream.

And there was there with us a young man, an Hebrew, servant to the captain of the guard; and we told him, and he interpreted to us our dreams; to each man according to his dream he did interpret.

And it came to pass, as he interpreted to us, so it was; me he restored unto mine office, and him he hanged.

The ungrateful butler had forgotten Joseph—God had not. For a third time in Joseph's life a set of two dreams would prove important to his future.

Pharaoh, the powerful ruler of Egypt, had two dreams that puzzled him greatly. Intuitively he saw them as a message for himself and the land of Egypt. The superstitious king feared such a dream to be an omen of evil. The inability of the wise men in his court to interpret the dreams brought him greater consternation.

When God is speaking to a man the wisdom of the world cannot help him understand. Pharaoh needed a man of God to interpret his dreams. Only as the butler observed the king's concern did he remember his friend Joseph in the prison. He advised the king of Joseph's ability to interpret dreams and confessed his negligence both to the king and to Joseph.

Joseph's Testimony

41:14-16 *Then Pharaoh sent and called Joseph, and they brought him hastily out of the dungeon: and he shaved himself, and changed his raiment, and came in unto Pharaoh.*

And Pharaoh said unto Joseph, I have dreamed a dream, and there is none that can interpret it: and I have heard say of thee, that thou canst understand a dream to interpret it.

And Joseph answered Pharaoh, saying, It is not in me: God shall give Pharaoh an answer of peace.

Immediately upon hearing the butler's story Pharaoh called for Joseph to be brought from the prison. The details of his preparation evidenced the unusual privileges he enjoyed as a prisoner. God had blessed Joseph through all the sufferings of his thirteen years as a slave. Joseph shaved himself to comply with Egyptian custom. The Hebrew custom would have been to retain the beard as a symbol of respect. Joseph had learned the wisdom of conforming to cultural practices that do not compromise the law of God.

Pharaoh asked Joseph when he appeared before him if he could understand dreams. As a servant of God, Joseph wanted the king to know that he was not a magician like the wizards of Pharaoh's court. Joseph gave God the glory and told the king that any understanding of the dreams he gave him would come from God.

The second part of Joseph's testimony to Pharaoh related to the king himself. God would give Pharaoh "an answer of peace." Joseph witnessed to the goodness of God and emphasized that the divine understanding of his dreams would be for Pharaoh's welfare.

Too little attention is given to the testimony God's people gave to the pagan world in Old Testament times. At every stage of history the nations were exposed to the word of God. Israel was the Old Testament witness to the world. Joseph brought the testimony of the God of Abraham, Isaac, and Jacob to the most powerful nation on earth in his day.

Joseph's Interpretation of the Dreams

41:17-45 *And Pharaoh said unto Joseph, In my dream, behold, I stood upon the bank of the river:*

239

And, behold, there came up out of the river seven kine, fatfleshed and well favoured; and they fed in a meadow:

And, behold, seven other kine came up after them, poor and very ill favoured and leanfleshed, such as I never saw in all the land of Egypt for badness:

And the lean and ill favoured kine did eat up the first seven fat kine:

And when they had eaten them up, it could not be known that they had eaten them; but they were still ill favoured, as at the beginning. So I awoke.

And I saw in my dream, and, behold, seven ears came up in one stalk, full and good:

And, behold, seven ears, withered, thin, and blasted with the east wind, sprung up after them:

And the thin ears devoured the seven good ears: and I told this unto the magicians; but there was none that could declare it to me.

And Joseph said unto Pharaoh, The dream of Pharaoh is one: God hath shewed Pharaoh what he is about to do.

The seven good kine are seven years; and the seven good ears are seven years: the dream is one.

And the seven thin and ill favoured kine that came up after them are seven years; and the seven empty ears blasted with the east wind shall be seven years of famine.

This is the thing which I have spoken unto Pharaoh: What God is about to do he sheweth unto Pharaoh.

Behold, there come seven years of great plenty throughout all the land of Egypt:

And there shall arise after them seven years of famine; and all the plenty shall be forgotten in the land of Egypt; and the famine shall consume the land;

And the plenty shall not be known in the land by reason of that famine following; for it shall be very grievous.

And for that the dream was doubled unto Pharaoh twice; it is because the thing is established by God, and God will shortly bring it to pass.

Now therefore let Pharaoh look out a man discreet and wise, and set him over the land of Egypt.

Let Pharaoh do this, and let him appoint officers over

*the land, and take up the fifth part of the land of Egypt
in the seven plenteous years.*

*And let them gather all the food of those good years
that come, and lay up corn under the hand of Pharaoh,
and let them keep food in the cities.*

*And that food shall be for store to the land against the
seven years of famine, which shall be in the land of
Egypt; that the land perish not through the famine.*

*And the thing was good in the eyes of Pharaoh, and in
the eyes of all his servants.*

*And Pharaoh said unto his servants, Can we find
such a one as this is, a man in whom the Spirit of God is?*

*And Pharaoh said unto Joseph, Forasmuch as God
hath shewed thee all this, there is none so discreet and
wise as thou art:*

*Thou shalt be over my house, and according unto thy
word shall all my people be ruled: only in the throne will
I be greater than thou.*

*And Pharaoh said unto Joseph, See, I have set thee
over all the land of Egypt.*

*And Pharaoh took off his ring from his hand, and put
it upon Joseph's hand, and arrayed him in vestures of
fine linen, and put a gold chain about his neck;*

*And he made him to ride in the second chariot which
he had; and they cried before him, Bow the knee: and he
made him ruler over all the land of Egypt.*

*And Pharaoh said unto Joseph, I am Pharaoh, and
without thee shall no man lift up his hand or foot in all
the land of Egypt.*

*And Pharaoh called Joseph's name Zaphnath-
paaneah; and he gave him to wife Asenath the daughter
of Poti-pherah priest of On. And Joseph went out over
all the land of Egypt.*

The biblical record does not indicate the spiritual
preparation Joseph made for meeting Pharaoh, but it can
be assured that he committed himself to the Lord in
prayer for the ministry. As soon as Pharaoh finished
reciting the facts of his two dreams Joseph began to interpret them. It must have amazed Pharaoh as he observed
the calm intelligent way in which Joseph proceeded to
give him an understanding of the dreams. There was

nothing of emotional and psychological manipulations so common to the wise men of his court. Joseph explained that the two dreams contained only one message. Egypt was to enjoy seven years of abundant harvest followed by seven years of famine. The advance warning of national disaster was an act of divine mercy so that Egypt could wisely prepare for the coming famine. The prediction was providential for the welfare of the covenant family. The same famine was to strike the land of Canaan.

The Lord advised Pharaoh through Joseph to select an officer to oversee the storage of grain during the good years. All Joseph said pleased the king and his advisors. They concluded that no one in Egypt was better qualified to take charge of this program than Joseph. He was invested with authority second only to the Pharaoh.

To give Joseph credibility with the people of Egypt, Pharaoh changed his name and gave him an Egyptian wife. The level of exposure Joseph had to Egyptian paganism would have been more than most men could survive. God had strengthened Joseph through thirteen years of adversity. His consecration to Jehovah was complete and he lived a godly life, therefore, in the midst of the spiritual darkness of that land.

Some Bible scholars see in Joseph a type of Christ. He was the savior and the sustainer of life as his Egyptian name suggests. His life provides many parallels to Christ. This becomes more evident as the story of his rule in Egypt unfolds.

Joseph the Ruler

41:46-57 *And Joseph was thirty years old when he stood before Pharaoh king of Egypt. And Joseph went out from the presence of Pharaoh, and went throughout all the land of Egypt.*

And in the seven plenteous years the earth brought forth by handfuls.

And he gathered up all the food of the seven years, which were in the land of Egypt, and laid up the food in cities: the food of the field, which was round about every city, laid he up in the same.

And Joseph gathered corn as the sand of the sea, very

much, until he left numbering; for it was without number.

And unto Joseph were born two sons before the years of famine came, which Asenath the daughter of Potipherah priest of On bare unto him.

And Joseph called the name of the firstborn Manasseh: For God, said he, hath made me forget all my toil, and all my father's house.

And the name of the second called he Ephraim: For God hath caused me to be fruitful in the land of my affliction.

And the seven years of plenteousness, that was in the land of Egypt, were ended.

And the seven years of dearth began to come, according as Joseph had said: and the dearth was in all lands; but in all the land of Egypt there was bread.

And when all the land of Egypt was famished, the people cried to Pharaoh for bread: and Pharaoh said unto all the Egyptians, Go unto Joseph; what he saith to you, do.

And the famine was over all the face of the earth: And Joseph opened all the storehouses, and sold unto the Egyptians; and the famine waxed sore in the land of Egypt.

And all countries came into Egypt to Joseph for to buy corn; because that the famine was so sore in all lands.

Pharaoh was not disappointed in Joseph's performance as a manager. His diligence and faithfulness won Joseph not only the trust of government but of the people as well.

Verses 50-57 have sometimes been called "the Song of an Exile." The exalted slave was now surrounded with the comforts of the ruling class and the joys of home life. God was fulfilling His word and the granaries of Egypt were filling up.

During the first seven years of Joseph's administration the Lord gave him two sons. He named the first Manasseh, meaning "forgetting," and the second Ephraim, meaning "fruitful." These names were chosen to symbolize the goodness of God to him. The years of suffering were past and he now enjoyed years of fruitfulness.

Now began a systematic absorption of the wealth of Egyptian people by Joseph on behalf of the king. Joseph did not give the grain away. He made the people pay for it with everything they had. He also sold to people in surrounding lands, but they had to pay dearly, too (Gen. 47:13-36). We will study this in more detail later.

22

Joseph Tests His Brothers

Genesis 42:1—44:34

The sudden rise of this Hebrew slave from prison to prime minister of Egypt entailed more than the work of fate. Joseph came to power because he had a special mission in the plan of God for the preservation of His people, the family of Jacob.

The scene shifts from Egypt to Canaan. The famine was threatening the survival of Jacob and his household. The patriarch's occupation compounded the danger he faced. As he and his sons were shepherds they must find food for their livestock as well as their family. Canaan had no reserves of grain. When news came of grain supplies in Egypt, Jacob dispatched his ten older sons to bring back food for the family. This journey was to have far reaching implications as far as Jacob was concerned.

Joseph's Brothers Come to Egypt

42:1-8 *Now when Jacob saw that there was corn in Egypt, Jacob said unto his sons, Why do ye look one upon another?*

And he said, Behold, I have heard that there is corn in Egypt: get you down thither, and buy for us from thence; that we may live, and not die.

And Joseph's ten brethren went down to buy corn in Egypt.

But Benjamin, Joseph's brother, Jacob sent not with his brethren; for he said, Lest peradventure mischief befall him.

And the sons of Israel came to buy corn among those that came: for the famine was in the land of Canaan.

And Joseph was the governor over the land, and he it was that sold to all the people of the land: and Joseph's brethren came, and bowed down themselves before him with their faces to the earth.

And Joseph saw his brethren, and he knew them, but made himself strange unto them, and spake roughly unto them; and he said unto them, Whence come ye? And they said, From the land of Canaan to buy food.

And Joseph knew his brethren, but they knew not him.

Jacob had become more mature and wiser in the way of faith but there lay ahead of him one more major crisis of faith. The loss of Joseph had not been forgotten. He cherished Benjamin, Joseph's younger brother and protected him against any possible threat. Benjamin was all Jacob had left of his relationship to Rachel. He could not bear the thought of losing Benjamin and for that reason kept him home when the older sons went to Egypt.

When Jacob's sons arrived in Egypt, they negotiated directly with Joseph for a sale of grain from the government storehouses. They showed the proper respect for Joseph and bowed low before him. Joseph recognized them immediately, but they were unable to recognize him because of his Egyptian clothing, and his fluent use of the Egyptian language.

He spoke roughly to his brothers so as not to betray his identity. Jacob's sons expected such treatment since they were shepherds and Egyptians had no regard for shepherds.

Joseph Shows Mercy

42:9-24 *And Joseph remembered the dreams which he dreamed of them, and said unto them, Ye are spies; to see the nakedness of the land ye are come.*

And they said unto him, Nay, my lord, but to buy food are thy servants come.

We are all one man's sons; we are true men, thy servants are no spies.

And he said unto them, Nay, but to see the nakedness of the land ye are come.

And they said, Thy servants are twelve brethren, the sons of one man in the land of Canaan; and, behold, the youngest is this day with our father, and one is not.

And Joseph said unto them, That is it that I spake

unto you, saying, Ye are spies:

Hereby ye shall be proved: By the life of Pharaoh ye shall not go forth hence, except your youngest brother come hither.

Send one of you, and let him fetch your brother, and ye shall be kept in prison, that your words may be proved, whether there be any truth in you: or else by the life of Pharaoh surely ye are spies.

And he put them all together into ward three days.

And Joseph said unto them the third day, This do, and live; for I fear God:

If ye be true men, let one of your brethren be bound in the house of your prison: go ye, carry corn for the famine of your houses:

But bring your youngest brother unto me; so shall your words be verified, and ye shall not die. And they did so.

And they said one to another, We are verily guilty concerning our brother, in that we saw the anguish of his soul, when he besought us, and we would not hear; therefore is this distress come upon us.

And Reuben answered them, saying, Spake I not unto you, saying, Do not sin against the child; and ye would not hear? therefore, behold, also his blood is required.

And they knew not that Joseph understood them; for he spake unto them by an interpreter.

And he turned himself about from them, and wept; and returned to them again, and communed with them, and took from them Simeon, and bound him before their eyes.

The true character of Joseph shows through in his attitude toward his brothers who had wronged him. How he could have gloated over their prostrate forms but his thoughts were on higher things as he recalled his boyhood dream now come true. Joseph had no interest in vengeance. His actions were controlled by love.

The apparent harshness of Joseph was with design. He knew the guilt that must have been condemning their hearts. His strategy was to promote true repentance in his brothers by slowly forcing them to face up to their heinous crime.

In a desperate effort to clear themselves they gave a complete account of Jacob and his entire family. Their deception with regard to Joseph must have convinced him they had not yet truly repented. Joseph used Benjamin to prod them. He insisted that he be brought to Egypt. He then imprisoned all ten of them for three days. Those days must have caused some soul-searching among Jacob's sons. When Joseph released them he gave them a clue to his identity but they were too spiritually dull to apprehend it. Joseph said that he feared God.

It must have been extremely difficult for Joseph to act with propriety under the emotional pressure of that meeting with his brothers. Self-control is a mark of spiritual maturity. Joseph knew that if he were to reach the hearts of his brothers he must carry through the plan to demand Simeon be retained while they take grain to Jacob's household and then return with Benjamin.

Because of Joseph's knowledge of Hebrew, he understood the conversation between his brothers. When Reuben rebuked the others for their rash act of selling Joseph into slavery, Joseph knew that the process of true repentance had started. There can be no repentance without the inward admission of wrong and the outward confession of it. What terror would have filled their souls had they known that the Egyptian knew every word they spoke and was indeed the brother they had wronged.

Joseph is the model of mercy. He turned aside to weep in private and for the sake of his brethren would wait until the appropriate time to reveal his true identity to them. Love would not allow him to crush their wounded souls. It is the qualities of character displayed by Joseph in this scene that cause Bible students to see in him a type of Christ.

The Brothers Journey Home

42:25-38 *Then Joseph commanded to fill their sacks with corn, and to restore every man's money into his sack, and to give them provision for the way: and thus did he unto them.*

And they laded their asses with the corn, and departed thence.

And as one of them opened his sack to give his ass provender in the inn, he espied his money; for, behold, it was in his sack's mouth.

And he said unto his brethren, My money is restored; and, lo, it is even in my sack: and their heart failed them, and they were afraid, saying one to another, What is this that God hath done unto us?

And they came unto Jacob their father unto the land of Canaan, and told him all that befell unto them; saying,

The man, who is the lord of the land, spake roughly to us, and took us for spies of the country.

And we said unto him, We are true men; we are no spies:

We be twelve brethren, sons of our father; one is not, and the youngest is this day with our father in the land of Canaan.

And the man, the lord of the country, said unto us, Hereby shall I know that ye are true men; leave one of your brethren here with me, and take food for the famine of your households, and be gone:

And bring your youngest brother unto me: then shall I know that ye are no spies, but that ye are true men: so will I deliver you your brother, and ye shall traffick in the land.

And it came to pass as they emptied their sacks, that, behold, every man's bundle of money was in his sack: and when both they and their father saw the bundles of money, they were afraid.

And Jacob their father said unto them, Me have ye bereaved of my children: Joseph is not, and Simeon is not, and ye will take Benjamin away: all these things are against me.

And Reuben spake unto his father, saying, Slay my two sons, if I bring him not to thee: deliver him into my hand, and I will bring him to thee again.

And he said, My son shall not go down with you; for his brother is dead, and he is left alone: if mischief befall him by the way in the which ye go, then shall ye bring down my gray hairs with sorrow to the grave.

Joseph shows further mercy to his brothers by giving

them provisions for their journey home. But evidently he detected the need for complete repentance on the part of his brothers and, therefore, placed the money they had given for the grain in their sacks. By this device he hoped to give them anxiety over their past sins. It had the desired effect for Joseph's brothers discerned the hand of God in this turn of events. Conviction for their sins was deepening. They now knew that God was dealing with them.

When the brothers of Joseph reached Canaan they reported their strange experiences in Egypt and with great trepidation told of Simeon's imprisonment and the governor's request that Benjamin be brought on their next trip to Egypt.

Jacob resented the loss of Simeon and refused to entertain the idea of sending Benjamin to Egypt. The abundant supply of grain did little to relieve Jacob's anxiety. The possible loss of Benjamin became an obsession with him. He lost his objectivity in the struggle to keep the control of his circumstances.

Jacob Gives up Benjamin

43:1-15   *And the famine was sore in the land.*

And it came to pass, when they had eaten up the corn which they had brought out of Egypt, their father said unto them, Go again, buy us a little food.

And Judah spake unto him, saying, The man did solemnly protest unto us, saying, Ye shall not see my face, except your brother be with you.

If thou wilt send our brother with us, we will go down and buy thee food:

But if thou wilt not send him, we will not go down: for the man said unto us, Ye shall not see my face, except your brother be with you.

And Israel said, Wherefore dealt ye so ill with me, as to tell the man whether ye had yet a brother?

And they said, The man asked us straitly of our state, and of our kindred, saying, Is your father yet alive? have ye another brother? and we told him according to the tenor of these words: could we certainly know that he would say, Bring your brother down?

And Judah said unto Israel his father, Send the lad with me, and we will arise and go; that we may live, and not die, both we, and thou, and also our little ones.

I will be surety for him; of my hand shalt thou require him: if I bring him not unto thee, and set him before thee, then let me bear the blame for ever:

For except we had lingered, surely now we had returned this second time.

And their father Israel said unto them, If it must be so now, do this; take of the best fruits in the land in your vessels, and carry down the man a present, a little balm, and a little honey, spices, and myrrh, nuts, and almonds:

And take double money in your hand; and the money that was brought again in the mouth of your sacks, carry it again in your hand; peradventure it was an oversight:

Take also your brother, and arise, go again unto the man:

And God Almighty give you mercy before the man, that he may send away your other brother, and Benjamin. If I be bereaved of my children, I am bereaved.

And the men took that present, and they took double money in their hand, and Benjamin; and rose up, and went down to Egypt, and stood before Joseph.

As time passed by the grain supply dwindled and Jacob grew concerned for replenishing it. When he suggested a second trip to Egypt he was reminded of the governor's terms for one further trading. God was dealing with Jacob through this situation. He wanted first place in Jacob's heart and that could not be as long as Jacob gave Benjamin that first place in his affections. Jacob could not be blessed until he gave up Benjamin. The struggle through which the patriarch passed was a spiritual one. At the time Jacob yielded to God on this issue he had no idea of the unspeakable blessing he would enjoy as a result of his submission to God.

Jacob's experience is an illustration of the death to self-interest that must take place in every believer before there can be fullness of blessing.

The Second Encounter with Joseph

43:16-23 *And when Joseph saw Benjamin with them, he said to the ruler of his house, Bring these men home, and slay, and make ready; for these men shall dine with me at noon.*

And the man did as Joseph bade; and the man brought the men into Joseph's house.

And the men were afraid, because they were brought into Joseph's house; and they said, Because of the money that was returned in our sacks at the first time are we brought in; that he may seek occasion against us, and fall upon us, and take us for bondmen, and our asses.

And they came near to the steward of Joseph's house, and they communed with him at the door of the house,

And said, O sir, we came indeed down at the first time to buy food:

And it came to pass, when we came to the inn, that we opened our sacks, and, behold, every man's money was in the mouth of his sack, our money in full weight: and we have brought it again in our hand.

And other money have we brought down in our hands to buy food: we cannot tell who put our money in our sacks.

And he said, Peace be to you, fear not: your God, and the God of your father, hath given you treasure in your sacks: I had your money. And he brought Simeon out unto them.

The guilt ridden brothers found it difficult to understand the tokens of mercy Joseph gave them. Joseph had instructed the steward as to how he should respond if his brothers admitted they had found the money bags in the grain sacks. Joseph wanted his brothers to tell the truth about the money. They had been honest and with this Joesph was pleased for he was testing them. Mercy comes with its healing touch to those who truly repent and are completely truthful with God.

With each unfolding of this remarkable narrative there is more evidence that Joseph is a type of Christ our Savior. The methods of Joseph with his conscienceless brothers are much like the methods of the Holy Spirit in His dealing with a troubled heart.

The Feast in Joseph's House

43:24-34 *And the man brought the men into Joseph's house, and gave them water, and they washed their feet; and he gave their asses provender.*

And they made ready the present against Joseph came at noon: for they heard that they should eat bread there.

And when Joseph came home, they brought him the present which was in their hand into the house, and bowed themselves to him to the earth.

And he asked them of their welfare, and said, Is your father well, the old man of whom ye spake? Is he yet alive?

And they answered, Thy servant our father is in good health, he is yet alive. And they bowed down their heads, and made obeisance.

And he lifted up his eyes, and saw his brother Benjamin, his mother's son, and said, Is this your younger brother, of whom ye spake unto me? And he said, God be gracious unto thee, my son.

And Joseph made haste; for his bowels did yearn upon his brother: and he sought where to weep; and he entered into his chamber, and wept there.

And he washed his face, and went out, and refrained himself, and said, Set on bread.

And they set on for him by himself, and for them by themselves, and for the Egyptians, which did eat with him, by themselves: because the Egyptians might not eat bread with the Hebrews; for that is an abomination unto the Egyptians.

And they sat before him, the firstborn according to his birthright, and the youngest according to his youth: and the men marvelled one at another.

And he took and sent messes unto them from before him: but Benjamin's mess was five times so much as any of their's. And they drank and were merry with him.

For the first time in twenty years the twelve sons of

253

Jacob were seated together. Joseph exercised unusual self-control in that he played the role of the tough governor until he was certain of the change of heart in his brethren. When the brothers gathered for the meal they were amazed that the seating arrangement placed them in order of their age. Joseph again showed mercy and cultivated in the heart of his brothers the realization that God was intervening in their lives. At that time Joseph's brothers knew not if the intervention would be for judgment or for blessing.

As the meal progressed Joseph tested his brethren with regard to their feelings toward Benjamin. In accordance with Egyptian custom, portions of food were taken from the master's table and served to the guest. Benjamin's portion was five times as large as the others. By this Joseph made Benjamin the guest of honor. He wanted to see if the same evil jealousy that sold him into slavery still existed in the hearts of his older brothers.

The Intercession of Judah

44:1-34 *And he commanded the steward of his house, saying, Fill the men's sacks with food, as much as they can carry, and put every man's money in his sack's mouth.*

And put my cup, the silver cup, in the sack's mouth of the youngest, and his corn money. And he did according to the word that Joseph had spoken.

As soon as the morning was light, the men were sent away, they and their asses.

And when they were gone out of the city, and not yet far off, Joseph said unto his steward, Up, follow after the men, and when thou dost overtake them, say unto them, Wherefore have ye rewarded evil for good?

Is not this it in which my lord drinketh, and whereby indeed he divineth? ye have done evil in so doing.

And he overtook them, and he spake unto them these same words.

And they said unto him, Wherefore saith my lord these words? God forbid that thy servants should do according to this thing:

Behold, the money, which we found in our sacks'

mouths, we brought again unto thee out of the land of Canaan: how then should we steal out of thy lord's house silver or gold?

With whomsoever of thy servants it be found, both let him die, and we also will be my lord's bondmen.

And he said, Now also let it be according unto your words: he with whom it is found shall be my servant; and ye shall be blameless.

Then they speedily took down every man his sack to the ground, and opened every man his sack.

And he searched, and began at the eldest, and left at the youngest: and the cup was found in Benjamin's sack.

Then they rent their clothes, and laded every man his ass, and returned to the city.

And Judah and his brethren came to Joseph's house; for he was yet there: and they fell before him on the ground.

And Joseph said unto them, What deed is this that ye have done? wot ye not that such a man as I can certainly divine?

And Judah said, What shall we say unto my lord? what shall we speak? or how shall we clear ourselves? God hath found out the iniquity of thy servants: behold, we are my lord's servants, both we, and he also with whom the cup is found.

And he said, God forbid that I should do so: but the man in whose hand the cup is found, he shall be my servant; and as for you, get you up in peace unto your father.

Then Judah came near unto him, and said, Oh my lord, let thy servant, I pray thee, speak a word in my lord's ears, and let not thine anger burn against thy servant: for thou art even as Pharaoh.

My lord asked his servants, saying, Have ye a father, or a brother?

And we said unto my lord, We have a father, an old man, and a child of his old age, a little one; and his brother is dead, and he alone is left of his mother, and his father loveth him.

And thou saidst unto thy servants, Bring him down unto me, that I may set mine eyes upon him.

And we said unto my lord, The lad cannot leave his father: for if he should leave his father, his father would die.

And thou saidst unto thy servants, Except your younger brother come down with you, ye shall see my face no more.

And it came to pass when we came up unto thy servant my father, we told him the words of my lord.

And our father said, Go again, and buy us a little food.

And we said, We cannot go down: if our youngest brother be with us, then will we go down: for we may not see the man's face, except our youngest brother be with us.

And thy servant my father said unto us, Ye know that my wife bare me two sons:

And the one went out from me, and I said, Surely he is torn in pieces: and I saw him not since:

And if ye take this also from me, and mischief befall him, ye shall bring down my gray hairs with sorrow to the grave.

Now therefore when I come to thy servant my father, and the lad be not with us; seeing that his life is bound up in the lad's life;

It shall come to pass, when he seeth that the lad is not with us, that he will die: and thy servants shall bring down the gray hairs of thy servant our father with sorrow to the grave.

For thy servant became surety for the lad unto my father, saying, If I bring him not unto thee, then I shall bear the blame to my father for ever.

Now therefore, I pray thee, let thy servant abide instead of the lad a bondman to my lord; and let the lad go up with his brethren.

For how shall I go up to my father, and the lad be not with me? lest peradventure I see the evil that shall come on my father.

At the conclusion of the feast in Joseph's home the eleven brothers laden with grain set out for home. They did not know that the most difficult of their encounters with Joseph lay ahead of them. Joseph had planted a silver cup in Benjamin's bag so that he could apprehend them and further test the attitude of his brothers toward Benjamin.

This whole narrative gives insights into the character traits of Jacob's sons. Reuben, though weak in many ways, showed a desire to do right by Joseph. Simeon, who was retained in prison, seems to have been extremely wicked in heart but melts under the dealings of God. In this passage Judah steps into the foreground. He becomes the intercessor in Benjamin's behalf. This is significant in that Messiah was to come from the family of Judah. Judah like the coming Savior was willing to bear Benjamin's guilt and take his place in punishment.

For the first time the virtue of love can be seen in one of Joseph's older brethren. Judah's love for Benjamin and for Jacob, his aged father, touched Joseph. He was satisfied that his brothers were now changed men. The chastenings were yielding the peaceable fruit of righteousness. The season of testing was over.

23

The Covenant Family Moves to Egypt

Genesis 45:1—46:34

The carnal believer has little appreciation for deeper truth. Joseph's older brothers found it difficult to comprehend his explanation of divine intervention. Only those who walk close to God learn the meaning of Romans 8:28. After years of treachery, hatred, and jealousy these men marveled that anything good could come out of Joseph's unfortunate life. It was probably harder for them to believe this than to believe that this Egyptian official was their brother Joseph whom they sold into slavery. Sinners always find it hard to believe the love of God.

Joseph Identifies Himself

45:1-8 *Then Joseph could not refrain himself before all them that stood by him; and he cried, Cause every man to go out from me. And there stood no man with him, while Joseph made himself known unto his brethren.*

And he wept aloud: and the Egyptians and the house of Pharaoh heard.

And Joseph said unto his brethren, I am Joseph; doth my father yet live? And his brethren could not answer him; for they were troubled at his presence.

And Joseph said unto his brethren, Come near to me, I pray you. And they came near. And he said, I am Joseph your brother, whom ye sold into Egypt.

Now therefore be not grieved, nor angry with yourselves, that ye sold me hither: for God did send me before you to preserve life.

For these two years hath the famine been in the land: and yet there are five years, in the which there shall neither be earing, nor harvest.

And God sent me before you to preserve you a

posterity in the earth, and to save your lives by a great deliverance.

So now it was not you that sent me hither, but God: and he hath made me a father to Pharaoh, and lord of all his house, and a ruler throughout all the land of Egypt.

The distance between Joseph and his brothers had been fixed by protocol and by their fear of this Egyptian officer. The fear must have turned into amazement when they were left alone with Joseph and he began to weep. Fear became terror when this supposed Egyptian began speaking to them in Hebrew. Joseph identified himself to his brothers and immediately assured them that he sought no revenge for their mistreatment of him.

He then invited them to come near as he told them of God's plan in overruling the difficult circumstances that had come upon him. This passage is a graphic lesson in the sovereignty of God in the affairs of His people. The difficult can be turned by God to blessing and comfort and such was the case with Joseph. The grace with which Joseph speaks to his brethren is a beautiful type of the mercy of Christ.

Joseph Shows Mercy

45:9-15 *Haste ye, and go up to my father, and say unto him, Thus saith thy son Joseph, God hath made me lord of all Egypt: come down unto me, tarry not:*

And thou shalt dwell in the land of Goshen, and thou shalt be near unto me, thou, and thy children, and thy children's children, and thy flocks, and thy herds, and all that thou hast:

And there will I nourish thee; for yet there are five years of famine; lest thou, and thy household, and all that thou hast, come to poverty.

And, behold, your eyes see, and the eyes of my brother Benjamin, that it is my mouth that speaketh unto you.

And ye shall tell my father of all my glory in Egypt, and of all that ye have seen; and ye shall haste and bring down my father hither.

And he fell upon his brother Benjamin's neck, and

wept; and Benjamin wept upon his neck.

Moreover he kissed all his brethren, and wept upon them: and after that his brethren talked with him.

Joseph's gracious words of forgiveness were immediately followed by an offer to care for all of Jacob's family. He explained the revelation he had received from God as to the duration of the famine and urged his brethren to return and bring the family to Egypt until this calamity subsided.

Joseph was especially concerned about Jacob and instructed his brothers to tell their father of Joseph's glory as prime minister of Egypt. Verses 12 and 13 provide a type of evangelistic witness.

Joseph's triumph over all his trials is an illustration of Christ. The glory of Joseph is a type of the glory of the resurrected and enthroned Christ. Joseph's brothers were to convey the message to Jacob and must overcome the suspicion and unbelief such a message would provoke in the heart of the patriarch. How would they overcome his unbelief? Joseph said that they should tell as eyewitnesses what they had seen of Joseph's position of power and glory. Modern day witnesses do well to follow the same formula when telling an unbelieving world about Christ.

Pharaoh's Invitation

45:16-24 *And the fame thereof was heard in Pharaoh's house, saying, Joseph's brethren are come: and it pleased Pharaoh well, and his servants. And Pharaoh said unto Joseph, Say unto thy brethren, This do ye; lade your beasts, and go, get you unto the land of Canaan;*

And take your father and your households, and come unto me: and I will give you the good of the land of Egypt, and ye shall eat the fat of the land.

Now thou art commanded, this do ye; take you wagons out of the land of Egypt for your little ones, and for your wives, and bring your father, and come.

Also regard not your stuff; for the good of all the land of Egypt is your's.

*And the children of Israel did so: and Joseph gave
them wagons, according to the commandment of
Pharaoh, and gave them provision for the way.*

*To all of them he gave each man changes of raiment;
but to Benjamin he gave three hundred pieces of silver,
and five changes of raiment.*

*And to his father he sent after this manner; ten asses
laden with the good things of Egypt, and ten she asses
laden with corn and bread and meat for his father by the
way.*

*So he sent his brethren away, and they departed: and
he said unto them, See that ye fall not out by the way.*

Pharaoh was pleased that Joseph's brothers had come
to Egypt. He was so grateful to Joseph for the preservation of his kingdom and the lives of his people that
nothing was too good for Joseph and his family. The
Pharaoh directed them to take their beasts laden with
grain back to Canaan and notify Jacob to bring the whole
Hebrew clan down to Egypt. He ordered that Egyptian
wagons, loaded with supplies, accompany them, so that
those who needed rides could come back in comfort. They
were not to be concerned about leaving anything behind,
because the best Egypt had to offer them would be theirs
upon arrival.

Joseph again tested his brothers as they prepared to go
back to Canaan. He gave each of his older brothers a
change of fine raiment, but he gave his full brother,
Benjamin, five changes of raiment and three hundred
pieces of silver besides. He sent his father a present of
twenty asses loaded with Egyptian gifts and plenty of
grain, bread, and other food (not meat as we define it).
Joseph's farewell warning to his brothers, not to argue on
their journey must have cut them deeply. Their guilty
hearts understood the import of Joseph's words. This
exhortation was essential to their repentance. Joseph by
this device reminded them of their weakness.

Israel's New Hope

*45:25-28 And they went up out of Egypt, and came
into the land of Canaan unto Jacob their father,*

And told him, saying, Joseph is yet alive, and he is governor over all the land of Egypt. And Jacob's heart fainted, for he believed them not.

And they told him all the words of Joseph, which he had said unto them: and when he saw the wagons which Joseph had sent to carry him, the spirit of Jacob their father revived:

And Israel said, It is enough; Joseph my son is yet alive: I will go and see him before I die.

When Jacob's sons returned the old patriarch was confronted with one of the greatest spiritual conflicts in his life. He had walked by faith for a long time but the sorrows and disappointments of his life had dulled his faith. The good news from Egypt seemed unbelievable. The struggle almost overwhelmed him. It was not until the sons presented him with the evidence of the wagons from Egypt that Jacob could believe. Faith gave birth to new hope and vitality. He would see Joseph before he died.

Jacob Meets God at Beersheba

46:1-7 *And Israel took his journey with all that he had, and came to Beer-sheba, and offered sacrifices unto the God of his father Isaac.*

And God spake unto Israel in the visions of the night, and said, Jacob, Jacob. And he said, Here am I.

And he said, I am God, the God of thy father: fear not to go down into Egypt; for I will there make of thee a great nation:

And I will go down with thee into Egypt; and I will also surely bring thee up again: and Joseph shall put his hand upon thine eyes.

And Jacob rose up from Beer-sheba: and the sons of Israel carried Jacob their father, and their little ones, and their wives, in the wagons which Pharaoh had sent to carry him.

And they took their cattle, and their goods, which they had gotten in the land of Canaan, and came into Egypt, Jacob, and all his seed with him:

His sons, and his sons' with him, his daughters, and

his sons' daughters, and all his seed brought he with
him into Egypt.

The interlude at Beersheba was an important step in the
aged Jacob's journey of faith to see his long-lost son. The
Lord put His divine approval on the move to Egypt and
gave Jacob prophetic assurance that his seed would
return to Canaan so the covenant might be fulfilled. This
experience may have brought to Jacob's memory the
revelation passed down from Abraham that his seed
would be afflicted for four hundred years in a strange land
(Gen. 15:12-16). This was exactly what was going to
happen to the Hebrews, but it was God's plan to make of
Israel a great nation in Egypt. Jacob was assured that his
remains would be brought back to Canaan and that his
son, Joseph, would perform the last rites at his death. By
this prediction he knew that Israel's return to Canaan
would be after his death.

Leaning on the promises of God, Jacob performed what
he was expected to do. Children, wives, and the infants
rode in the wagons. Servants drove beasts of burden,
flocks of sheep, and herds of goats ahead of them. They
moved from oasis to oasis through the hot and dusty
terrain. The signs of famine and death were all around
them, but they were well-supplied with food. God
protected them against marauders during their entire trip
into Egypt.

A Census of Israel

46:8-27 *And these are the names of the children of
Israel, which came into Egypt, Jacob and his sons:
Reuben, Jacob's firstborn.*

*And the sons of Reuben; Hanoch, and Phallu, and
Hezron, and Carmi.*

*And the sons of Simeon; Jemuel, and Jamin, and
Ohad, and Jachin, and Zohar, and Shaul the son of a
Canaanitish woman.*

And the sons of Levi; Gershon, Kohath, and Merari.

*And the sons of Judah; Er, and Onan, and Shelah,
and Pharez, and Zarah: but Er and Onan died in the
land of Canaan. And the sons of Pharez were Hezron*

and Hamul.

And the sons of Issachar; Tola, and Phuvah, and Job, and Shimron.

And the sons of Zebulun; Sered, and Elon, and Jahleel.

These be the sons of Leah, which she bare unto Jacob in Padan-aram, with his daughter Dinah: all the souls of his sons and his daughters were thirty and three.

And the sons of Gad; Ziphion, and Haggi, Shuni, and Ezbon, Eri, and Arodi, and Areli.

And the sons of Asher; Jimnah, and Ishuah, and Isui, and Beriah, and Serah their sister: and the sons of Beriah; Heber, and Malchiel.

These are the sons of Zilpah, whom Laban gave to Leah his daughter, and these she bare unto Jacob, even sixteen souls.

The sons of Rachel Jacob's wife; Joseph, and Benjamin.

And unto Joseph in the land of Egypt were born Manasseh and Ephraim, which Asenath the daughter of Poti-pherah priest of On bare unto him.

And the sons of Benjamin were Belah, and Becher, and Ashbel, Gera, and Naaman, Ehi, and Rosh, Muppim, and Huppim, and Ard.

These are the sons of Rachel, which were born to Jacob: all the souls were fourteen.

And the sons of Dan; Hushim.

And the sons of Naphtali; Jahzeel, and Guni, and Jezer, and Shillem.

These are the sons of Bilhah, which Laban gave unto Rachel his daughter, and she bare these unto Jacob; all the souls were seven.

All the souls that came with Jacob into Egypt, which came out of his loins, besides Jacob's sons' wives, all the souls were threescore and six;

And the sons of Joseph, which were born him in Egypt, were two souls: all the souls of the house of Jacob, which came into Egypt, were threescore and ten.

Sixty-six descendants of Jacob came with him from Canaan to Egypt. No explanation is given for not counting Dinah. Jacob, himself, plus Joseph, and Joseph's two sons, Manasseh and Ephraim bring the total number of the clan to seventy. Incidentally, Rachel and Leah had died in Canaan (Gen. 35:19; 49:31), and perhaps Zilpah and Bilhah had, too, since they are not mentioned again.

Jacob and. . .

Leah		Zilpah		Rachel		Bilhah	
Reuben	Judah	Gad	Asher	Joseph	Benjamin	Dan	Naphtali
Hanoch	Er	Ziphion	Jimnah	Manasseh	Belah	Hushim	Jahzeel
Phallu	Onan	Haggi	Ishuah	Ephraim	Becher		Guni
Hezron	Shelah	Shuni	Isui		Ashbel		Jezer
Carmi	Zarah	Ezbon	Serah		Gera		Shillem
	Pharez	Eri	Beriah		Naaman		
Simeon		Arodi			Ehi		
	Hezron	Areli	Heber		Rosh		
Jemuel	Hamul		Malchiel		Muppim		
Jamin					Huppim		
Ohad	Issachar				Ard		
Jachin							
Zohar	Tola						
Shaul	Phuvah						
	Job						
Levi	Shimron						
Gershon	Zebulun						
Kohath							
Merari	Sered						
	Elon						
(Dinah)	Jahleel						
33 (+ Dinah)		16		14		7 = 70	

Reunion with Joseph

46:28-30 *And he sent Judah before him unto Joseph, to direct his face unto Goshen; and they came into the land of Goshen.*

And Joseph made ready his chariot, and went up to meet Israel his father, to Goshen, and presented himself unto him; and he fell on his neck, and wept on his neck a good while.

And Israel said unto Joseph, Now let me die, since I have seen thy face, because thou art yet alive.

Jacob received the reward of his journey to Egypt when with his own eyes he saw Joseph. All the grief of twenty-two years was healed in an instant. Above the joy the reunion brought was the realization that God had worked all things out according to His perfect will for the covenant people.

Joseph Instructs His Brethren

46:31-34 *And Joseph said unto his brethren, and unto his father's house, I will go up, and shew Pharaoh, and say unto him, My brethren, and my father's house, which were in the land of Canaan, are come unto me;*

And the men are shepherds, for their trade hath been to feed cattle; and they have brought their flocks, and their herds, and all that they have.

And it shall come to pass, when Pharaoh shall call you, and shall say, What is your occupation?

That ye shall say, Thy servants' trade hath been about cattle from our youth even until now, both we, and also our fathers: that ye may dwell in the land of Goshen; for every shepherd is an abomination unto the Egyptians.

Joseph's position in Egypt made it possible for him to secure permission for his family, now refugees from Canaan, to settle in Goshen. He was well acquainted with the country and knew that the area of Goshen was suited to the needs of Israel's family. It was a good grazing country and their flocks could prosper there when the famine ended. Until that time they would be sustained from Joseph's granaries.

Understanding the nature of the covenant Jacob had with God, Joseph probably thought it best that the clan be isolated from Egyptian culture as much as possible. No one knew better than Joseph the paganism of Egypt. He wanted to protect the covenant people from the spiritual darkness that prevailed in the land.

Joseph said that when he presented them to the king, they would be asked what their occupation was. They were to report that they had been shepherds from their youth onward, and they were to say that they came from ancestors who were shepherds.

24

God's Care for Israel in Egypt

Genesis 47:1-31

Custom demanded that Joseph present the members of his family to the Pharaoh. He took five of his brothers and his father to see the king. While they were in Pharaoh's presence Joseph asked for the land of Goshen as a dwelling place for his people. this request was readily granted and the security of Jacob's family for the immediate future was sure. Goshen, later called the land of Rameses (v. 11) was located in the eastern part of the Nile Delta and was known for its fertile soil. It had access to the Nile River with its supply of fish and the land with abundant pastures for their livestock.

Jacob Blesses the King

47:1-12 *Then Joseph came and told Pharaoh, and said, My father and my brethren, and their flocks, and their herds, and all that they have, are come out of the land of Canaan: and, behold, they are in the land of Goshen.*

And he took some of his brethren, even five men, and presented them unto Pharaoh.

And Pharaoh said unto his brethren, What is your occupation? And they said unto Pharaoh, Thy servants are shepherds, both we, and also our fathers.

They said moreover unto Pharaoh, For to sojourn in the land are we come; for thy servants have no pasture for their flocks; for the famine is sore in the land of Canaan: now therefore, we pray thee, let thy servants dwell in the land of Goshen.

And Pharaoh spake unto Joseph, saying, Thy father and thy brethren are come unto thee:

The land of Egypt is before thee; in the best of the land make thy father and brethren to dwell; in the land of Goshen let them dwell: and if thou knowest any men of activity among them, then make them rulers over my cattle.

And Joseph brought in Jacob his father, and set him before Pharaoh: and Jacob blessed Pharaoh.

And Pharaoh said unto Jacob, How old art thou?

And Jacob said unto Pharaoh, The days of the years of my pilgrimage are an hundred and thirty years: few and evil have the days of the years of my life been, and have not attained unto the days of the years of the life of my fathers in the days of their pilgrimage.

And Jacob blessed Pharaoh, and went out from before Pharaoh.

And Joseph placed his father and his brethren, and gave them a possession in the land of Egypt, in the best of the land, in the land of Rameses, as Pharaoh had commanded.

And Joseph nourished his father, and his brethren, and all his father's household, with bread, according to their families.

The Pharaoh thought so highly of Joseph that he was quick to grant his family permission to live in Goshen. An unusual feature of this account was Pharaoh's request that some skilled husbandmen from among the Israelites be put in charge of his own cattle. On the surface this request seems inconsistent with the Egyptian traditional disregard for shepherds. Why then did this Pharaoh have cattle? The answer has been found in the relatively recent discovery that the Pharaohs ruling at Joseph's time in history were of the Hyksos Dynasty. They had at an earlier date invaded Egypt and taken over the kingdom. They were not typical Egyptians. The Hyksos were a shepherd people themselves. This accounts for their ready acceptance of Jacob and his sons along with their flocks and herds.

One of the highlights of the Old Testament is the scene of aged Jacob before the great Egyptian Pharaoh. The old patriarch had peace with God. He had learned to walk by faith and at this time in his life he was not impressed with the grandeur and wealth of Pharaoh's court. Jacob stood before this mighty earthly ruler as a Prince with God. He sensed spiritually that his power was superior and had the audacity to bless the most powerful ruler on earth with the simple benediction of the people of God.

The Hard Years of the Famine

47:13-22 *And there was no bread in all the land; for the famine was very sore, so that the land of Egypt and all the land of Canaan fainted by reason of the famine.*

And Joseph gathered up all the money that was found in the land of Egypt, and in the land of Canaan, for the corn which they bought: and Joseph brought the money into Pharaoh's house.

And when money failed in the land of Egypt, and in the land of Canaan, all the Egyptians came unto Joseph, and said, Give us bread: for why should we die in thy presence? for the money faileth.

And Joseph said, Give your cattle; and I will give you for your cattle, if money fail.

And they brought their cattle unto Joseph: and Joseph gave them bread in exchange for horses, and for the flocks, and for the cattle of the herds, and for the asses: and he fed them with bread for all their cattle for that year.

When that year was ended, they came unto him the second year, and said unto him, We will not hide it from my lord, how that our money is spent; my lord also hath our herds of cattle; there is not ought left in the sight of my lord, but our bodies, and our lands:

Wherefore shall we die before thine eyes, both we and our land? buy us and our land for bread, and we and our land will be servants unto Pharaoh: and give us seed, that we may live and not die, that the land be not desolate.

And Joseph bought all the land of Egypt for Pharaoh; for the Egyptians sold every man his field, because the famine prevailed over them: so the land became Pharaoh's.

And as for the people, he removed them to cities from one end of the borders of Egypt even to the other end thereof.

Only the land of the priests bought he not; for the priests had a portion assigned them of Pharaoh, and did eat their portion which Pharaoh gave them: wherefore they sold not their lands.

With the passing of each year the effect of the famine produced more and more hardships on the people of Egypt. Their money was soon depleted and they appealed to Joseph for help. The Egyptians then bartered their livestock to Joseph for grain until they were all gone. He then shrewdly devised a system of payment from their land holdings that eventuated in all of the land of Egypt becoming the property of the Pharaoh. When the land was gone the Egyptians had no alternative but to give themselves in servitude to Pharaoh in exchange for food.

Unable to work their fields because of the drought, and unable to tend their livestock because they had sold them to Joseph for grain, the common people had little to do on their farms. Joseph ordered them to move into the settled areas where they could be better controlled and fed with the grain from the royal storehouses. Perhaps he used them to take care of the royal livestock which he had acquired.

The pagan priests of Egypt were not subjected to the same treatment, for they were able to retain their lands. The king made sure that they received enough food to survive. He evidently did not want to offend the religious leaders, for he wanted their blessing, and he found them useful in keeping control of the people. We have no way of knowing how Joseph felt about these priests, but he was married to Asenath, daughter of the priest of On, and thus had a personal interest in their welfare. He also realized that he could not force the Pharaoh to abandon those on whom he had long relied for advice in the royal court.

Joseph's Recovery Program

47:23-26 *Then Joseph said unto the people, Behold, I have bought you this day and your land for Pharaoh: lo, here is seed for you, and ye shall sow the land.*

And it shall come to pass in the increase, that ye shall give the fifth part unto Pharaoh, and four parts shall be your own, for seed of the field, and for your food, and for them of your households, and for food for your little ones.

And they said, Thou hast saved our lives; let us find grace in the sight of my lord, and we will be Pharaoh's servants.

And Joseph made it a law over the land of Egypt unto this day, that Pharaoh should have the fifth part; except the land of the priests only, which became not Pharaoh's.

Joseph while conforming to the absolutism of Egyptian government, nevertheless, had true compassion for the needs of the people. Toward the close of the famine he wisely worked out a recovery program. Each family was given seed and instructed to sow the land. He established a law that 20 percent of the harvest went to Pharaoh. In terms of modern taxation this was a rather modest levy. By Joseph's wise and merciful program the Egyptian people could once again hope for prosperity.

The Blessing of God on Israel

47:27-31   And Israel dwelt in the land of Egypt, in the country of Goshen; and they had possessions therein, and grew, and multiplied exceedingly.

And Jacob lived in the land of Egypt seventeen years: so the whole age of Jacob was an hundred forty and seven years.

And the time drew nigh that Israel must die: and he called his son Joseph, and said unto him, If now I have found grace in thy sight, put, I pray thee, thy hand under my thigh, and deal kindly and truly with me; bury me not, I pray thee, in Egypt:

But I will lie with my fathers, and thou shalt carry me out of Egypt, and bury me in their buryingplace. And he said, I will do as thou hast said.

And he said, Swear unto me. And he sware unto him. And Israel bowed himself upon the bed's head.

This was not the announcement of his death, but it did bring the Genesis account up to the final year of Jacob's life. He had expected to pine away with grief at the age of one hundred and eight years, after his older sons returned from Dothan with the blood-spattered robe of Joseph (Gen. 37:31-35). He had expected to die after going down to be reunited with Joseph in Egypt at the age of one hundred and thirty years (Gen. 45:28). The Lord gave him seventeen good years in Goshen. He had his whole family around him. He had all the material things he needed. He was able to see the rapid multiplication of his descendants and envision them becoming a great nation, just as God had promised (Gen. 46:3).

Jacob appreciated the blessings he had enjoyed in Egypt but he did not want to be buried there. This was not just an old man's dying wish but a desire that had deep covenant implications. Jacob wanted to be buried in the land of Canaan as a solemn reminder to his descendants of God's promise to them. Since Joseph was the most powerful leader among his sons and had the political connections to assure Jacob that his will would be carried out, Jacob asked an oath of Joseph that he would bury him among his fathers.

There are different interpretations of this statement. Some say that Jacob bowed upon his bed and others say that he bowed "upon the top of his staff" (Heb. 11:21). The problem is that the Hebrew words for "bed" and "staff" use the same consonants. Different systems for vowel markings account for the difference in interpretation. The details of the action are not so important as the purpose of Jacob's action. He was bowing to worship in gratitude for God's goodness to him. He was comforted by the confidence that Joseph would carry out the oath to bury his father in Canaan.

25

The Close of the Patriarchal Age

Genesis 48:1—50:26

The death of Jacob brought to a close a long epoch of redemptive history. Abraham, Isaac, and Jacob all heard God's call to live as pilgrims awaiting the fulfillment of God's promise to Abraham. God had declared that from the loins of the patriarchs would come a great nation. The side trip of the covenant family into Egypt proved a part of God's overall plan to accomplish His purpose. As aliens in Egypt they grew in number in anticipation of the creation of the covenant nation.

Joseph's Last Visit with Jacob

48:1-7   *And it came to pass after these things, that one told Joseph, Behold, thy father is sick: and he took with him his two sons, Manasseh and Ephraim.*

And one told Jacob, and said, Behold, thy son Joseph cometh unto thee: and Israel strengthened himself, and sat upon the bed.

And Jacob said unto Joseph, God Almighty appeared unto me at Luz in the land of Canaan, and blessed me,

And said unto me, Behold, I will make thee fruitful, and multiply thee, and I will make of thee a multitude of people; and will give this land to thy seed after thee for an everlasting possession.

And now thy two sons, Ephraim and Manasseh, which were born unto thee in the land of Egypt before I came unto thee into Egypt, are mine; as Reuben and Simeon, they shall be mine.

And thy issue, which thou begettest after them, shall be thine, and shall be called after the name of their brethren in their inheritance.

And as for me, when I came from Padan, Rachel died by me in the land of Canaan in the way, when yet there was but a little way to come unto Ephrath: and I buried her there in the way of Ephrath; the same is Beth-lehem.

Sometime after Joseph promised to take Jacob's body back to Canaan for burial after he died, the old patriarch became ill and a message was sent to Joseph. Joseph's sons, who were probably in their twenties, came with him to visit Jacob.

When Joseph and his sons arrived Jacob readied himself to receive them. This was to be an important meeting for everyone concerned. Jacob was not only the beloved father and grandfather but he was the prophet and spiritual leader of the covenant family. The words Jacob was about to speak would effect many succeeding generations of his descendants.

Jacob began with a review of his personal history. He recalled the glorious experience he had at Luz (Bethel) and the vision of the staircase leading up to heaven and God at the top of it. He carefully restated that the covenant which had originally been given to his grandfather Abraham, and then to his father Isaac, had been given to him, as well (Gen. 12:2-3, 7; 26:1-5; 28:13-15).

Jacob must have had new hope in the promise as he saw the Hebrews (Israelites) multiplying in Goshen. But Jacob understood that they could not become a nation in Egypt. They must return to Canaan. His faith was strong, and he believed what God had promised him at Bethel the first time (Gen. 28:13-15), at Bethel the second time (Gen. 35:11-12), and at Beersheba just before coming to Egypt (Gen. 46:3-4). Jacob would not live to see this covenant fulfilled, but his descendants would. For that reason Jacob wanted Joseph's sons to be a part of this wonderful spiritual inheritance. As a prophet he declared their place in the nation.

The Blessing on Ephraim and Manasseh

48:8-22 *And Israel beheld Joseph's sons, and said, Who are these?*

And Joseph said unto his father, They are my sons, whom God hath given me in this place. And he said, Bring them, I pray thee, unto me, and I will bless them.

Now the eyes of Israel were dim for age, so that he

could not see. And he brought them near unto him; and he kissed them, and embraced them.

And Israel said unto Joseph, I had not thought to see thy face: and, lo, God hath shewed me also thy seed.

And Joseph brought them out from between his knees, and he bowed himself with his face to the earth.

And Joseph took them both, Ephraim in his right hand toward Israel's left hand, and Manasseh in his left hand toward Israel's right hand, and brought them near unto him.

And Israel stretched out his right hand, and laid it upon Ephraim's head, who was the younger, and his left hand upon Manasseh's head, guiding his hands wittingly; for Manasseh was the firstborn.

And he blessed Joseph, and said, God, before whom my fathers Abraham and Isaac did walk, the God which fed me all my life long unto this day,

The Angel which redeemed me from all evil, bless the lads; and let my name be named on them, and the name of my fathers Abraham and Isaac; and let them grow into a multitude in the midst of the earth.

And when Joseph saw that his father laid his right hand upon the head of Ephraim, it displeased him: and he held up his father's hand, to remove it from Ephraim's head unto Manasseh's head.

And Joseph said unto his father, Not so, my father: for this is the firstborn; put thy right hand upon his head.

And his father refused, and said, I know it, my son, I know it: he also shall become a people, and he also shall be great: but truly his younger brother shall be greater than he, and his seed shall become a multitude of nations.

And he blessed them that day, saying, In thee shall Israel bless, saying, God make thee as Ephraim and as Manasseh: and he set Ephraim before Manasseh.

And Israel said unto Joseph, Behold, I die: but God shall be with you, and bring you again unto the land of your fathers.

Moreover I have given to thee one portion above thy brethren, which I took out of the hand of the Amorite with my sword and with my bow.

Jacob evidently could make out light and shadow, but he was too blinded by age to distinguish more than that. After Joseph assured him that they were his two sons, Jacob asked that they be brought close to him for his final blessing.

Jacob remembered the sad years when he thought Joseph to be dead and rejoiced that God had been so good as to not only allow him to see Joseph again but his children as well.

Joseph, the mighty governor of Egypt, prostrated himself before his aged father because he knew who the real Source of his blessing was. Jehovah in heaven was a King above all kings. Jehovah blessed Jacob and gave him the covenant. Joseph wanted his sons to have the blessing of that covenant more than any of the riches of Egypt.

Joseph was very careful to see that his father put his hands upon the right sons as the time for conferring the blessing came. However, Jacob deliberately switched his hands so that his right hand rested on the head of Ephraim, the younger brother, and his left hand rested on the head of Manasseh, the older brother.

Jacob blessed Joseph by blessing his two sons. He called on the Lord, of course, to do the blessing. Jacob described the Lord in three ways—the God of his fathers Abraham and Isaac, the God who fed him all of his life, and the "Angel" who redeemed him from all harm. The angel of the Lord is generally considered to be a reference to Jehovah himself. Jacob wanted Ephraim and Manasseh to be a credit to his name and to the names of Abraham and Isaac. He wanted them to have many descendants on the earth.

Such blessings by the ancient patriarchs had a prophetic element to them. They were apparently irrevocable once they were pronounced. They were taken very seriously by those involved.

None of Joseph's political power mattered to Jacob on this occasion. God had spoken to the old patriarch and had predicted who would be greatest among Joseph's sons. Jacob predicted that in years to come the Israelites would develop a saying when they wished others well. They would say, "May God make you as blessed as the tribes of Ephraim and Manasseh!" Thus it was that Jacob

276

set Ephraim ahead of Manasseh, although he spoke a blessing on both of them.

Jacob seemed to have a premonition of imminent death and wanted everything set in order. After blessing the sons, he addresses Joseph. Jacob referred to his own imminent death. He had a certainty that it was coming. That is something many people near death seem to get. Perhaps the Lord gives it to them, so that they can set things in order before they pass away from this life.

In the second part of this verse, Jacob referred to God's blessing upon Joseph while he lived, but he also looked beyond Joseph's death to the time that his body would be returned to Canaan. We know from other Scripture references what happened to Joseph. He died at the age of one hundred and ten. He was embalmed and put into a coffin in Egypt. His bones were taken by Moses when the Israelites left Egypt. The Israelites buried those bones at Shechem in the land which Jacob had bought from the sons of Hamor (Gen. 50:26; Exod. 13:19; Josh. 24:32). Keep this in mind as we consider the last verse.

This was obviously a reference to the property bought by Jacob from the children of Hamor, including the man named Shechem who raped Jacob's daughter Dinah (Gen. 33:18—34:2). We recall that the sons of Jacob persuaded Hamor and Shechem to have the males of Shalem circumcised, and then Simeon and Levi slaughtered them on the third day afterward, enslaved the women and children, and looted the houses and fields (Gen. 34:3-29). Not long after that, the Hebrews left that area for Bethel, and evidently the pagan Amorites in Canaan took over Jacob's property at Shechem. This later was part of the inheritance given to the descendants of Joseph when Canaan was conquered and divided among the various tribes of Israel (Josh. 16:1-4; 17:7).

Jacob's Prophecy

49:1-2 *And Jacob called unto his sons, and said, Gather yourselves together, that I may tell you that which shall befall you in the last days.*

Gather yourselves together, and hear, ye sons of Jacob; and hearken unto Israel your father.

After Jacob had pronounced special blessings on his two grandsons, Ephraim and Manasseh, he called all his sons to his bedside to give them his dying blessings.

There are slight differences between the listing of Jacob's descendants in this chapter and the lists in chapters 29:32—30:24. This arrangement observes the order of Jacob's blessings on his sons.

Order of Birth			Order of Blessing		
1. Reuben			1. Reuben		
2. Simeon			2. Simeon		
3. Levi	Leah		3. Levi		
4. Judah			4. Judah	Leah	
5. Dan			5. Zebulun		
6. Naphtali	Bilhah		6. Issachar		
7. Gad			7. Dan		
8. Asher	Zilpah		8. Gad		
9. Issachar			9. Asher	Concubines	
10. Zebulun	Leah		10. Naphtali		
11. Joseph			11. Joseph		
12. Benjamin	Rachel		12. Benjamin	Rachel	

49:3-4 *Reuben, thou art my firstborn, my might, and the beginning of my strength, the excellency of dignity, and the excellency of power:*

Unstable as water, thou shalt not excel; because thou wentest up to thy father's bed; then defiledst thou it: he went up to my couch.

Jacob begins the prophecy with a lamentation for the spiritual loss Reuben suffered as a result of his indiscretion. As the firstborn son, he could have succeeded his father and had the privileges of the birthright blessing (a double portion), but this went to Joseph's sons (1 Chron. 5:1). By committing sexual sin with Bilhah, his father's concubine (secondary wife), Reuben forfeited this blessing (Gen. 35:22). Jacob's words give insight into the weaknesses of Reuben's character. He was both unstable and lawless by nature.

49:5-7 *Simeon and Levi are brethren; instruments of cruelty are in their habitations.*

O my soul, come not thou into their secret; unto their

278

*asembly, mine honour, be not thou united: for in their
anger they slew a man, and in their selfwill they digged
down a wall.*

*Cursed be their anger, for it was fierce; and their
wrath, for it was cruel: I will divide them in Jacob, and
scatter them in Israel.*

Jacob recalling the murder of the Shechemites led by
Simeon and Levi predicted that their descendants would
not enjoy an inheritance in Canaan and that they would
be scattered among the other tribes. This prophecy came
true in the subsequent history of the nation Israel.

49:8-12 *Judah, thou art he whom thy brethren shall
praise: thy hand shall be in the neck of thine enemies;
thy father's children shall bow down before thee.*

*Judah is a lion's whelp: from the prey, my son, thou
art gone up: he stooped down, he couched as a lion, and
as an old lion; who shall rouse him up?*

*The sceptre shall not depart from Judah, nor a law-
giver from between his feet, until Shiloh come; and unto
him shall the gathering of the people be.*

*Binding his foal unto the vine, and his ass's colt unto
the choice vine; he washed his garments in wine, and
his clothes in the blood of grapes:*

*His eyes shall be red with wine, and his teeth white
with milk.*

The prophecy pronounced on Judah is exceeded only by
Jacob's prophecy given to Joseph. From the line of Judah
would come the Messiah. Judah was to be the kingly line
in the nation. The triumph described in verses 11 and 12
forecast the glorious coming kingdom when Israel shall
enjoy the literal reign of Messiah.

49:13-15 *Zebulun shall dwell at the haven of the sea;
and he shall be for an haven of ships; and his border
shall be unto Zidon.*

*Issachar is a strong ass couching down between two
burdens:*

And he saw that rest was good, and the land that it

was pleasant; and bowed his shoulder to bear, and became a servant unto tribute.

The descendants of Zebulun would live between the Sea of Galilee and the Mediterranean Sea and were to be a sea-going people.

The descendants of Issachar were to be strong, patient people with a love for their inheritance in the land. They were later subjugated to servitude as Jacob's prophecy had indicated.

49:16-18 *Dan shall judge his people, as one of the tribes of Israel.*

Dan shall be a serpent by the way, an adder in the path, that biteth the horse heels, so that his rider shall fall backward.

I have waited for thy salvation, O Lord.

Dan, like Reuben, would yield to the weaknesses of his character and fall short of his potential place of leadership.

49:19 *Gad, a troop shall overcome him: but he shall overcome at the last.*

This was a play on words. Gad meant "troop," and Jacob said that a troop (of enemies) would attack and conquer the descendants of this son. Gad would fight back and eventually conquer. They settled east of the Jordan River and helped protect the nation against marauders out of the Arabian Desert to the east of them.

49:20 *Out of Asher his bread shall be fat, and he shall yield royal dainties.*

The descendants of Asher settled along the Mediterranean coast from Mount Carmel to Tyre. Their fertile land produced good food fit for kings, such as those ruling over Tyre and Sidon.

49:21 *Naphtali is a hind let loose: he giveth goodly words.*

This verse is translated in several ways. The descendants of Naphtali are likened to wild deer having spreading antlers or lovely fawns, or they are likened to trees with spreading or lovely branches. Some think that the last part of the verse should be taken literally, meaning that great speakers were produced by this tribe. The territory of Naphtali was in the north between the Sea of Galilee and the territory of Asher on the Mediterranean coast.

> 49:22-26 *Joseph is a fruitful bough, even a fruitful bough by a well; whose branches run over the wall:*
> *The archers have sorely grieved him, and shot at him, and hated him:*
> *But his bow abode in strength, and the arms of his hands were made strong by the hands of the mighty God of Jacob; (from thence is the shepherd, the stone of Israel:)*
> *Even by the God of thy father, who shall help thee; and by the Almighty, who shall bless thee with blessings of heaven above, blessings of the deep that lieth under, blessing of the breasts, and of the womb:*
> *The blessings of thy father have prevailed above the blessings of my progenitors unto the utmost bound of the everlasting hills: they shall be on the head of Joseph, and on the crown of the head of him that was separate from his brethren.*

Jacob abundantly praised Joseph, his son, who became fruitful in spite of bitter jealousy from others both inside and outside of his family. The source of Joseph's strength in resisting his enemies was Almighty God, the Shepherd, the Rock of Israel. The Lord had blessed Joseph in Egypt, and He would bless his descendants through Ephraim and Manasseh in Canaan. Ephraim's territory was north of Judah and Benjamin, and Manasseh's territory was on both sides of the Jordan River north and east of the territory of Ephraim. The prediction was that these tribes would be blessed with abundant fruit of the womb and of the soil. Joseph's position as "prince" among the tribes of Israel was to be perpetuated in the descendants of Ephraim and Manasseh.

49:27 Benjamin shall ravin as a wolf: in the morning he shall devour the prey, and at night he shall divide the spoil.

The descendants of Benjamin were known for their ferocious warriors. They even went to war with the other tribes of Israel. In time they were absorbed by the tribe of Judah and the record of them dies out after the Babylonian captivity.

The Death of Jacob

49:28-33 All these are the twelve tribes of Israel: and this is it that their father spake unto them, and blessed them; every one according to his blessing he blessed them.

And he charged them, and said unto them, I am to be gathered unto my people: bury me with my fathers in the cave that is in the field of Ephron the Hittite,

In the cave that is in the field of Machpelah, which is before Mamre, in the land of Canaan, which Abraham bought with the field of Ephron the Hittite for a possession of a buryingplace.

There they buried Abraham and Sarah his wife; there they buried Isaac and Rebekah his wife; and there I buried Leah.

The purchase of the field and of the cave that is therein was from the children of Heth.

And when Jacob had made an end of commanding his sons, he gathered up his feet into the bed, and yielded up the ghost, and was gathered unto his people.

The blessings of Jacob on his sons is a remarkable prophetic passage. The predictions given here have been vindicated in Israel's history.

Jacob again gave instructions regarding his burial. He was to be taken to the family burial plot purchased by Abraham from Ephron, the Hittite.

After taking care of the necessary details Jacob laid down in his bed and died with the same dignity that characterized this whole final scene with his sons and grandsons. The expression in verse 33, "was gathered unto his people," is a clear testimony to the hope of immortality that was a part of Israel's faith.

The Burial of Jacob

50:1-14 *And Joseph fell upon his father's face, and wept upon him, and kissed him.*

And Joseph commanded his servants the physicians to embalm his father: and the physicians embalmed Israel.

And forty days were fulfilled for him; for so are fulfilled the days of those which are embalmed: and the Egyptians mourned for him threescore and ten days.

And when the days of his mourning were past, Joseph spake unto the house of Pharaoh, saying, If now I have found grace in your eyes, speak, I pray you, in the ears of Pharaoh, saying,

My father made me swear, saying, Lo, I die: in my grave which I have digged for me in the land of Canaan, there shalt thou bury me. Now therefore let me go up, I pray thee, and bury my father, and I will come again.

And Pharaoh said, Go up, and bury thy father, according as he made thee swear.

And Joseph went up to bury his father: and with him went up all the servants of Pharaoh, the elders of his house, and all the elders of the land of Egypt,

And all the house of Joseph, and his brethren, and his father's house: only their little ones, and their flocks, and their herds, they left in the land of Goshen.

And there went up with him both chariots and horsemen: and it was a very great company.

And they came to the threshingfloor of Atad, which is beyond Jordan, and there they mourned with a great and very sore lamentation: and he made a mourning for his father seven days.

And when the inhabitants of the land, the Canaanites, saw the mourning in the floor of Atad, they said, This is a grievous mourning to the Egyptians: wherefore the name of it was called Abel-mizraim, which is beyond Jordan.

And his sons did unto him according as he commanded them:

283

For his sons carried him into the land of Canaan, and buried him in the cave of the field of Machpelah, which Abraham bought with the field for a possession of a buryingplace of Ephron the Hittite, before Mamre.

And Joseph returned into Egypt, he, and his brethren, and all that went up with him to bury his father, after he had buried his father.

Joseph wanted his father's body preserved for the time of mourning and for the long trip to Canaan for burial. The embalming process took forty days to complete. We are not told if the seventy days included those forty days, or if they were in addition to them, but both the Hebrews and the Egyptians mourned for Jacob as they would for royalty, probably out of respect for Joseph.

A huge caravan formed to carry Jacob's body back to Canaan. It included the Pharaoh's chief counselors, Egyptian officials from throughout the country, and the grown members of the Hebrew clan. Only the children and domestic animals were left behind, probably in the care of Egyptian servants. The array of chariots and horsemen must have been of considerable interest to observers along the three-hundred-mile route.

The Test of Joseph's Love

50:15-21 *And when Joseph's brethren saw that their father was dead, they said, Joseph will peradventure hate us, and will certainly requite us all the evil which we did unto him.*

And they sent a messenger unto Joseph, saying, Thy father did command before he died, saying,

So shall ye say unto Joseph, Forgive, I pray thee now, the trespass of thy brethren, and their sin; for they did unto thee evil: and now, we pray thee, forgive the trespass of the servants of the God of thy father. And Joseph wept when they spake unto him.

And his brethren also went and fell down before his face; and they said, Behold, we be thy servants.

And Joseph said unto them, Fear not: for am I in the place of God?

But as for you, ye thought evil against me: but God

meant it unto good, to bring to pass, as it is this day, to save much people alive.

Now therefore fear ye not: I will nourish you, and your little ones. And he comforted them, and spake kindly unto them.

Joseph's older brothers felt that the only thing restraining him from getting revenge on them for their mistreatment of him as a teen-ager was the fact that Jacob was alive. Now that their father was gone, their fear of Joseph returned. Joseph wept when he received word of their fear for he did not want his brothers to doubt the permanence of his forgiveness.

Patiently and lovingly Joseph allayed their fears and did what he could to encourage them. The evidence of his love continued as Joseph watched over them and supplied their needs.

Joseph's Prophecy

50:22-26 And Joseph dwelt in Egypt, he, and his father's house: and Joseph lived an hundred and ten years.

And Joseph saw Ephraim's children of the third generation: the children also of Machir the son of Manasseh were brought up upon Joseph's knees.

And Joseph said unto his brethren, I die: and God will surely visit you, and bring you out of this land unto the land which he sware to Abraham, to Isaac, and to Jacob.

And Joseph took an oath of the children of Israel, saying, God will surely visit you, and ye shall carry up my bones from hence.

So Joseph died, being an hundred and ten years old: and they embalmed him, and he was put in a coffin in Egypt.

Before his death, Joseph proclaimed to his brethren the future deliverance of the tribes of Israel from Egyptian rule and the planting of Israel in the land of promise. Joseph described this event as a divine visitation. So strong was his own faith in the fulfillment of this prophecy, Joseph asked his brethren to swear by an oath that his body would be taken with them when they left Egypt so that he might be finally buried in Canaan, God's gift to Israel, His covenant people.

Bibliography

Barnhouse, Donald G. *Genesis: A Devotional Commentary in One Volume.* Grand Rapids: Zondervan Publishing House, 1973.

Baughen, Michael. *The Moses Principle: Leadership and the Venture of Faith.* Wheaton: Harold Shaw Publishers, 1979.

Candlish, Robert S. *Studies in Genesis.* Grand Rapids: Kregel Publications, 1979.

DeHaan, Martin R. *Portraits of Christ in Genesis.* Grand Rapids: Zondervan Publishing House, 1978.

Delitzsch, Franz. *A New Commentary on Genesis.* Minneapolis: Klock and Klock Christian Publishers, 1978.

Fritsch, Charles T. *Genesis.* Atlanta: John Knox Press, 1959.

Fromer, Margaret and Keyes, Sharrel. *Genesis One to Twenty-Five: Walking with God* and *Genesis Twenty-Five to Fifty: Called by God.* Wheaton: Harold Shaw Publishers, 1979.

Green, William H. and Youngblood, Ronald. *The Unity of Genesis.* Grand Rapids: Baker Book House, 1979.

Gutzke, Manford G. *Plain Talk on Genesis.* Grand Rapids: Zondervan Publishing House, 1975.

Hargreaves, John. *Guide to the Book of Genesis.* Naperville: Alec R. Allenson, Inc., 1969.

Hartley, William. *In the Beginning God: Jottings from Genesis.* Grand Rapids: Baker Book House, 1975.

Heslop, W. G. *Gems from Genesis.* Grand Rapids: Kregel Publications, 1975.

Hobbs, Herschel H. *The Origin of All Things: Studies in Genesis.* Waco: Word Books, 1976.

Jensen, Irving L., ed. *Genesis.* Chicago: Moody Press, 1967.

Kidner, F. Derek. *Genesis.* Downers Grove: InterVarsity Press, 1968.

Lentz, Thomas W. *Studies in Genesis: How It All Began*. Lima: C.S.S. Publishers, Inc., 1970.

MacKintosh, Charles H. *Genesis to Deuteronomy: Notes on the Pentateuch*. Neptune: Loizeaux Brothers, Inc., 1973.

Morris, Henry M. *The Beginning of the World*. Denver: Accent Books, 1977.

Morris, Henry M. and Whitcomb, John C. *The Genesis Flood*. San Diego: Creation-Life Publishers.

Morrison, G. H. *In the Beginning God*. Chattanooga: AMG Publishers, 1976.

Owens, John J. *Genesis*. New York: Harper and Row Publishers, 1978.

Pink, Arthur W. *Gleanings in Genesis*. Chicago: Moody Press, 1964.

Schultz, Samuel J. *The Gospel of Moses*. Chicago: Moody Press, 1979.

Speiser, E. A., ed. *Genesis*. Garden City: Doubleday and Co., Inc., 1964.

Stedman, Ray. *The Beginnings (Genesis Four to Eleven and Twenty-Six)*. Waco: Word Books, 1977.

Stevens, Sherrill. *Layman's Bible Book Commentary: Genesis*. Nashville: Broadman Press, 1978.

Stigers, Harold G. *A Commentary on Genesis*. Grand Rapids: Zondervan Publishing House, 1975.

Thomas, W. Griffith. *Genesis: A Devotional Commentary*. Grand Rapids: Wm. B. Eerdmans Publishing Co., 1946.

Unger, Merrill F. *Unger's Bible Commentary: Pentateuch*. Chicago: Moody Press, 1979.

Vawter, Bruce. *On Genesis*. Garden City: Doubleday and Co., Inc., 1977.

Von Rad, Gerhard. *Genesis, A Commentary*. Philadelphia: Westminster Press, 1973.

Wood, Leon J. *Genesis: A Study Guide Commentary*. Grand Rapids: Zondervan Publishing House, 1975.